THE CULTURE OF TERRORISM

THE CULTURE OF
TERRORISM

NOAM CHOMSKY

BLACK
ROSE
BOOKS

Montréal - New York

Black Rose Books No. Q 129

Canadian Cataloguing in Publication Data

Chomsky, Noam
    The culture of terrorism

Includes index.

ISBN 0-921689-29-2 (bound). — ISBN 0-921689-28-4 (pbk.).

1. United States — foreign relations — 1981-
2. United States — military policy
3. Terrorism — government policy — United States
4. Iran-Contra affair, 1985-
 I. Title

E876.C45 1988   327.73   C88-090322-8

Cover design: Richard Parent

BLACK ROSE BOOKS

C.P. 1258	2250 Military Road	99 Wallis Road
Succ. Place du Parc	Tonawanda, NY	London, E9 5LN
Montréal, H2X 4A7	14150	England
Canada	USA	UK

Printed and bound in Quebec, Canada

Table of Contents

Part II Further Successes of the Reagan Administration

Part III The Current Agenda

Preface

This essay on the culture of terrorism is based on a December 1986 "postscript" for several foreign editions of my book *Turning the Tide*.[1] I had originally intended to update the same material for a new U.S. edition, carrying it through the Iran-contra hearings, but it took on a rather different character in the course of rewriting, so I have prepared it for separate publication. I will, however, generally assume the discussion in *Turning the Tide* and the further elaboration in *On Power and Ideology* as background, without specific reference.

This earlier material dealt with several topics: the travail ① of Central America; the principles that underlie U.S. policy planning as revealed by the documentary record; the application of these principles in Third World intervention, primarily with regard to Central America and the Caribbean; the application of the same principles to national security affairs and interactions among the industrial powers; and some relevant features of domestic U.S. society. The central—and not very surprising—conclusion that emerges from the documentary and historical record is that U.S. international and security policy, rooted in the structure of power in the domestic society, has as its primary goal the preservation of what we might call "the Fifth Freedom," understood crudely but with a fair degree of accuracy as the freedom to rob, to exploit and to dominate, to undertake any course of action to ensure that existing privilege is protected and advanced. This guiding principle was overlooked when Franklin Delano Roosevelt announced the Four Freedoms that the U.S. and its allies would uphold in the conflict with fascism: freedom of speech, freedom of worship, freedom from want, and freedom from fear.

1

The internal documentary record of U.S. planning and, more importantly, the unfolding historical events themselves yield ample evidence to evaluate the significance attached to the Four Freedoms in doctrine and in practice, and to demonstrate their subordination to the Fifth Freedom, the operative principle that accounts for a substantial part of what the U.S. government does in the world. When the Four Freedoms are perceived to be incompatible with the Fifth, a regular occurrence, they are set aside with little notice or concern.

To pursue programs that are conceived and applied in these terms, the state must spin an elaborate web of illusion and deceit, with the cooperation of the ideological institutions that generally serve its interests—not at all surprisingly, given the distribution of domestic wealth and power and the natural workings of the "free market of ideas" functioning within these constraints. They must present the facts of current history in a proper light, conducting exercises of "historical engineering," to use the term devised by American historians who offered their services to President Wilson during World War I: "explaining the issues of the war that we might the better win it," whatever the facts may actually be. It has commonly been understood that the responsibility of the serious academic historian and political scientist, as of political leaders, is to deceive the public, for their own good. Thus the respected historian Thomas Bailey explained in 1948 that "Because the masses are notoriously short-sighted and generally cannot see danger until it is at their throats, our statesmen are forced to deceive them into an awareness of their own long-run interests," a view recently endorsed by the director of Harvard University's Center of International Affairs, Samuel Huntington, who wrote in 1981 that "you may have to sell [intervention or other military action] in such a way as to create the misimpression that it is the Soviet Union that you are fighting. That is what the United States has done ever since the Truman Doctrine." An accurate assessment, which applies very aptly to Central America today. The academic world too must be rallied to the cause. In his presidential address to the American Historical Association in 1949, Conyers Read explained that

> we must clearly assume a militant attitude if we are to survive.... Discipline is the essential prerequisite of every effective army whether it march under the Stars and Stripes or under the Hammer and Sickle... Total war, whether it be hot or cold, enlists everyone and calls upon everyone to assume his part. The

historian is no freer from this obligation than the physicist.. This sounds like the advocacy of one form of social control as against another. In short, it is.[2]

In general, it is necessary to ensure that the domestic population remains largely inert, limited in the capacity to develop independent modes of thought and perception and to formulate and press effectively for alternative policies—even alternative institutional arrangements—that might well be seen as preferable if the framework of ideology were to be challenged.

Subsequent events illustrate very well the theses developed in the earlier material to which I referred above. I will review a number of examples, including the "scandals" that erupted in late 1986 and their consequences, and the new demands that these developments posed for the ideological system. The scandals elicited a good deal of commentary and reflection on our political institutions and the way they function. Much of it, I think, is misguided, for reasons that I will try to explain as we proceed. My main concern will be to assess what we can learn about ourselves, particularly about the dominant intellectual culture and the values that guide it,[3] from an inquiry into recent events and the reaction to them at a critical moment of American life.

Dedication to the Fifth Freedom is hardly a new form of social pathology. Nor, of course, was it an invention of the "white hordes" who, "fortified in aggressive spirit by an arrogant, messianic Christianity" and "motivated by the lure of enriching plunder,...sallied forth from their western European homelands to explore, assault, loot, occupy, rule and exploit the rest of the world" during the nearly six centuries when "western Europe and its diaspora have been disturbing the peace of the world"—as the advance of European civilization is perceived, not without reason, by a perceptive African commentator.[4] But this vocation of the powerful constantly assumes new forms—and new disguises, as the supportive culture passes through varying stages of moral cowardice and intellectual corruption.

As the latest inheritors of a grim tradition, we should at least have the integrity to look into the mirror without evasion. And when we do not like what we see, as we most definitely will not if we have the honesty to face reality, we have a far more serious moral responsibility, which should be obvious enough.

Cambridge, Massachusetts
October 1987

Notes Preface

1. *Turning the Tide* (South End, 1985), henceforth *TTT*. The "postscript" has appeared in the Canadian and Italian editions (Black Rose (Montreal), 1987; Eleuthera (Milan), 1987). See also my *On Power and Ideology* (Black Rose 1987; henceforth, *PI*), a series of lectures delivered in Managua in 1986, dealing with similar themes.

2. For sources and more general discussion, see my *Towards a New Cold War* (Pantheon, 1982), chapter 1, drawing particularly on Jesse Lemisch, *On Active Service in War and Peace: Politics and Ideology in the American Historical Profession* (New Hogtown Press (Toronto), 1975), an important study, unread for the usual reasons: wrong message. Lemisch was one of the many young scholars eliminated from the universities during the little-known but extensive academic repression of the left during the 1960s, on the grounds that his "political concerns interfered with his scholarship"—meaning, he failed to adopt the proper "political concerns." Many illusions have been fostered about what happened in the universities in those years of conflict, when the rigid ideological barriers were breached to a limited extent, but at a serious cost to many of the young people who achieved this important result. Huntington, in *International Security*, Summer, 1981.

3. A related and very significant question, which I do not attempt to address, is the shaping of the popular culture for the general public in television, cinema, mass circulation journals, educational practice, and so on.

4. Chinweizu, *The West and the Rest of Us: White Predators, Black Slavers and the African Elite* (Vintage, 1975), 3.

INTRODUCTION

The Public and State Violence

The 1986 "scandals" and their aftermath are instructive for those who are concerned to understand American society, and particularly, for those who hope to change its character and course. Temporarily at least, the scandals caused some disarray and retreat among state planners and ideologists, discrediting certain of the more violent policies as they were partially exposed. These developments encouraged moves within Central America towards the kind of political settlement that would long have been possible had it not been for the commitment of the United States to establish its own terms by force. Even if successful, these steps could not in themselves lay the groundwork for confronting the deep-seated problems facing the societies of Central America, problems that result in no small measure from earlier U.S. intervention in the region, where the U.S. has been the dominant outside influence through the century. But if domestic inhibitions suffice to constrain the advocates of force in Washington, then there might be a respite from the worst terror, and a small window of opportunity might open for constructive efforts to overcome the legacy of a bitter past.

The scandals of 1986, in turn, are a tribute to the popular movements that developed in the 1960s and that have not been tamed, despite major efforts by business, government and intellectual elites in the post-Vietnam period. This important fact will not be the topic of books and articles, and indeed will not penetrate to official history, just as the comparable lesson of the Vietnam years can hardly be recognized within an ideological system dedicated to the service of power. It is important, however, for concerned citizens to think through the matter for themselves, and to understand just how the public was able to influence state policy.

During the Vietnam years, the public played a significant though indirect role in influencing policy. Evidently, the influence was not expressed through the electoral system; a 2-1 vote for the "peace candidate" in 1964 did not deter Lyndon Johnson and his associates from carrying out the plans for escalation they were in the process of developing while the election was won on the promise that we do not want a wider war. But as the Vietnam war escalated through the stages of subversion, state terrorism, and outright U.S. aggression,[1] disaffection and protest among the public became a significant force, preventing the government from declaring the national mobilization that would have been required to win what was becoming a major war. The effort to fight a "guns and butter war" so as to pacify an increasingly restive public gave rise to severe economic problems. These were a factor in leading elite elements to urge that the enterprise be reduced in scale or liquidated by early 1968. The general dissidence, particularly among the youth, was perceived in elite circles as a serious problem in itself by 1968, while within the Pentagon, there was concern that sufficient military force be held in reserve to control domestic disorder if the U.S. aggression visibly increased. The key phrase is "visibly"; it was fear of the public that led to the expansion of clandestine operations in those years, on the usual principle that in our form of democracy, if the public escapes from passivity, it must be deceived—for its own good. The collapse of will among the troops in the field, influenced by rising dissidence at home, also became a matter of elite concern, teaching the lesson that it was a mistake to employ a citizen's army to fight a brutal colonial war rather than mercenary forces, foreign or locally recruited, as has been traditional practice. These problems convinced economic and political elites to change course after the Tet offensive of January 1968 made it clear that military victory remained a distant prospect without escalation of the sort that the population would not easily tolerate.

Similar factors inhibited U.S. intervention in Central America in the 1980s. The scale of domestic dissidence was greater and it was more broadly based than at comparable stages of the Indochina wars. The Reagan administration was therefore unable to carry out the Kennedy-Johnson transition from state terrorism to direct aggression. Had the public been quiescent, it would have been possible for Reagan to send the Marines in the style of Lyndon Johnson when it became necessary to avert the threat of democracy in the Dominican Republic in 1965, or to emulate John F. Kennedy, who sent the U.S. Air Force to bomb and defoliate South Vietnam to counter what his administration called "internal aggression" there. Much to the dismay of U.S. elites, direct aggression is now impeded by the enemy of the state at home, the domestic population, and the resort to indirect means brings with it inevitable problems. Devious means are less efficient than the direct exercise of violence. Furthermore, despite the general loyalty of the ideological institutions, there is a risk of exposure. When suppression is no longer possible, some opposition will be aroused among groups that are concerned to protect their own power and prerogatives (Congress, in the present case). And no less seriously, the exposures tend to undermine the rhetoric that is used to pacify the general population—in particular, the hypocritical pose of "combating terrorism" regularly affected by some of the world's leading terrorist commanders, but difficult to sustain when they are found to be dealing with Iran.

Domestic dissidence was the essential factor that forced state terror underground in the 1980s, leading to problems when certain of its facets were exposed to a broad public during the scandals of 1986. I will return to these recent developments and their immediate background, but it is important not to allow the central conclusion to be effaced in a welter of detail.

The most important conclusion to be drawn from these events is that they demonstrate, once again, that even in a largely depoliticized society such as the United States, with no political parties or opposition press beyond the narrow spectrum of the business-dominated consensus, it is possible for popular action to have a significant impact on policy, though indirectly. That was an important lesson of the Indochina wars. It is underscored, once again, by the experience of the 1980s with regard to Central America. And it should be remembered for the future.

Notes Introduction

1. Needless to say, these are not the conventional terms used to describe what happened during those years. But they are the accurate terms. For discussion, see several essays in my *Towards a New Cold War*, and sources cited there. On the conventional interpretation as the war progressed and since, particularly in the media, see Edward Herman and Noam Chomsky, *The Political Economy of the Mass Media* (Pantheon, 1988), chapters 5, 6.

PART ONE

The Scandals of 1986

1

The Challenge

The scandals that erupted in the Fall of 1986 and the reaction to them cast a revealing light on the political system and the intellectual culture that interprets and sustains it. As we shall see in detail below, these events demonstrated that the United States remains dedicated to the rule of force, that political elites agree and indeed insist that it must remain so, and that, furthermore, the commitment to violence and lawlessness frames their self-image as well, barely concealed beneath deceptive rhetoric. These conclusions can readily be drawn from the actual record, if we face it honestly and without illusion. They have serious implications for the future, just as the same conclusions in earlier days, no less readily established, no less regularly suppressed, have had profound consequences in the past.

With regard to Central America, the scandals disrupted a tacit elite consensus, troubled by some tactical disagreements over generally shared goals. They imposed new demands for the ideological system, which must control the domestic damage and ensure that it is confined within narrow and politically meaningless bounds while dedicating itself anew to the major and continuing task: to fashion an appropriate version of the real scandals of the 1980s so as to place U.S. actions in a favorable light and thus to ensure that similar policies can proceed without serious impediment when they are considered necessary.

This task gained new urgency in June 1986, as the World Court issued its long-expected judgment condemning the United States for its attack against Nicaragua, and Congress voted aid for the contras, endorsing the illegal use of force while "asserting that it

11

was the only way to get the Sandinistas to negotiate seriously"—five days after Nicaragua had accepted the latest draft of the Contadora treaty, rejected by the U.S. and its clients.[1] "This is for real. This is a real war," a U.S. government official commented, confirming the judgment of Nicaraguan President Daniel Ortega that the congressional vote "amounted to a declaration of war."[2]

The media and the general intellectual community had largely accepted and internalized the basic framework of government doctrine throughout, but with the virtual declaration of war, under these circumstances, it became necessary to pursue the task of imposing a suitable doctrinal structure with renewed vigor. Specifically, since we have declared war against Nicaragua and established a functioning terrorist state in El Salvador, it must be true—and therefore it *is* true—that Nicaragua is a brutal one-party dictatorship devoted to torture and oppression while the resistance who courageously fought "the *former* dictator" Somoza[3] now fight for freedom and democracy against the new dictator Ortega imposed by Soviet imperalism; correspondingly, it is necessarily the case that El Salvador, like Guatemala and Honduras, is a "fledgling democracy" marching forward towards the Four Freedoms thanks to our fervent love of liberty. If the facts show otherwise, then so much the worse for the facts.

The task of constructing a usable version of history and the current scene confronted further obstacles in the summer of 1987. Despite a substantial military effort by the United States, the much-heralded Spring Offensive of "the sons of Reagan," as the marauders of the proxy army announce themselves when swooping down on barely defended farms and villages to kill and destroy, achieved no military victories that could be flaunted to convince wavering legislators that the exercise of violence might succeed; organizing achievements among the Nicaraguan populace are not even a topic for consideration. What was worse, the disarray caused by the scandals encouraged U.S. allies, Costa Rica in particular, to risk the wrath of Washington and proceed in the course of diplomacy.

The Reagan administration had succeeded in undermining the initiatives of the major Latin American governments, expressed through the efforts of the Contadora nations, to find a way to a political settlement, and the commitment to obstruct these efforts persisted through 1987. Nevertheless, Costa Rican President Oscar Arias, with the support of Guatemala, continued to press a plan unacceptable to Washington, which responded by repeated efforts to undermine it to which we return, and direct punishment of Costa Rica for its transgressions. U.S. assistance to the ailing Costa Rican economy was suspended in March 1987 as Arias proceeded with his plan over Washington's objections, along with commercial U.S. bank loans to Costa Rica, as Washington refused, for the first time, to intervene on Costa Rica's behalf, prejudicing Costa Rican efforts to obtain other international loans as well; Costa Rican exports to the U.S. were cut by government bans and restrictions; and U.S. diplomatic pressures forced the resignation of an adviser to President Arias who had been instrumental in formulating the peace plan, according to Costa Rican officials. While Costa Rica was lined up in Washington's crusade to overthrow the Sandinistas, two reporters in San José observe, "U.S. aid soared to more than $200 million annually. 'Costa Rica has not received a penny [of U.S. aid] since almost the beginning of the peace plan effort. That, of course, is purely coincidental,' one Arias insider remarked sarcastically." The Council on Hemispheric Affairs reports that "According to Costa Rican officials, the Reagan Administration's delay in recently appointing a new ambassador for more than seven months is a sign of its displeasure with Arias's diplomatic moves in the region. One Arias aide said that for Washington 'this embassy is not here for dialogue or political development in Costa Rica. It's still here with the aim of creating a southern front [for the contras]'."[4]

These topics are generally ignored, despite their obvious significance, in conformity with the principle that the state sets the agenda of concern for respectable opinion. Within that framework, tactical debate is legitimate, but the bounds must not be transgressed. This principle is a corollary to the requirement that the public must be deceived, if it is not quiescent. We shall see many further instances as we proceed.

Despite extreme U.S. hostility, the efforts to achieve a diplomatic settlement persisted through 1987. With the support of the Contadora nations, serving as crucial intermediaries, the Central American presidents reached a tentative peace agreement in August 1987, shocking the administration and threatening to undercut its efforts throughout the past years to prevent a diplomatic settlement. Given that the comparative advantage of the United States lies in its unparalleled means of violence, while it lacks any political appeal in the region apart from favored military and wealthy elites to whose rule and privilege it is committed, it is natural that the U.S. government should consistently prefer the arena of force to that of diplomacy, and so it has. In contrast, Nicaragua has sought throughout to pursue the path of diplomacy, calling for international monitoring of borders, elimination of foreign bases and advisers so as to reduce security concerns, etc., while accepting proposals for a general (Contadora-initiated) treaty, taking the conflict to the International Court of Justice and the United Nations Security Council and General Assembly as required by international convention, and so on.

We return to the specifics, but there is no real question that these are the essential facts, and they are plainly unacceptable.

To face the task of purification of history posed by the Central American accords of August 1987, it was necessary to adopt a new stance, outlined with precision by Robert Hunter, senior fellow at the Center for Strategic and International Studies, consultant for the National Bipartisan (Kissinger) Commission on Central America, and respected commentator on international affairs. We must regretfully concede that the contras proved an inadequate instrument for "forcing pluralism on the Sandinistas" and that the "price of democracy in Nicaragua" can only be paid "by sacrificing American lives," too great a sacrifice even for a state so caring and benevolent as ours:

> By contrast, the contras seem to have been instrumental in achieving another, less noticed goal of US policy: acceptance by Nicaragua of a peace process that can be used to reduce security threats in the region. This goal, less ambitious than a Sandinista overthrow, has the virtue of broad support across the US political spectrum.[5]

This explanation of the virtues of the less noticed-goal, however, overlooks one slight flaw in the argument: the goal could readily have been achieved at any time in the preceding years by accepting the diplomatic options urged and pursued by the Nicaraguan enemy, adamantly rejected at every turn by the Reagan administration. This perception being entirely unacceptable, it must be exorcised, and a more fitting history must be enshrined along the lines that Hunter outlines. As explained by James Rohwer in the *New York Times*, it was "America's pugnacity over the last several years" that compelled Nicaragua to accept the conditions of the peace settlement (namely, those it had been requesting for six years against unceasing U.S. opposition), conditions that will secure borders and remove security threats and thus will prevent

Nicaragua from overrunning its neighbors, if not threatening the
United States itself, and will compel these Hitlerian aggressors to
"keep Nicaragua's miseries to itself"—these miseries, of course,
being entirely their responsibility, having nothing to do with
"America's pugnacity."[6] This "pugnacity" and its effects merit only
admiration and approval, within the culture of terrorism.

While the standard argument offered by Robert Hunter is
transparently absurd, and the variant offered by James Rohwer
merits somewhat harsher terms, one might imagine a more
sophisticated version: "America's pugnacity" compelled the
totalitarian Sandinistas to accept terms that call for their internal
democratization, along with a lessening of their threat to their
neighbors, namely, the terms of the August 1987 accords, which
previously they refused to accept. It is noteworthy that the
argument is not offered, but that is for other reasons: no arguments
are required during the incantation of state propaganda. But let us
consider this argument nonetheless. It is readily tested. We simply
inspect the diplomatic record to determine when the United
States, or anyone else, offered Nicaragua the option of accepting a
treaty which terminated U.S. support for its proxy army in return
for the internal moves called for in the August accords in all
countries of the region, and we ask when Nicaragua rejected this
option, compelling the United States to resort to "pugnacity" to
achieve these long-desired goals. We quickly discover, again, that
the United States never contemplated such a proposal, and has
undermined the diplomatic process from the start, and still does:
the Reagan administration at once demonstrated the hostility
towards the August 1987 agreements that is traditional when
diplomacy or international law interfere with the preferred route
of violence. The real reasons for "America's pugnacity" lie
elsewhere, and they are obvious enough, but, being unacceptable,
they cannot be considered in the cultural mainstream.

There can be little doubt that this enterprise of historical
engineering will succeed, just as similar ones have in the past. Its
manifest absurdity is unlikely to prove an impediment for the
dominant intellectual culture. We return to a closer look at how
these problems have evolved and have been addressed, and how
the basis has been laid for assuring that they will be successfully
solved, as in the past, with impressive consistency and a regular
display of piety and self-righteousness.

The doctrinal truths must be driven home forcefully and
incessantly, because more is at stake than merely providing a

justification for what has been done. A basis must be laid for the continuing resort to violence in the likely event that a political settlement will not suit U.S. demands and will therefore be undermined—by enemy treachery, the required conclusion whatever the facts, therefore the one that must be established as doctrine. And what more fitting argument could there be than the "historical fact" that only through the use of force was it possible to drive the enemy to the bargaining table in the first place. Furthermore, similar situations are bound to arise in the future, and historical engineering must ensure, without delay, that the proper arsenal of lessons will be available, to be deployed when needed.

In pursuit of these objectives, the current situation may be obscured by the usual technique of selective focus and interpretation that adheres to approved principles, or simply by outright falsification or suppression of unacceptable fact. As for the past, it is plainly irrelevant, since we have undergone a miraculous conversion and have changed course—despite the fact that the institutional structures and planning system that lie behind past atrocities remain intact and unchallenged, and there is little recognition in the intellectual or popular culture of what has happened in reality, apart from those (not insignificant) sectors of popular nonelite opinion that remain stricken by the "Vietnam syndrome."

The doctrine of "change of course," which allows any past horror to be cheerfully dismissed, is highly functional within a terrorist culture. It is presented in its most vulgar form by 1987 Pulitzer Prize winner Charles Krauthammer, who assures us that "today's America is not Teddy Roosevelt's or Eisenhower's or even that imagined by Ronald Reagan, the candidate." Now "democracy in the Third World has become, for the right as well as the left, a principal goal of American foreign policy." While it is true that "liberty has not always been the American purpose," now all has changed: "We believe in freedom," and the past can be consigned to oblivion along with all that it teaches us about American institutions and the way they operate.[7] As for the present, it will be rendered with the same scrupulous concern for accuracy and honest self-criticism that was exhibited during past eras when, we now concede in retrospect, there may have been an occasional blemish.

A more sophisticated version of this valuable doctrine is offered by the editors of the conservative London *Spectator*, who are able to perceive that "the sudden attachment of the United States to pluralist democracy in Central America in general, and Nicaragua in particular, may seem a little strange" in the light of the historical record, and that "this hypocrisy, as some see it, has deprived the Americans of credibility." But, they continue, such a reaction is improper, because it "assumes no nation has a right to act unless it has been perfectly consistent through the ages"; "cases have to be decided on their own merits," and the case for a war against Nicaragua is "apparent to all but western *marxistant* visitors, dazzled as they always are by the glories of low-cost housing projects, women's groups and universal measles vaccination." In contrast, wealthy and privileged sectors of the West show proper contempt for such absurdities, preferring the wise reflections of Winston Churchill, who observed to his colleague Joseph Stalin in 1943 that

> the government of the world must be entrusted to satisfied nations, who wished nothing more for themselves than what they had. If the world-government were in the hands of hungry nations, there would always be danger. But none of us had any reason to seek for anything more. The peace would be kept by peoples who lived in their own way and were not ambitious. Our power placed us above the rest. We were like rich men dwelling at peace within their habitations.

Enjoying this happy state as a result of our virtue and good works, we are entitled to sneer disdainfully at ridiculous attempts to save children dying of disease, provide housing for the poor and starving, offer women the possibility of escaping from slavery and degradation, and other such childish nonsense in "hungry nations" unsatisfied with their proper lot.[8]

For all their astuteness, however, the editors still miss a few small points: (1) contrary to what they allege, the United States (along with "satisfied nations" generally) is quite consistent in its choice of targets of violence and its selective concerns, as the historical record shows, and the reasons are explained with sufficient clarity in internal documents; (2) ideological managers are equally consistent in concealing these striking regularities, which can readily be grasped once we escape the confines of convenient dogma; (3) the United States has no commitment "to pluralist democracy in Central America," but, rather, has dedicated itself, particularly in the 1980s, to demolishing any possibility that it might arise.[9] It makes perfect sense for the United States to develop a "sudden attachment" to its particular conception of "democracy" in Nicaragua from the moment of the overthrow of the Somoza regime in July 1979, though not before, while undertaking programs of ruthless savagery to destroy popular organizations that might lay the basis for meaningful democracy in El Salvador in the very same years. There is no inconsistency, apart from the constructions of the commissars, striving to adapt to changing events.

One useful consequence of the doctrine of "change of course" is that all analytic work devoted to the study of American society and history is entirely irrelevant, no matter what it reveals. Since we have now changed course, we may dismiss the lessons of history and begin afresh, unburdened by any understanding of the nature of American society or the documentary and historical record. All studies of these topics may be shelved, as now irrelevant, apart from their antiquarian interest. Furthermore, analysis of current developments may also be dismissed when the conclusions are unacceptable, since we can, after all, always change course once again and set forth anew on the path of righteousness when the truth about the world is too obvious to suppress. The highest value proclaimed in the intellectual culture, if it is to serve its functions, must be total ignorance about who we are and what we do in the world, for Ignorance is Strength. Given the facts and what they reveal, this is a doctrine of no little utility and significance.

The extraordinary efficiency of the doctrine of willful ignorance of ourselves, which allows a convenient "change of course" whenever it becomes necessary to dispose of inconvenient facts, is revealed at every turn. During the 1987 Iran-contra hearings, for example, the country and the media were exposed to a record of duplicity that demonstrated beyond any question that the Reagan administration cannot be trusted to adhere to congressional directives, and surely not to international agreements. The point was hammered home with particular intensity, day after day, with regard to its operations in Central America. This much, at least, is not even in dispute. The public hearings came to an end on August 3, and two days later, the Reagan administration proposed a "peace plan" for Central America. I will return to its timing and the background, but consider just its basic contents. The Reagan plan called for dismantling of the political system in Nicaragua along with the scheduled elections and suspension of emergency regulations instituted in response to U.S.-organized attacks, a "demobilization of Sandinista and insurgent forces," and a halt in arms shipments to Nicaragua from "Communist countries," which means a total halt in arms shipments, since the U.S. had succeeded years earlier in ensuring that Nicaragua would be forced to rely solely on the Soviet bloc for defense. In return, the U.S. would pledge to halt arms shipments to the contra army it formed in Honduras to attack Nicaragua.[10]

Let us put aside the question of why Nicaragua alone in Central America should be called upon to undergo a form of unilateral disarmament and internal changes dictated by U.S. power, and consider just the cancellation of arms shipments to "both sides": the government of Nicaragua, and the U.S. proxy army attacking Nicaragua from foreign bases. If Nicaragua were to accede to these dictates, its adherence to the agreement would be easily monitored. Furthermore, Washington can readily contrive non-compliance with the agreement on the part of Nicaragua, confident that its fabrications will be prominently displayed on the front pages, as frequently in the past. Familiar examples include the allegations about Sandinista support for Salvadoran guerrillas, a doctrinal truth presupposed as proven in media commentary despite the complete failure to provide credible evidence; and the disinformation operation with regard to Soviet MIGs timed carefully to overcome the (minimal) danger of honest coverage of the unwanted Nicaraguan elections of 1984 —one of Oliver North's capers, so it appears[11]—these elections being a non-event according to official doctrine and media commentary.[12] Adherence to the agreement by the Reagan administration, in contrast, would be completely unverifiable, and as the hearings on which all eyes had been focused had demonstrated beyond any conceivable doubt, the administration could proceed as before, if it chose, to provide new armaments to its proxy forces and to direct continuing attacks against Nicaragua, whatever agreements were reached on paper. The suggestion that the U.S. media or Congress would expose such operations is too ludicrous to merit comment, in the light of the record that had just been revealed. Hence Nicaragua was expected to disarm, subject to severe sanctions, while the U.S. could proceed to maintain or accelerate the attack against Nicaragua as it chooses, independently of what may be stipulated in an agreement which, in the real world, requires compliance only by Nicaragua.

All of this is transparent. It is the conclusion that anyone who gave the matter a moment's thought would at once draw from the story that had been displayed on the television screen and the front pages for the preceding months. But the media were oblivious to these truisms. Doves and hawks alike pondered the prospects in ways to which I will return, but without any recognition of the fundamental absurdity of a "peace plan" under which Nicaragua disarms in exchange for a pledge of good behavior from Ronald Reagan and his cohorts.[13] It was assumed on all sides that the Reagan administration would undergo the familiar miraculous conversion, that it would suddenly change course, would become law-abiding and would comply with agreements without monitoring or any meaningful supervision. There were concerns that Nicaragua would lie and cheat in the manner of all Communists, but no questions about the likelihood that the United States would live up to an unverifiable commitment. When the Central American states reached their own tentative agreement a few days later, rejecting the Reagan plan, the director of the Latin American program at the Council on Foreign Relations issued a solemn warning of "a very serious flaw in the agreement: the absence of penalties in the event of noncompliance." A problem no doubt, but why? The sole reason offered is that the "Marxist-Leninist regime" of Nicaragua might "violate the agreement."[14] No other difficulty comes to mind.

Critics of Reaganite aggressiveness can perceive that Nicaragua may also have some concerns. Discussing the diplomatic alternative that he favors, Wayne Smith, one of the strongest and most consistent critics of the contra option, urges that we enter into a bilateral security pact with Nicaragua as "a corollary to the Central American treaty itself":

> Of course, we would want adequate means of verification. So would the Sandinistas, who have no more reason to trust us than we have to trust them. Compliance would be assured not by the contras but by the strength and honor of the United States.[15]

In short, our strength will assure *their* compliance, and our honor will assure *our* compliance, thus allaying Nicaraguan concerns. Recall that we are inspecting the outer limits of expressible dissent.

It is too much to expect the media or the intellectual culture generally to consider the earlier record of U.S. adherence to agreements: the Geneva accords of 1954 or the Paris peace agreements of 1973, for example, both immediately disrupted by the United States.[16] Perhaps it is also too much to expect a question about such exotic topics as whether the provisions of the

Central American agreement on internal freedoms could possibly be honored in the U.S. client state of El Salvador, still effectively ruled by the same military forces that carried out a major slaughter and physically destroyed the independent media and political opposition. What is particularly noteworthy, however, is that the doctrine of willful self-ignorance is so deeply rooted that it can efface, instantaneously, the news story that had been the major preoccupation for ten months up to the very day of the new promise of miraculous conversion. The grip of the doctrine is so powerful that the question is not even open to discussion. Even the simplest observations lie beyond awareness. The United States is Good, its leaders are Good, the facts are irrelevant, no matter how prominently displayed.

The levelling of discourse within the ideological system is an extremely important matter. Part of the genius of American democracy has been to ensure that isolated individuals face concentrated state and private power alone, without the support of an organizational structure that can assist them in thinking for themselves or entering into meaningful political action, and with few avenues for public expression of fact or analysis that might challenge approved doctrine. The significance of these achievements of thought control is highlighted by the experience of the loosely-knit communities that have succeeded in escaping them, for example, through listener-supported radio, which has helped to create and sustain small subcultures with regular access to information and a range of opinion and analysis that is unimaginable within highly indoctrinated elite circles and the information and doctrinal system they control.

Adherence to doctrinal truth confers substantial reward, not only acceptance within the system of power and a ready path to privilege, but also the inestimable advantage of freedom from the onerous demands of thought, inquiry and argument. Conformity frees one from the burden of evidence, and rational argument is superfluous while one is marching in an approved parade. In contrast, those who dare to question are required to meet high standards of evidence and argument, often standards unattainable in the soft disciplines. These difficulties are compounded by the isolation and lack of resources that are a natural concomitant of dissidence. Apart from this, independent minds appear exotic and are readily ignored or misrepresented, since, after all, their conclusions are unconventional and rarely heard; we are not dealing here with the sciences, where it is at least an ideal, and one often honored, that ideas are to be judged by their merits rather than their utility within a system of power. And if no other measures suffice, dissidents can be dismissed as Stalinist apologists, evidence and argument always being superfluous in the service of power.[17] Failure to observe doctrinal purity with regard to Nicaragua proves that one is "pro-Sandinista," therefore unreliable and unobjective; only those who are properly anti-Sandinista and thus conform to the demands of American power qualify as objective and may therefore enter the arena of public discourse. With regard to El Salvador, the same failure proves that one is "pro-guerrilla," therefore unreliable and unobjective; only those who are properly supportive of the U.S. project escape these defects. A variety of rhetorical devices have been constructed to exorcise independent thought: "Marxist," "radical," "useful idiot" (and other fabrications attributed to Lenin), and other terms which, like these, have lost whatever meaning they might once have had, serving now merely as terms of generalized abuse to guarantee that the bounds of propriety will not be transgressed. But the devices need rarely be used, since the difficulty of escaping the rigidities of the ideological system with its narrow certainties is so great as to marginalize any serious challenge to acceptable thought.

Let us see how these various tasks are currently addressed, and what we can learn about our own society and intellectual culture from observing the performance.

Notes Chapter One

1. Wayne Smith, "Lies about Nicaragua," *Foreign Policy*, Summer 1987; Smith was chief of the U.S. interests Section in Havana prior to his resignation from the State Department in 1982 in protest over Reagan's foreign policy, after 24 years in the Foreign Service, where he was considered the Department's leading expert on Cuba. See chapter 3 on the World Court decision and the reaction to it, and chapter 7 for more on the diplomatic record.

2. James LeMoyne, Linda Greenhouse, Week in Review, *New York Times*, June 29, 1986.

3. Peter Jennings, ABC News, May 20, 1987; his emphasis.

4. Martha Honey and Tony Avirgan, San José, Costa Rica, *In These Times*, Sept. 2, *Nation*, Sept. 12, 1987; COHA's *Washington Report on the Hemisphere*, Sept. 30, 1987. The six-month aid suspension ended in September 1987, though only after President Arias acceded to such U.S. demands as strengthening private banks at the expense of the state banking system; *Nation*, Sept. 19, 1987.

5. "Waking up from the dream of the 'victorious' contras," *Christian Science Monitor*, Aug. 24, 1987.

6. Rohwer, deputy foreign editor of the London *Economist*, *New York Times Book Review*, Sept. 20, 1987; I rephrase his rhetorical question. Rohwer is much in favor of the use of violence to "keep Marxists out of power" in the U.S. crusade for "democracy, human rights and economic growth" in Latin America, to which it has been dedicated for a century with such impressive results, just as Britain was in Africa and India in its day in the sun.

7. *New Republic*, September 8, 1986.

8. *Spectator*, Aug. 15, 1987; Churchill, *The Second World War*, vol. 5 (Houghton Mifflin, 1951), 382.

9. See *TTT, PI*.

10. *NYT*, Aug. 6, 1987.

11. Alfonso Chardy, *Miami Herald*, July 5, 1987.

12. I put aside here two reasonable questions that cannot be raised in the U.S. cultural climate: whether it would be legitimate for Nicaragua to obtain aircraft to defend itself from U.S. terrorism and aggression; and whether it would be proper to provide arms to people driven to the hills by U.S.-organized state terror to help them defend themselves, as in El Salvador; see *TTT*, 126f., 137. Comparable questions are permitted, and readily answered, with regard to U.S. support for its allies, or for victims

of state terror and aggression by official enemies, the guerrillas in Afganistan, for example.

13. A unique exception, to my knowledge, was Alexander Cockburn, *Wall St. Journal*, Aug. 13, 1987. See also the forthright criticism by Randolph Ryan, "Hollow talk of peace," *Boston Globe*, Aug. 8, 1987, noting that Nicaragua "cannot reasonably be expected to demobilize until the attack ends"—in fact, until the threat of attack ends, as we would agree in the case of any ally subject to threat of superpower violence, or even lesser threat.

14. Susan Kaufman Purcell, *NYT*, Aug. 12, 1987.

15. Wayne Smith, "How to Deal with Managua," *NYT*, Sept. 24, 1987.

16. See chapter 7 for further comment.

17. Consider, for example, Dennis Wrong's allegation (*New Republic*, Sept. 7, 1987) that the *Nation* features some "pro-Soviet writers," "notably Alexander Cockburn," who qualifies for the epithet because he is critical of the pieties of apologists for U.S. violence and sometimes refutes the propaganda devised to mobilize public support for U.S. repression and atrocities, thus challenging the important right to lie in service to the state. By the same logic, a Soviet dissident critical of the violence and repression of all sides who refutes lies about the United States in Soviet propaganda would be condemned by Party Liners as a "pro-American writer." Wrong adds that "'Zionism', of course, is a negative epithet in today's *Nation*," a journal that would be regarded as dovish Zionist by Israeli standards, but exhibits insufficient loyalty to Israel by the standards of this author or the journal in which he writes. It is unnecessary to comment on the irony of these paired accusations, the latter reflecting the familiar Stalinist caste of mind.

2

The Cultural-Historical Context

It is commonly supposed that the two Reagan "landslides" of the 1980s reflected a significant "right turn" in American politics and society, a rejection of the "disruptive" and "anarchic" mood of the sixties. In contrast to the war protestors, two commentators explain, "decent, patriotic Americans demanded—and in the person of Ronald Reagan have apparently achieved—a return to pride and patriotism, a reaffirmation of the values and virtues that had been trampled upon by the Vietnam-spawned counter-culture."[1] These "values and virtues," we are to understand, are exemplified in the Reagan Doctrine abroad and the Reaganite socioeconomic programs at home.

The "right turn" during the Reagan years is not unreal, but it is also not quite what it is often thought to be. Let us briefly consider two questions: first, what the "right turn" really is; and second, how it fits into deeper and more enduring features of American society and state policy. I will keep to foreign policy for the most part, though that is only one part of a much larger story.

To begin with, what is the "right turn"? Specifically, what are the policies of the Reagan administration, which are thought to exemplify them? Basically, they fall into three categories:

Transfer of resources from the poor to the wealthy

Increase in the state sector of the economy, and growth of state power in general

An "activist" foreign policy

The first of these goals was substantially achieved by fiscal measures and an attack on labor and the welfare system, both

already weak by international standards. The second program on
the agenda was conducted in the traditional way, by expanding the
protected state market for high technology waste production and
thus forcing a public subsidy to advanced sectors of industry; what
is called euphemistically "defense spending."[2] This has been the
most rapid military build-up in U.S. peacetime history.
Concomitantly, state spending increased more rapidly than at any
time since World War II, and the administration moved to protect
the more powerful state from public scrutiny by such measures as
censorship, limiting access to documents, and an enormous
increase in clandestine activities designed to diminish still further
any influence of the annoying public on affairs of state. It is
entirely in keeping with this commitment to state power that the
president should nominate for the Supreme Court a man described
as "critical of virtually every Supreme Court case protecting
individual liberties," whose "constitutional decisions can be
explained by a single principle: where there's government versus
the individual, the government always wins."[3]

The third plank in the program, the "activist" foreign policy, is
also of the traditional variety though again at an extreme of the
spectrum: intervention, subversion, aggression, international
terrorism, and general gangsterism and lawlessness, the essential
content of the highly-praised "Reagan doctrine." Its central
achievement was the organization of an onslaught of state
terrorism in El Salvador, which achieved its major goal: to avert
the threat of democracy and social reform by destroying "the
people's organizations fighting to defend their most fundamental
human rights," in the words of Archbishop Romero (soon to be
assassinated by elements of the U.S.-backed security forces) as he
pleaded with President Carter not to send military aid to the junta,
which would, of course, use it for exactly these purposes. Carter's
limited war was rapidly expanded under Reagan, yielding a
notable increase in the level of slaughter and general terror. The
operations were carried out by a U.S. mercenary army, trained,
supplied and directed by the United States. U.S. forces also
participated directly. U.S. air force units flying from foreign bases
coordinated air strikes, an innovation that yielded an immediate
improvement in the "kill rate" among defenseless villagers and
fleeing peasants. Long-range reconnaissance patrols were
conducted by CIA paramilitary agents who led and accompanied
Salvadoran units, allowing "the Reagan administration to secretly
exceed its publicly declared limit of 55 military advisers in El

Salvador" and to overcome the ban on participation by U.S. personnel in field operations; these operations were "spectacularly successful," according a U.S. official, in calling in "aircraft to hit the targets."[4]

When the savage terror had achieved its aims, and was becoming an impediment to further funding for the U.S. mercenary army, Washington ordered that the scale be restricted and removed further from public view, as was done, demonstrating with great clarity just who was controlling the process from the outset. The commanders in Washington are much lauded for this display of moderation.

Reagan also launched a war against Nicaragua with another mercenary army, an operation that at the very least must be "characterized as terrorism, as State-sponsored terrorism" (former CIA director Stansfield Turner, testifying before Congress in April 1985[5]), and possibly as the more serious crime of aggression, as implied in the World Court judgment. The general goal was to "fit Nicaragua back into a Central American mode" and compel it to observe the "regional standard," as advocated by the doves who are critical of Reagan's excessive zeal.[6]

The maximal objective in Nicaragua was to replace the Sandinista government by one more attuned to traditional U.S. standards for the region, one that will uphold the "Fifth Freedom," a crucial doctrine well-illustrated in the historical and documentary record.[7] The minimal objective, largely achieved, is dual: (1) to block and reverse social reform and diversion of resources to the needs of the poor majority, such measures as improvement of health services and production for domestic needs, involvement of the poor in the development process, literacy programs, and so on; (2) to force Nicaragua to rely on the Soviet Union for survival and thus to provide retrospective justification for the attack launched against it as punishment for the crime of undertaking social reforms. It was evident from the first days of the Reagan administration that its policies were designed to ensure that "Nicaragua will sooner or later become a Soviet client, as the U.S. imposes a stranglehold on its reconstruction and development, rebuffs efforts to maintain decent relations, and supports harassment and intervention," the standard policy adopted in the case of an enemy the U.S. undertakes to subvert or destroy.[8]

To attain the second of these goals, the U.S. rejected a Sandinista request for arms and training and pressured its allies to do the same, thereby ensuring that Nicaragua, lacking any other source, would become entirely dependent on Soviet arms; the U.S. blocked aid from international lending institutions to the same end. When the U.S. embargo was declared in May 1985, Nicaraguan trade with the Soviet bloc was about 20%, roughly the same as the U.S. and far less than Europe and the Third World, an intolerable situation that must be overcome so as to allow apologists for U.S. international terrorism to justify it as defense against Soviet imperialism.[9] The same U.S. policies, with their predictable effects, enable the Free Press to refer to "the Moscow-backed Government in Nicaragua," a phrase with appropriately ominous overtones and one that is literally correct, given the success of the Reagan administration in ensuring that Nicaragua must turn to the Soviet Union for defense against U.S. international terrorism. The Free Press may also proceed to characterize the U.S. war against Nicaragua as a conflict between "the Soviet-supported Sandinista regime" and "the United States backed rebels," thus establishing the framework of East-West confrontation required by state propaganda.[10] And it may invoke the frightening specter of "Soviet-supplied armaments" while bemoaning the fate of the poor contras, trying to fight "Soviet helicopters" with only "boots and bandages" (we return to the realities). These images help to instill the proper mood of fear and concern at home, even among liberal critics of the means adopted by the Reagan administration to defend ourselves from Soviet expansionism. Meanwhile commentators sagely ponder the Nicaraguan threat to conquer Central America as agents of Soviet imperialism, if not to invade Texas (as Reagan intimated) or provide bases for Soviet bombers attacking the United States (General John Singlaub).[11]

Elsewhere in the region, the "activist" policy included enthusiastic support for atrocities in Guatemala at a level unprecedented even by the standards that the U.S. has helped maintain since overthrowing Guatemalan democracy in 1954; the conversion of Honduras into a military base for U.S.-directed international terrorism; and the subversion of Costa Rican democracy by pressures upon Costa Rica, on pain of economic collapse, to line up in U.S. crusades against democracy and social reform in the region.

In Central America, the Reagan Doctrine deserves a large share of the credit for a most impressive slaughter. The death toll under Reagan in El Salvador passed 50,000 and in Guatemala it may approach 100,000. In Nicaragua, the terror was less successful, amounting to only some 11,000 civilians killed under Reagan by 1986[12]; the problem is that in Nicaragua the population has an army to defend it from the U.S.-organized terrorist forces, whereas in El Salvador and Guatemala the terrorist force attacking the civilian population *is* the army. The death toll under Reagan in this region alone thus amounts to 150,000 or more. This was, furthermore, not ordinary killing, but rather Pol Pot-style atrocities, with extensive torture, rape, mutilation, "disappearance," and similar measures to ensure that the populations would be properly traumatized. We may add over 20,000 killed during the U.S.-backed Israeli invasion of Lebanon in 1982, mostly civilians, and untold additional victims of international terrorism, starvation, disease and brutal labor.

Other exercises of the "activist" policy include the bombing of Libya in April 1986 with about 100 reported killed, the worst single act of international terrorism of the year; steps to ensure that South Africa would be able to maintain its illegal control over Namibia (virtually never discussed in the media) while disrupting its neighbors and preventing them from escaping the dependence on South Africa that is a legacy of the colonial system; support for continued Israeli terrorism in Lebanon, and so on.

In essence, that is the "right turn." Now three observations.

First, these policies are as far from "conservatism" as one can imagine. We might refer to them as "reactionary jingoism," or perhaps harsher terms are appropriate. There are few genuine conservatives within the U.S. political system, and it is a sign of the intellectual corruption of the age that the honorable term "conservatism" can be appropriated to disguise the advocacy of a powerful, lawless, aggressive and violent state, a welfare state for the rich dedicated to a lunatic form of Keynesian economic intervention that enhances state and private power while mortgaging the country's future.

Second, this "right turn" is generally supported by elite opinion across the political spectrum, apart from tactical disagreements. The policies were initiated by the liberal Carter administration, including the military build-up which largely follows its projections, the dismantling of the welfare state, the terrorist slaughter in El Salvador, and so on. There are differences, but they are within a general tendency that has won wide agreement. The Democratic opposition has broadly supported these policies, even the attack against Nicaragua, the most

controversial element of the Reagan program because of concern
that it might prove costly to the United States. U.S. international
terrorism in El Salvador also raised doubts when there was fear
that it might be unsuccessful and too costly to us, but such
criticism waned, replaced by avid enthusiasm, when the violence
began to achieve its goals and could be concealed behind an
electoral charade that merits comparison to the exercises in
"democracy" in the Soviet sphere that are lauded by *Pravda*,
though even this comparison may be too kind in the light of the
circumstances.[13]

We should also bear in mind that the second and third plank
of the Reagan program follow lines laid down by John F. Kennedy,
whose administration did not have to adopt Reagan's first plank
because U.S. power led them to believe that the U.S. could
construct "great societies at home and grand designs abroad"
(Presidential adviser Walter Heller). With the relative decline in
U.S. power, the great societies at home must now be abandoned, a
fact recognized by Kennedy's "neoliberal" descendants. Among
these descendants are some of the most enthusiastic supporters of
Reaganite atrocities, for example, the editors of the *New Republic*,
still the major organ of American liberalism, who urged Reagan to
proceed with the slaughter in El Salvador "regardless of how many
are murdered" and now congratulate him, and themselves, on the
successes achieved in this endeavor,[14] a performance that passes
without comment in a terrorist culture.

Third, the "right turn" is opposed by the general public. The
vote for Reagan in his "landslide" victories reached some 30% of
the electorate, and even that was largely an expression of
discontent with things as they were and with the pallid
Democratic alternatives; most voters hoped that Congress would
not enact Reagan's legislative program and a tiny percentage (about
1% of the electorate in 1984, down from 4% in 1980) voted for
him because they took him to be a true "conservative." As polls
have consistently shown, the public has continued a slow drift
towards support for New Deal-style policies, much preferring
social to military spending, supporting the rights of women,
workers, minorities and the poor, and so on.[15] The public also
overwhelmingly supports a nuclear freeze, and if more than a
small fraction had been aware of such Soviet initiatives as their
unilateral freeze, the public would undoubtedly have strongly
advocated U.S. participation. Opposition to the attack against
Nicaragua has also been high,[16] even though there is an elite

consensus on "containing Nicaragua" and positive comments about the Sandinistas have long been effectively barred from mainstream discourse, an important matter to which I return. By 1987, polls indicate, the public want "their next President to distance himself from President Reagan's policies" by more than 2 to 1, "by a significant margin think Vice President Bush's association with Reagan will hurt rather than help his chances to become President," and "trust Congress over Reagan when it comes to solving the nation's major problems by nearly a 2-1 margin"; and by a similar margin the public says that things in this country "have gotten pretty seriously off on the wrong track," with "a resurgence of the cynicism and negativism that marked the Watergate/oil embargo/inflation-scarred years of the past decade."[17]

In summary, the "Right Turn" surely exists, but it represents an elite consensus, tactical considerations aside, with few and scattered exceptions. And throughout, it has been in large measure inconsistent with the public mood. Furthermore, it is anything but "conservative."

The "right turn" among elites began in the early 1970s, in response to problems caused in large measure by the Vietnam war. These problems fell into two major categories: economic and disciplinary.

The economic problem was that the war proved costly to the United States and beneficial to its industrial rivals. Canada, for example, became the largest per capita war exporter, enriching itself on the destruction of Indochina while deploring American brutality.[18] The most important case was Japan. The Japanese economy began to recover with the stimulus of the Korean war, but it was the Vietnam war that really moved it into high gear thanks to U.S. military procurements. The Kennedy administration was concerned to find ways to ensure the viability of the Japanese economy, but that has not been the problem in the post-Vietnam years. In 1965, the trade balance shifted in favor of Japan, reaching serious proportions by the 1980s. As for Europe, the trade balance began to shift in Europe's favor in the late 1950s,[19] and the relative decline in U.S. power became noticeable, and disturbing to elite opinion, as a consequence of the Vietnam war. South Korean "take-off" also dates from that period, with the Vietnam war responsible for some 20% of its foreign exchange earnings during the war, including pay for some 300,000 Korean mercenaries introduced from January 1965 to "defend South Vietnam" by terrorizing its population.[20]

It was therefore necessary for the government to undertake measures to restore the profitability and power of U.S. business. Nixon began the process by suspending the convertibility of the dollar and imposing a 10% surcharge on imports, in violation of international commitments. These steps were unpopular among some business and financial circles, but the domestic measures of the following years received wide elite support: the attack on labor and social programs, the forced subsidy to advanced industry through the Pentagon system, and the other programs instituted as the Reagan administration undertook the required "right turn."[21]

The disciplinary problems were of two types: international and domestic. Parts of the Third World were out of control with the collapse of the Portuguese Empire and the growing ferment in Latin America. These problems require an "activist" foreign policy, which in turn requires a jingoist consensus, at least among the elite and politically active segments of the population.

There were also disciplinary problems at home, where much of the population was also out of control. The Vietnam war contributed to the politicization of American society. The naive might call this democracy, but sophisticated Western thinkers understand that it is, as they called it, a "crisis of democracy," which must be overcome by returning the generally marginalized population to the passivity that is their proper state. This is necessary if "democracy" is to survive in the Orwellian sense of proper discourse, where the term refers to unhampered rule by business-based sectors, a system of elite decision with periodic public ratification, but, crucially, no significant public role in the formation of state policy. It was thus necessary to return the population to apathy and obedience, to restore discipline in the institutions responsible for "the indoctrination of the young," to exclude the limited forms of dissent that had appeared in the media, and in general, to bar any serious challenge to elite rule. These problems, in fact, had arisen worldwide. They were addressed in the first major publication of the Trilateral Commission, formed at the initiative of David Rockefeller to bring together liberal elites from the United States, Europe and Japan; it is their 1975 study of "the crisis of democracy" that I have been quoting and paraphrasing.[22]

Every major war of this century has evoked a similar reaction on the part of dominant social groups: business, the political elites that are primarily business-based, the corporate media, and the privileged intelligentsia generally, serving as ideological managers. During and after World War I, the Wilson administration, under the pretext of a Bolshevik threat, launched a "Red Scare" that succeeded in deterring the threat of democracy (in the true sense of the word) while reinforcing "democracy" in the technical Orwellian sense. With broad liberal support, the Red Scare succeeded in undermining the labor movement and dissident politics, and reinforcing corporate power. Two lasting institutional developments from that period, of great consequence, are the rise of the Public Relations industry, dedicated quite openly to controlling "the public mind," and the national political police (the FBI). It was also at that time that liberal democratic theorists such as Walter Lippmann began to discuss the importance of "the manufacture of consent" as a means of controlling the population in societies in which the state lacks the requisite force for internal coercion. These ideas were to become a major theme in the academic social sciences and the Public Relations industry.

World War II had similar consequences, the most familiar being the phenomenon mislabelled "McCarthyism"—in fact, a broad-based effort spearheaded by business, its Public Relations industry and liberal Democrats to overcome the "crisis of democracy" then brewing. In 1938, the National Association of Manufacturers Board of Directors had observed that "the hazard facing industrialists" is "the newly realized political power of the masses"; "unless their thinking is redirected," they warned, "we are definitely headed for adversity." Substantial efforts were undertaken to overcome this threat, with considerable success. In 1947, State Department public relations officer Melton Davis commented that "smart public relations [has] paid off as it has before and will again," moving "the public opinion climate" sharply to the right—"anti-social change, anti-economic change, anti-labor," at the same time that "the rest of the world," including Europe, "has moved to the left, has admitted labor into the government [and] passed liberalized legislation." The climate in the United States "is not moving to the right, it has been moved—cleverly—to the right," he observed, in contrast to Europe. These developments in the rest of the world caused much concern, and U.S. power was applied to reverse them.[23]

The point is that wars and other periods of turmoil tend to make people think, to involve them in social and political action, creating a "crisis of democracy," that is, a threat that there might be meaningful steps towards democracy. Dominant elites must rally to prevent this threat to their privilege and power. The current "Right Turn" thus falls into a regular and natural pattern. It has been highly successful among educated elites, but much less so among the general population, in contrast to earlier exercises. Some of the central features of the Reagan Doctrine are a response to this problem, to which we now turn.

Notes Chapter Two

1. Allan Goodman and Seth Tillman, *NYT*, March 24, 1985.

2. True believers in Reaganomics are dissatisfied, though budget deficits "have at least restrained Congress from launching big new domestic spending programs"—meaning, programs directed to the needs of the poor, rather than the wealthy, for whom state spending has vastly increased through the military system. They complain that "there has been some deregulation—but less than in the Carter administration. International trade is more regulated than it was 10 years ago" (William Niskanen, formerly of the Council of Economic Advisers under Reagan). Treasury Secretary James Baker commented that "President Reagan has granted more import relief to U.S. industry than any of his predecessors in more than half a century." Lindley Clark, *Wall Street Journal*, Sept. 24, 1987. In short, not a limited state, but a more powerful one, which serves the wealthy and privileged.

3. Erwin Chemerinsky, professor of constitutional law at the University of Southern California, speaking for a group of lawyers opposing the nomination of Judge Robert Bork, reflecting the views of civil libertarians rather generally; Bernard Weinraub, *NYT*, Aug. 29, 1987. A principle that emerges with still greater clarity is that where there's business versus anyone, business wins. On Bork's muddled thinking and "fake" scholarship, see Ronald Dworkin, *New York Review*, Aug. 13, 1987; Arthur Schlesinger, *WSJ*, Sept. 24, 1987. Perhaps the most remarkable feature of his hearings was his bland dismissal of his academic work, as not to be taken seriously, an interesting attitude towards the profession, and towards integrity.

4. Doyle McManus, *MH*, *Los Angeles Times* news service, July 9, 1987. These CIA operations were revealed in the Iran-contra hearings by the committee counsel, from Oliver North's notes of a discussion with Gen. Paul Gorman, then commander of the U.S. Southern Command. See also Frank Smyth, *Village Voice*, Aug. 11, 1987, with evidence from War College documents and military sources on participation by U.S. Special Forces, including combat operations.

5. Cited by Peter Kornbluh in Thomas Walker, ed., *Reagan vs. the Sandinistas* (Westview, 1987), from testimony before the House Subcommittee on Western Hemispheric Affairs, April 16, 1985.

6. Editorial, *Washington Post*, weekly edition, March 31, 1986.

7. See Preface, and *TTT*, chapter 2.

8. Chomsky, *Towards a New Cold War*, 51; this went to press a few months after the Reagan inauguration, when the policy outlines were already entirely clear.

9. See *TTT*, 54; Bradford Burns, *At War in Nicaragua* (Harper & Row, 1987), 34; Theodore Schwab and Harold Sims, in Thomas Walker, ed., *Nicaragua: The First Five Years* (Praeger, 1985); Walker, *Nicaragua* (Westview, 1986), 67. See *TTT*, chapter 2.2, for futher discussion.

10. Neil Lewis, Sept. 13, 1987 (we return to the context of these particular warnings in chapter 7); James LeMoyne, *NYT*, Aug. 10, 1987; and innumerable other examples. These have been, in fact, the standard and virtually invariant terms of news reporting and commentary as the U.S. attack intensified.

11. Testifying in the Iran-contra hearings. See also Bernard Trainor, "U.S. Fears Soviet Use of New Nicaraguan Airfield," *NYT*, July 26, 1987, replaying the Grenadan farce. For details on the media version of the "Soviet helicopters" versus "boots and bandages" struggle, and media coverage of Nicaragua generally, see Jack Spence, in Walker, *Reagan vs. the Sandinistas*.

12. Estimates for Guatemala and Nicaragua are by Piero Gleijeses and John Booth, respectively, *Current History*, Dec. 1986.

13. See Edward Herman and Frank Brodhead, *Demonstration Elections* (South End, 1984), and for foreign reactions, *TTT*, 117f. See Herman and Brodhead for a detailed comparison with "a Soviet-sponsored demonstration election" in Poland, which did not deter Robert Leiken, attempting to evade their critique of his distortion of their concept of "demonstration elections" in the course of his pro-contra crusade, from accusing them of designing the concept "as a way of focusing attention on Western imperialism while diverting it from Soviet imperialism," a standard reflex when deceit is exposed. *New York Review of Books*, Dec. 5, 1985.

14. We return to the matter, p. 226-7.

15. For details, see *TTT*, chapter 5; Thomas Ferguson and Joel Rogers, *Right Turn* (Hill & Wang, 1986).

16. An apparent shift towards contra support after Oliver North's testimony at the Iran-contra hearings proved temporary; see *NYT*, August 7, 1987. Note that as in the case of the Vietnam war, at certain stages, much of the popular opposition may well be of the "win or get out" variety. For people to gain a rational understanding of what their government is doing is very difficult, given the character of the ideological system.

17. David Lamb, *Los Angeles Times*, Feb. 26, 1987, reporting an *LA Times* poll; David Broder, *WP weekly*, July 27, 1987, reporting a *WP*-ABC poll.

18. On the Canadian role, see my "Towards Global War," *Studies on Political Economy* (Ottawa), Summer 1985; Victor Levant, *Quiet Complicity* (Between the Lines, Toronto, 1986).

19. Alfred Grosser, *The Western Alliance* (Continuum, 1980), 8, 178.

20. Bruce Cumings, "The origins and development of the Northeast Asia political economy," *International Organization*, Winter 1984. On some of the Korean exploits, see Chomsky and Edward Herman, *Political Economy of Human Rights* (South End, 1979), I, 5.1.4.

21. See Ferguson and Rogers, *Right Turn*.

22. M. J. Crozier, S. P. Huntington and J. Watanuki, *The Crisis of Democracy* (New York U. press, 1975).

23. See Alex Carey, "Managing Public Opinion: the Corporate Offensive," ms., New South Wales, 1986. On the measures taken to deal with the problems in Japan and Europe, see my paper "The 'Right Turn' in American Politics and the Decline of the Grand Area," ms., May 1987, delivered at the conference on Switzerland, the United States and the Third World, Fribourg, May 1987, from which some of these remarks are taken.

3

The Problems of Clandestine Terrorism

Four important features of domestic U.S. society relevant to the issues we are considering are: (1) the effective exclusion of the majority of the population from meaningful participation in the political system; (2) the subordination of the intellectual establishment to the system of state-private power; (3) the limits on the capacity of the state to control its citizens by force; (4) the substantial improvement in the moral and intellectual level of the general population resulting from the mass popular movements of the 1960s and the 1970s.[1] The interplay of these factors has complex effects.

Consider the attack against Nicaragua by the U.S.-organized contra armies. The public generally opposes aid to the contras, just as it opposed virtually every major program of the Reagan administration. But central policy issues are largely excluded from the corporate media and barely arise in the political system, one reason why voting continues to decline, to barely 37% in the November 1986 elections.

Nevertheless, popular dissidence remains significant and cannot be controlled by force. Congress, which is somewhat responsive to the public mood, raised a number of barriers to direct U.S. aggression against Nicaragua. This compelled the Reagan administration to devise a complex array of covert means to maintain its mercenary army attacking Nicaragua. Arms were sent to the contras through a shadowy network of CIA subsidiaries and "private" organizations controlled by U.S. ex-generals in close coordination with the White House.[2] Notorious international terrorists were enlisted in the cause, for example, Luis Posada Carriles, a CIA-trained Cuban exile sprung from a Venezuelan prison where he was charged with planning the 1976 bombing of a Cubana airliner with 73 civilians killed, then taken to El Salvador to help organize the contra supply network from the U.S.-controlled Ilopango Air Base.[3] The Reagan administration took over the World Anti-Communist League, a collection of Nazis who had been recruited by the U.S. as part of its global campaign against the anti-fascist resistance in the immediate post-World War II period, fanatic anti-Semites, death squad assassins, torturers and killers from around the world, backed by U.S. client states such as South Korea and Taiwan. This organization was converted into an instrument of international terrorism from Mozambique to Nicaragua.[4] Profits from U.S. arms sales to Iran via Israel with Saudi Arabian funding, undertaken for entirely different purposes to which we return, were diverted to the contras through Swiss banks, along with tens of millions of dollars from long-term clients such as Taiwan and Saudi Arabia, and targets of opportunity such as the Sultan of Brunei. In what the *Far Eastern Economic Review* describes as a particularly "remarkable case of arms diplomacy," the U.S. succeeded in arranging a cooperative effort of China and Taiwan "to help the anti-Communist Nicaraguan resistance [sic]," in a November 1984 deal arranged by Oliver North whereby China shipped arms to the contras through Canadian arms dealers and Portugal, funded by Taiwan.[5] The level of support developed through these state-private networks was so large that when $10 million solicited by the State Department from the Sultan was misplaced, the loss was not even noticed. Such machinations provided the contra armies with an air force and military equipment in violation of explicit congressional legislation and U.S. laws going back to the 18th century Neutrality Act, enabling them to maintain some forces within Nicaragua and to continue the terrorist activities that are generally ignored by the U.S. media and dismissed by apologists as "Sandinista atrocity allegations."[6]

In such ways, the Reagan administration constructed an international terrorist network of impressive sophistication, without parallel in history to my knowledge, and used it for a variety of purposes in conformity with the Reagan Doctrine, as already discussed.

Some eyebrows were raised when it was disclosed, after the public phase of the Iran-contra hearings concluded, that "Senior

Reagan administration officials approved a plan in early 1984," with the agreement of Secretary of State George Shultz (as a CIA cable indicated), to enlist South Africa too in contra support operations, and that Edén Pastora's forces in the south received 200,000 pounds of equipment from South Africa, so the CIA reported in February 1985. But after what Duane Clarridge, the CIA official in charge of the agency's covert support for the contras, called the "hullabaloo" over the CIA mining of the harbors, there were "some second thoughts around town as to the wisdom" of involving South Africa (John McMahon, CIA deputy director, in an April 1984 cable), and the plan was shelved. As the *Times* puts it, the administration "explicitly ruled out any countries with human rights problems or those dependent on American aid"; the State Department solicited aid only "from countries that had good human rights records," such as "South Korea, Saudi Arabia and Singapore," also Taiwan, China, Israel, all with "good human rights records" by *Times* standards and "not dependent on American aid."[7]

It is important to bear in mind that the reliance on clandestine terrorism and proxy forces was undertaken to evade public opinion and its weak reflection in congressional legislation. Clandestine operations are not a secret to their victims, or, generally, to foreign powers and other groups, including business interests out to make a buck, foreign states, shady characters of the Manucher Ghorbanifar variety regarded by Oliver North as an Israeli agent as well as a "liar" and a "cheat" while North relied upon his advice as to how to evade congressional legislation, and so on. It is the domestic population which must be protected from knowledge of these operations, because it would not approve them; otherwise, they need not be secret. As we shall see, Congress and the media helped to conceal the operations until the task became virtually impossible, and now seek to limit any significant understanding of them. Such tactics are a natural feature of the "right turn," given its restricted nature as an elite phenomenon.

It is normal for the state to regard the domestic population as a major enemy, which must be excluded, repressed or controlled to serve elite interests. This contempt for the citizenry and for the democratic processes that to some extent reflect their concerns has been a notable feature of the Reagan administration, revealed with some clarity in the congressional hearings despite their narrow focus and evasion of such matters. An intriguing case arose when the questioning of Col. North by Rep. Jack Brooks touched upon his plan to suspend the Constitution and impose martial law in the event of "national crises" such as "violent and widespread internal dissent or national opposition to a U.S. military invasion abroad." In this event, control of the United States was to be turned over to the national crisis-management unit FEMA, directed by Louis Guiffrida. He is a close associate of Reagan and Edwin Meese who, while at the Army War College in 1970, wrote a memorandum recommending internment of all "American Negroes" in "assemble-centers or relocation camps," in the event of civil disorder. Chairman Daniel Inouye quickly intervened to terminate this line of questioning, and these crucial disclosures were also evaded by the national media, unreported in the *New York Times*, for example, apart from the few sentences in the aborted congressional questioning.[8]

The same fear of the domestic population is what lies behind the resort to a clandestine international terrorist network within the framework of the Reagan Doctrine. A central principle of a terrorist culture is that these crucial facts must be obscured, and indeed they are.

In the case of the contra armies, their massive support, supply system, training, access to U.S. intelligence, radio and TV penetration of Nicaragua, and foreign sanctuaries, are far beyond anything available to authentic guerrilla forces[9]; if a real guerrilla movement such as the one in El Salvador had a fraction of the support lavished on the contras, it would have quickly become a major military force and the U.S.-imposed regime would have long ago collapsed. Nevertheless, the CIA-directed proxy army proved unable to move beyond random terrorism, so that the CIA was once again compelled—as when it carried out the mining of harbors and attacks on oil installations—to employ its own commando groups, now parachuted into Nicaragua to conduct sabotage missions from aircraft piloted by mercenaries (including Belgians, former Rhodesian citizens and Americans) working under CIA contract. These operations are conducted from command centers in El Salvador and Honduras and U.S. ships off the Atlantic and Pacific coasts of Nicaragua.[10] The CIA is "choosing precise military targets for the rebels," the *New York Times* reports, providing them "with precise information on dams, bridges, electrical substations, port facilities," etc.; these "precise military targets" were built by the Army Corps of Engineers and other U.S. agencies that supply maps, blueprints and floor plans to facilitate missions by the commandos of the foreign power attacking Nicaragua.[11]

As the Spring Offensive of the refurbished proxy army began, its forces were directed by their U.S. controllers to "[go] after soft targets...not [try] to duke it out with the Sandinistas directly," so General John Galvin, commander of the U.S. Southern Command, explained to Congress and the media, adding that with these more sensible tactics, aimed at civilians lacking means of defense against armed terrorist bands, prospects for the contras would improve. Months later, U.S. and Western military observers noted that "the contras have yet to chalk up a major, atten tion-getting battle success anywhere in Nicaragua... [T]he offensive has not been able to get past Sandinista defenses to move down from the mountains to populous towns, let alone cities, or to strike critical objectives. 'They're still going after small, soft targets' like farmers' cooperatives, the U.S. military analyst says."[12]

Under the Reagan doctrine, the United States has created something new in the annals of international terrorism: a lavishly equipped army organized not for combat but for terror, maintained in the field through an extensive supply system provided and protected by the superpower sponsor, directed to attacking "small, soft targets," to bleeding the victim, which is far too weak to maintain a viable society, let alone persist in social reform, in the face of such a superpower assault. This achievement stands alongside the creation of a terrorist army dedicated to suppressing the population by massive violence in El Salvador, and support for a similar force, in part through the medium of mercenary states, in Guatemala. The program has largely been a success in its basic aims, not very surprisingly, given the balance of force. And there is every reason to expect it to continue, in one or another form, whatever agreements are written down on paper, just as there is little doubt that it will be criticized by responsible opinion only for occasional failings in the pursuit of a noble cause that reveals the benevolence of our intentions.

We should also not overlook the fact that the U.S. strategic weapons system and its intervention forces have constantly been used in the war against Nicaragua. The former serves its traditional function of "deterrence": namely, providing a "nuclear umbrella" to deter any interference with U.S. policies of subversion, aggression and international terrorism—the primary meaning of "deterrence," dismissing here familiar Orwellisms.[13] The threat of overwhelming U.S. force is a crucial factor in maintaining the proxy army attacking Nicaragua. As agreed on all sides, this military force does not remotely resemble guerrillas in any meaningful sense of the term. It has never attempted to formulate a political program or to construct a substantial popular base, even in areas where the government is highly unpopular. The civiliah front constructed by the United States to soften the terrorist image for domestic purposes has also lacked the interest or competence to attempt even perfunctory moves in this direction. The U.S.-controlled troops can survive in the field only with an extensive supply system, including daily air drops by mid-1987, an elaborate intelligence apparatus also provided by the foreign master, and armaments beyond the dreams of authentic guerrillas. We return to details, but again, the essential facts are not in doubt. It is therefore absolutely necessary to ensure that Nicaragua not be permitted to obtain the means to defend its territory from hostile penetration by a U.S. air supply operation, with an air force of its own, adequate anti-aircraft systems, and so on. That Nicaragua must remain defenseless is accepted across the U.S. political spectrum. Such liberal doves as Senators Paul Tsongas and Christopher Dodd agree that Nicaragua must not be permitted to defend its national territory; Tsongas went so far as to assert that the U.S. would have to bomb Nicaragua should it obtain jet planes, because "they're also capable against the United States," a remark too outlandish to merit comment, except insofar as it illuminates the hysterical intellectual climate in a terrorist superpower.[14] The threat of overwhelming U.S. violence in reserve serves to guarantee that U.S. directives in this regard will not be infringed, a crucial contribution to the survival of the mercenary forces attacking Nicaragua.

U.S. conventional forces are more directly engaged in Central America, not only in such operations as coordinating air strikes in El Salvador but also in the U.S. attack against Nicaragua. The regular maneuvers in Honduras have the dual purpose of creating a U.S. military base in defiance of congressional directives, and compelling Nicaragua to maintain a permanent state of mobilization against the regular threat of invasion. The deployment of 50,000 U.S. forces in maneuvers in May 1987 served a still more specific function. It was a crucial part of the Spring Offensive of the contra armies; the U.S. maneuvers were designed to draw the Nicaraguan army away from population defense so that the terrorist army could prove to Congress that it could achieve sufficient success in its attacks against "soft targets" so as to merit continued support.

When a U.S. ally is forced to mobilize by threatening actions, we regard this threat as tantamount to aggression, justifying a pre-emptive military strike in self-defense. When Israel was compelled to mobilize in late May 1967 as Arab armies were deployed in threatening positions, U.S. and Western opinion generally regarded this as intolerable—how can Israel be expected to sustain mobilization for more than a few days?—so that Israel's attack was therefore justified in self-defense. Israel was not an impoverished country under attack by a terrorist superpower, but when U.S. military threat compels Nicaragua to maintain permanent mobilization, and to remove its forces from defense of the civilian population so as to clear the way for U.S.-organized terrorists, there is barely a critical word in the media (or in the West rather generally)—except, of course, condemnation of Nicaragua for maintaining defensive military forces, and particularly, for obtaining Soviet arms after the Western allies have refused, under U.S. pressure, to provide them with means to withstand the U.S. terrorist assault, obviously the ultimate proof that they are mere Soviet clients, barely deserving to be called Nicaraguans, a major threat to our security. Putting aside the moral cowardice, the reaction is understandable within a terrorist culture, where it is, furthermore, a crucial obligation to feign ignorance of these obvious facts, systematically suppressed in the media and journals of opinion.

Although the toll of direct murder has been less satisfactory in Nicaragua than in El Salvador and Guatemala, it is a grand success of the Reagan Doctrine, and is no doubt celebrated as such, when thousands of children again die from epidemics that had been eradicated by the early reforms of the Sandinistas. These have been reversed, much to the relief of Washington, along with achievements in literacy and economic development, as a result of U.S.-organized terrorism aimed at "soft targets" accompanied with an embargo and pressures on allies and international lending institutions, and the constant threat of invasion. We read an occasional report that "in Nicaragua's remote countryside," the health care programs that had "dramatically lowered" infant mortality and preventable disease are deteriorating, now underfunded because the government has been forced to "put more of their meager resources into the war effort" and because the U.S. proxy forces have attacked such "soft targets" as health programs and schools, destroying over 60 health centers and killing or kidnapping large numbers of medical workers. In one village, 150 children died of measles because contras prevented government health workers, regular assassination targets, from reaching them; and tuberculosis and other diseases are again reaching epidemic proportions, while hospitals and health centers lack medicine and equipment and malnutrition is beginning to rise and might even return to its earlier levels if U.S. efforts succeed. Infant mortality, cut in half by Sandinista health reforms, is on the rise, and hospitals that had previously served only the richest 2% of the population but were opened without cost for the general public under the Sandinistas are now unable to function because of the "increasing demand for care" and the lack of supplies, thanks to the U.S. attack and embargo. Similarly, while the number of teachers has almost tripled, supplies are close to nonexistent. "The Contras Have Learned to Hit Where It Hurts," a headline in the *Washington Post* reads, with a report on how the contra army, "reportedly in high spirits and outfitted by the CIA," succeeded in burning down "a church-sponsored health clinic that had been the pride of the community" in the isolated village of Tapalse, proudly reported by the major contra military group (FDN) as "one of its 'most important operations'."[15]

These are among the consequences of the dedication of the United States to reducing Nicaragua to the zero grade of life. In assessing the crimes of Pol Pot, we rightly count not only those killed outright, but also the victims of disease, malnutrition, and harsh conditions of labor. Those capable of escaping the indoctrination system may recall that the chorus of protest over Khmer Rouge "genocide" or "autogenocide" reached its peak of outrage in early 1977, at a time when State Department intelligence—the only source with substantial information—estimated the toll at "tens if not hundreds of thousands" from all causes, primarily "disease, malnutrition or other factors" rather than outright killing—an estimate that stands up rather well in the light of subsequent scholarship.[16] But respectable opinion would never consider an assessment of the Reagan Doctrine or earlier exercises in terms of their actual human costs, and could not comprehend that such an assessment—which would yield a monstrous toll if accurately conducted on a global scale—might perhaps be a proper task in the United States. At the same level of integrity, disciplined Soviet intellectuals are horrified over real or alleged American crimes, but perceive their own only as benevolent intent gone awry, or errors of an earlier day, now overcome; the comparison is inexact and unfair, since Soviet intellectuals can plead fear as an excuse for their services to state violence.

In the real world, the people of Nicaragua must be punished for the criminal effort of the Sandinista government to divert resources to the poor majority. This crime explains "the firm belief" of the Reagan administration that "the Sandinistas must be overthrown or, at least, theirs must become a revolution of misery, a frightful object lesson to the people of the region,"[17] who must be deterred from similar heresies. We may then observe their "miseries" with undisguised pleasure, congratulating ourselves in the *New York Times* that "America's pugnacity" has compelled them to "keep their miseries to themselves."[18]

Much the same thinking lay behind the U.S. resort to large-scale terror against the rural population of South Vietnam. As Kennedy-Johnson adviser General Maxwell Taylor explained to Congress, "We intend to show that the 'war of liberation'...is costly, dangerous and doomed to failure,"[19] as is any attempt by suffering people to modify the rules of the international order maintained by its powerful beneficiaries, Winston Churchill's "rich men dwelling at peace within their habitations" who are to run the world by virtue of this status. The same reasons explain why this commitment of the Reagan administration represents an elite consensus, and why the plain and simple truth of the matter is barely expressible within the cultural mainstream.

It may also be recalled that the previous state of grim suffering and death in Nicaragua, to which we must again reduce them, elicited scarcely a flicker of interest among the educated classes in the United States, just as the perpetuation of these circumstances in Honduras and elsewhere evokes no concern today. Rather, it was the effort to overcome the grim consequences of a century of U.S. dominance that aroused horror and indignation (concealed in the usual "anti-Communist" disguise), along with a dedicated commitment to restore Nicaragua to the "Central American mode," in the approving words of the editors of the *Washington Post*, to which we return.

Terrorist attacks on "soft targets" such as health clinics and schools serve obvious purposes. The perceived threat of the Sandinistas was that despite their meager resources and the horrifying conditions left by the final phase of the U.S.-backed Somoza terror, they might be able to introduce the kinds of reforms that would have appeal both in neighboring countries, and in regions of Nicaragua where the Somoza regime maintained a degree of popular support within the peasant society and there was antagonism to Sandinista measures, sometimes conducted foolishly and even brutally, particularly in the early period. But the fear of successful reform can be overcome by destroying health services, schools and cooperative farms. It is, therefore, only rational to direct the proxy army to attack such "soft targets," and in the generally remote areas where the terrorist forces can penetrate, these policies have had some success in their aims, so the occasional press reports indicate. Thus in Jinotega province near the Honduran border, Peter Ford reports, contras have succeeded in terrorizing civilians by ambushing trucks with many civilian casualties, killing many doctors, health workers and teachers, forcing the government to close newly opened schools and clinics, and repeatedly burning down houses, educational facilities, cooperative stores, community kitchens and so on, causing such random destruction that cooperative "members barely manage to feed themselves, let alone make a profit from their harvests." The contra leaders also deliver what counts as a "political speech" by U.S. standards: namely, a warning to the cooperative members that if they rebuild their community "100 times, they would destroy it 100 times," so a peasant woman reports.[20] The expectation is that these tactics will abort measures of reform and national integration, fuel discontent, and, ultimately, bring the population to understand that only by a return to "the Central American mode" established by the United States will the terror come to an end.

Partisans of U.S. terror have constructed a special vocabulary to conceal their satisfaction with the achievements of the Reagan Doctrine despite its possible "flaws." Thus, *New Republic* editor Morton Kondracke warns us that failure to stay the course may "jeopardize all that has been achieved for democracy in recent years" in Central America.[21] Meanwhile, at the left-liberal extreme of the expressible spectrum, Charles Lane explains in the same journal, apparently without irony, that the Reagan Doctrine sought "a low-cost way to reconcile America's noble wish for democratic development in the Third World with its muscular desire to overcome the Vietnam syndrome." But while the Doctrine may have succeeded in El Salvador, he continues, it is threatened by American impatience in Nicaragua, where "the United States finds itself faced with a society and a culture that can't be made

democratic as quickly as it would like" by "armed rebel-
lion"—incidentally, supported by such stellar democracies as
Argentina under the rule of the neo-Nazi generals, Taiwan, Saudi
Arabia and South Korea, and organized at home by such
enthusiasts of democratic processes as William Casey, Edwin
Meese, John Poindexter, and the rest of the cabal. Critics of the
Reagan Doctrine are concerned that the Reagan administration's
"active promotion of democracy" may be too "aggressive" (John
Rielly), that our efforts "to force the Sandinista revolution into the
American democratic mold" may not be worth "the risk" (John
Oakes), and that Nicaragua may be "beyond the reach of our good
intentions" (Jefferson Morley).[22] Lane, Oakes and Morley are at the
outer limits of dissent within mainstream journalism. Beyond this
spectrum of respectable opinion, we have only those whom
McGeorge Bundy once described as "wild men in the wings,"
referring to people who dared to question the "first team" that was
in charge of our earlier crusade for democracy in Vietnam.[23]

Faith in our "good intentions" remains unimpaired by the
historical record in Central America and the Caribbean, not to
speak of Southeast Asia, Africa, the Middle East and elsewhere;
and properly so, given the irrelevance of the historical and
documentary record in a terrorist culture, which carefully avoids
any institutional critique and can always appeal to the doctrine of
"change of course" if nothing else avails. U.S. sponsorship in
Central America of some of the most horrendous atrocities of
recent years elicits only the thought that some problems there may
be "beyond the reach of our good intentions." The reaction was
similar when popular opposition to brutal dictatorship and state
terror in South Korea, long supported by the United States,
reached a level difficult to ignore by 1987; the resulting outburst of
anti-Americanism evoked the reflection that "imposing American
morality on other countries' political systems is a ticklish
business," nothing more.[24]

The doctrine of "good intentions" is beyond challenge, even
beyond awareness—at least at home. Others manage a clearer
view, even among our allies. As the U.S. was exploiting Britain's
travail to take over its traditional domains during World War II, the
British foreign services were able to penetrate the ideological
mask. In their wartime records, we read that "American
imperialism is in the forefront in the conduct of affairs in the Far
East," as elsewhere, "attempting to elbow us out." The High
Commissioners of the British Dominions warned of "the economic

imperialism of American business interests, which is quite active under the cloak of a benevolent and avuncular internationalism." As for the fabled "benevolence" of the United States, a staple of Western ideological systems, the Minister of State at the British Foreign Office, Richard Law, commented to his Cabinet colleagues that Americans believe "that the United States stands for something in the world—something of which the world has need, something which the world is going to like, something, in the final analysis, which the world is going to take, whether it likes it or not"[25]—a good succinct summary of U.S. foreign policy and its conventional disguise.

Such insights are commonly achieved by the victims: the British displaced by U.S. "economic imperialism"; the peasants subjected to somewhat more rigorous measures of discipline in Central America, Southeast Asia and elsewhere; or the European working classes who were called upon to bear the costs of the reconstruction of capitalism in the interests of U.S. investors and their local associates in the early postwar period. It is the task of the educated classes to conceal these facts as they discourse about the nobility of the "American purpose" and other familiar doctrines, a task that they have conducted with considerable success, and in the United States, with notable uniformity and devotion.

To maintain discipline abroad often proves a harder task. From early on, the Reagan administration has elicited criticism and serious concern, even in conservative circles, for heightening world tension and "debasing the language of international intercourse with feverish rhetoric," creating a "chasm" between "current American perceptions of the world and the world's perception of America" (David Watt, Director of the Royal Institute of International Affairs in London). While U.S. terrorism in Nicaragua was still "clandestine"—meaning well-known, but kept under cover—Canada's leading newspaper, generally restrained and pro-U.S., condemned the Reagan administration for acts of "madness" in organizing a "band of cutthroats" to attack Nicaragua under the direction of its "bizarre cowboy leader" in Washington. As Washington sought to undermine the Central American accords of August 1987, the centrist British press virtually pleaded with President Reagan to "come to terms with reality in Central America" and allow the peace plan to proceed instead of "financing a murderous and incompetent band of Contra mercenaries" in his "obsession with the overthrow of the elected government of Nicaragua," a crusade that "has brought dishonour to him and his Administration":

> It also flouts rulings by the International Court of Justice, and parallels the so-called Soviet 'Brezhnev doctrine' as applied in Afghanistan and Eastern Europe. Not least, it has caused the deaths of tens of thousands of men, women and children and million of pounds' worth of destruction in an already wretchedly poor area of the world.
>
> For all Washington's propaganda efforts, the US is seen internationally as the loser and the Sandinistas as one of the more genuinely popular regimes in Central America. Nicaragua is so weakly aligned to the Soviet Union that Mr Gorbachov has cut off its oil supplies. Meanwhile, the country that proclaims itself the world's greatest democracy aligns itself with regimes, such as those in Guatemala, Honduras and El Salvador, which are little more than façades for military rule... The symbol of the Republican Party has, of course, always been that of an elephant. It is dismaying to watch it behaving true to form with a gnat.[26]

Such perceptions would be difficult to find in the domestic counterparts of these national journals, though in a few U.S. client states there is a sympathetic popular response to Reaganite "madness."[27]

While exercises of international terrorism cause problems among the allies, there are compensations as well. The state managers are naturally not unaware of the image they present abroad, and they have sought to exploit it for the furtherance of their terrorist operations. A few weeks after its bombing of Libya in April 1986, the Reagan administration sought to line up the Western powers in its anti-Libyan crusade. To this end, it circulated a position paper at the Tokyo summit in May warning of "the need to do something so that the crazy Americans won't take matters into their own hands again." The strategy was successful, and Reagan's aides were quite clear about the reasons:

> "We've got the madman factor going for us," said one U.S. official, referring not to Kaddafi but to Reagan. "You know, 'Keep me from killing again'."[28]

Returning to terrorist operations closer to home, the media and other commentators assure us that the Sandinistas merely exploit the pretense that they are under attack and threatened by invasion to justify repression and to explain away the economic catastrophe that has been caused by their incompetence and evil nature. It is unnecessary to provide any factual basis or reasoned argument for these claims, since they are required by the propaganda system and are therefore true by definition. We may therefore cheerfully ignore the record of repression of other states in situations of conflict—clearly El Salvador must be avoided because the wrong conclusions will be too obvious, but we must also suppress the record of such states as Israel or the United States itself, in far less onerous circumstances.[29]

The well-behaved commentator must also dismiss the facts about economic performance: for example, the 1983 conclusion of the Inter-American Development Bank, now barred from offering loans to Nicaragua by U.S. pressure, that "Nicaragua has made noteworthy progress in the social sector, which is laying a solid foundation for long-term socio-economic development," a conclusion supported by the charitable development agency Oxfam and numerous others who are not properly disciplined; and the fact that Nicaragua's net increase in Gross Domestic Product "for 1980-1985 was 4.4 percent, almost double the rate of increase of the Latin American GDP as a whole" and well beyond that of any other country in Latin America. We must ignore or disparage the welfare programs, and the substantial increase in capital investment in agriculture, which threatened to allow Nicaragua to become self-sufficient in food while during the same years (early 80s), capital investment in agriculture dropped elsewhere in Central America, by 57% in Guatemala and 73% in Costa Rica. It would also be inappropriate to consider the figures on export production, increasing by over 11% in Nicaragua from 1979 through 1985 (while the value of these exports declined by almost 25% because of deterioration in terms of trade), in contrast to a 19% decline elsewhere in Central America. We must ignore the general economic crisis throughout Latin America, particularly severe in Central America, or the conclusion of Enrique Bolaños, chairman of the Council of Private Enterprise in Nicaragua and a leading opponent of the Sandinistas (hence a leading democrat in the U.S.), who attributes the economic crisis in Nicaragua to the war (60%), the international economic crisis (10%), the contraction of the Central American Common Market (10%), and decapitalization by the business sector and government errors (20%).[30]

It is also important to forget that the unacceptable achievements after the overthrow of the U.S.-backed Somoza regime took place against the background of the devastation it had left, and the final robbery of what remained, leaving the country in such a state that an October 1980 World Bank mission estimated that "per capita income levels of 1977 will not be attained, in the best of circumstances, until the late 1980s."[31] The actual circumstances were the escalating U.S. war against Nicaragua, requiring mobilization of population and resources at a level that would be unbearable even in a wealthy and well-functioning economy.

All other factors notwithstanding, the problems in Nicaragua must be the responsibility of the official enemy, and nothing more need be said to prove the point. The problems in neighboring countries enjoying bountiful U.S. aid rarely reach the threshold of attention and elicit no impassioned condemnation.

To maintain strict discipline on these matters is no easy task, one of the ancillary ideological problems of clandestine terrorism. But it must be done, and one will find few departures from the doctrinal requirements of the terrorist state.

Closer examination of the charges of Sandinista Marxist-Leninist dogmatism and its catastrophic effects helps illuminate the culture of terrorism from another standpoint. The *Wall St. Journal* headlines an article by Clifford Krauss: "Nicaragua is Getting Little Foreign Aid in Righting Economic Mess it Created."[32] Krauss concedes that the war may have "strained" the government budget, but dismisses the effects of the trade embargo and other U.S. measures, though these have plainly been severe in blocking natural markets and sources of supply, even spare parts, and forcing Nicaragua to rely on the Soviet Union in accordance with Reagan administration imperatives.[33] The real problem, he insists, is the "counterproductive government pricing policies," which lead to such "market absurdities" as an artificially low price for bananas, part of the effort to ensure that the urban poor will have access to food. Assume the criticism to be valid. One will search in vain, however, for derisive articles on the pricing policies based on market realities in U.S. domains, for example, Honduras, which exports crops while much of the population literally starves to death. These are simply the natural workings of the market, meriting only approbation for the rational policies that happen to benefit U.S. corporations and their local associates, if not the Honduran peasant.

Condemnation of the Sandinistas for the economic failures resulting from "Marxist-Leninist dogmatism" must also refrain from any comparison with the world's richest and most powerful state, where the brilliant economic management of the Reaganites, largely reflecting an elite consensus, is reviewed in an October

1986 report of the U.S. Department of Commerce that describes how, "in a few short years, a wealthy creditor nation has become the number one debtor" as "the United States has largely lost its ability to compete successfully in international trade."[34] "The United States required nearly 70 years to attain a creditor position of $150 billion, reached in 1982... As of now, the debtor status is about $250 billion. Some analysts project that the debtor position could approach or exceed $800 billion by 1990." That would constitute a shift of close to a trillion dollars within a decade in the relations of the world-dominant power to its rivals, a remarkable and unprecedented phenomenon in world affairs. The International Monetary Fund warns that the main danger to the world economy "lies in the huge US budget and trade deficits," which it considers "unsustainable" for the world's economy.[35] Plainly these achievements, only a part of the dismal Reaganite heritage, offer us a proper platform for contemptuous denunciation of the failings of the Sandinistas, in their far more favorable circumstances.

In extenuation of the Reaganite economic managers, one might argue that they have, after all, been dedicated to reducing the gap, or chasm, in living standards that separates the United States from the suffering people of the Third World. Thus we read that "Third world conditions have reached the Middle West," where "We're starting to see goiters and abscessed baby teeth in farm children, which indicates they are not getting adequate nutrition." "Hunger and malnutrition are a new phenomenon among Kansas farm families, experts say," a phenomenon of the 1980s, though not a new phenomenon among the urban power or elsewhere, conditions that have notably worsened during the Reagan years. "Ironically, experts explain, farmers today are suffering more than in the Great Depression" because of "modern practices aimed at increasing efficiency," so that farmers buy their food at supermarkets while producing corn, sorghum and wheat for sale.[36]

We might also take note of another and rather more serious debt crisis, namely, in the Third World. Since 1981, Third World countries have become net capital exporters as debt servicing exceeds new borrowing—to which we must add profit repatriations by transnational corporations and massive capital flight, which in Latin America approaches the scale of the debt itself. With non-oil commodity prices declining and the capital outflow rapidly increasing, there is "a historically unprecedented transfer of resources from the poor to the rich countries," a recent analysis observes.[37] This transfer of resources with the predictable human consequences is not regarded by elite opinion as a problem, though inability to pay the banks is a different matter.

The covert activities of the Reagan administration in violation of public opinion and congressional dictates were well-known all along. "Journalists in Central America knew long ago that somebody was flying supplies to the Contras inside Nicaragua," the right-wing correspondent of the London *Spectator* pointed out after the "scandals" had erupted.[38] "Captain Ricardo Wheelock, the head of the Sandinista military intelligence, was even able to give us fairly precise details of these flights, but nobody bothered to chase the story until Eugene Hasenfus was shot down and captured" in October 1986. Similarly, reporters failed to follow many leads indicating that "Oliver North was running the Contra operation from his office at the National Security Council." North's role was of course known,[39] and suppressed. Over a year before the scandals broke, the *New York Times* reported that the contras were "receiving direct military advice from White House officials" in an operation run by a military officer on the National Security Council staff who "briefs President Reagan," namely Oliver North, whose name they suppressed for fear of endangering his life, according to the editors. Shortly after, Reagan held a press conference in which the Washington press corps, which has concocted for itself a self-congratulatory image of aggressiveness that is generally laughable, raised 26 questions on 15 different subjects, asking nothing about these reports,[40] which were of no interest because the operations only endanger the lives of people who deserve to suffer for their sins.

It was also apparent that the contras were receiving arms from U.S. clients such as El Salvador, Honduras, and Israel, meaning that in effect they were receiving arms from the United States in violation of congressional directives.[41] Well before the "scandals" had erupted, CIA involvement in contra aid in violation of congressional restrictions was revealed to be at a level that "may astound even the most jaded observer," Congressman Sam Gejdenson commented, including funding of military operations and bribing of Honduran and Costa Rican officials.[42] The disclosures attracted little notice.

In general, the facts were known, but suppressible. The same was true of the disclosures concerning Iran, to which we return. In fact, the only really novel insight produced in the 1986-87 exposures is that these two clandestine operations were linked, although the scale and sophistication of the international terrorist network constructed during the Reagan years was not known in detail and is of no little interest. The same was true of the "secret wars" in Laos and Cambodia, known to the media throughout, but suppressible.[43]

Furthermore, it was entirely obvious, even without direct information, that a lawless administration would simply find other ways to pursue its goals if Congress were to bar direct takeover of the war. This is surely understood by the media and Congress as well as it is by the terrorist commanders supported under the Reagan Doctrine, for example, Jonas Savimbi, who remarked to journalists in 1982 that "A great country like the U.S. has other channels... The Clark Amendment [barring aid to Savimbi's UNITA] means nothing."[44] Those unable to draw the conclusion for themselves could turn to Reagan administration sources for enlightenment. Thus in a front-page story of March 9, 1986, the *Miami Herald* outlined Reagan's request to Congress for aid to the contra armies, quoting its crucial paragraph authorizing the CIA and any other "department or agency in the executive branch" to take over the war effort. "Officials said that if Congress rejects the package, then Reagan may feel free to use other measures to contain Nicaragua"[45]—the latter phrase serving as one of the euphemisms for international terrorism. When the "scandals" could no longer be suppressed, the press quoted officials who supervised the secret war as saying that "legality was viewed as an obstacle that had to be gotten around. That was the spirit of the program," then commenting that "the real wonder is that Congress, the Reagan administration and the public took so long to become concerned about the questionable activities and possible violations of law in contra funding that have been evident for several years."[46] A more pertinent question, unasked, is why it took the press so long to report what it had long known. There were numerous other indications of the obvious, but it was more convenient to disregard them, in the usual style of subordination to power.

The supply flights to the contras and other evidence ignored by the media were, of course, known to U.S. intelligence, hence to State Department intelligence; even if the flights had not been arranged by U.S. agencies, it is difficult to imagine that U.S. intelligence is so incompetent that it was unable to detect flights from U.S.-supervised military air bases in El Salvador and Honduras to Nicaragua, which is probably under more intense aerial surveillance than any other place in the world, or to learn what was familiar fare to journalists in Managua. All of this was therefore surely known to Elliott Abrams and George Shultz.[47] Their professions of ignorance and the perfunctory inquiry into these matters at the Iran-contra hearings merit no comment, nor need we tarry over "the refreshingly blunt candor of Secretary of State George Shultz, battling for his honor" at the hearings, which so impressed Congress and the media.[48]

But it proved impossible to maintain secrecy after the downing of the contra supply plane in Nicaragua and the revelation by a Beirut journal and by the Iranians of the visit to Teheran by former national security adviser Robert McFarlane. The partial unravelling of the complex web of deceit from October 1986 became a severe embarrassment to the terrorist commanders in Washington, who were forced to pretend that they knew nothing of the programs carried out under their general orders. These exposures might serve to limit their capacity to conduct the programs of international terrorism to which they are dedicated, at least temporarily. The exposures also slightly widened the opportunities for honest journalists to publish some of what they knew, not only with regard to Central America, much as happened during the Watergate period before the door was again slammed shut.

Notes Chapter Three

1. See *TTT* and *PI*, and sources cited there, for extensive discussion.

2. For extensive detail on these operations, and other exploits of Reagan's international terrorist network, see Jonathan Marshall, Peter Dale Scott, and Jane Hunter, *The Iran-Contra Connection: Secret Teams and Covert Operations in the Reagan Era* (Black Rose 1987).

3. Sam Dillon and Guy Gugliotta, *MH*, Nov. 2, 1986.

4. See *TTT*, 4.4; Scott Anderson and John Lee Anderson, *Inside the League* (Dodd, Mead, 1986). U.S. involvement in the League, now run by ex-general John Singlaub, received limited notice after the capture of U.S. mercenary Eugene Hasenfus when his supply plane was shot down in Nicaragua in October 1986. The press repeated as fact government claims that the League had been purged of Nazis and the most extreme terrorist fanatics (Robert Reinhold, *NYT*, Oct. 14, 1986). It did not, however, report that at the annual conference of the League in Europe a few weeks earlier, the same Nazis were present and were given "respectful applause" when they addressed the conference (Chris Horrie, *New Statesman* (London), Oct. 31, 1986); the continued presence of Latin American assassins after their alleged expulsion is noted by the Andersons. Horrie reports the praise of General Singlaub for the South-African backed RENAMO forces terrorizing Mozambique, who were also prominent at the conference. On the Reagan administration's contributions to terrorism in Mozambique, see Kevin Danaher, "Action Alert," Food First/Institute for Food and Development Policy, Summer, 1986. On the general background, see Joseph Hanlon, *Beggar Your Neighbors* (Catholic Institute for International Relations, Indiana U. Press, 1986).

5. Nayan Chanda, *FEER*, July 9, 1987.

6. Morton Kondracke, *New Republic*, Dec. 29, 1986; Robert Conquest dismisses Oxfam reports of atrocities as "silly," in the style of his Stalinist models, who are the subject of his historical work; *Daily Telegraph* (London), April 19, 1986.

7. Stephen Engelberg, *NYT*, Aug. 20, Aug. 21, 1987. Israel's abysmal civil and human rights record is quite inadequately covered in the media, and does not affect its image as a stellar democracy; see my *Fateful Triangle* (South End, 1983), chapter 4, for discussion, largely drawn from the Israeli press. The regular reports of such organizations as the Israeli League for Civil and Human Rights or the Palestine Human Rights Committee are also not a possible media source. Nevertheless, the reference to states "not dependent on American aid" is a little surprising, the facts not being unfamiliar. See Robert Gibson, "Israel: An Economic Ward of U.S.," *LAT*,

July 20, 1987, for a recent accounting of assistance for which "no parallel exists in the history of international capital flow," amounting to $1000 a year for each Israeli by his calculation, three-fourths from U.S. government aid (all grants, not repayable loans, since 1985), most of the rest from tax-free private donations. Israel was not recruited for financial contributions, from the U.S. Treasury in any event, but for quite different services. See pp. 53, 161, 177.

8. For details, see the front-page story by Alfonso Chardy, *MH*, July 5, 1987, who obtained a copy of the North-FEMA documents; Christopher Hitchens, *New Statesman*, July 17, 1987; Dave Lindorff, *Village Voice*, July 21, 1987, with further details on similar Reaganite enterprises as governor of California. See *Taking the Stand* (Pocket Books, 1987), the transcripts of North's testimony, 643, for the record.

9. For comic relief, we may turn to *Commentary*, December 1986, where Penn Kemble and Arturo Cruz, Jr. inform us that "the fact that the resistance survived for two years without the direct support of the United States government is especially galling to its opponents, and a source of enormous political strength. It is this transgression against the laws of history—rather than any violation of the laws of the United States—that accounts for the frenzied campaign to prove that such a thing in fact could not have happened." The article appeared after the first revelations of the extensive support for the contras by the U.S. government and its clandestine network. Note also the fantasies about the opposition, for which they require no evidence, in accordance with standard convention.

10. Alfonso Chardy and Sam Dillon, *MH*, April 1, 1987.

11. Joel Brinkley, *NYT*, March 19, 1987.

12. Fred Kaplan, *BG*, May 20, 1987; Julia Preston, *WP weekly*, Sept. 21, 1987.

13. On the real meaning of "deterrence," as understood by U.S. planners, see *TTT*, 207f. and *PI*, 105.

14. See *TTT*, 137.

15. Nancy Nusser, *BG*, April 21; Philip Bennett, *BG*, April 10; Stephen Kinzer, *NYT*, March 23; Julia Preston, *WP*, March 23, 1987.

16. On the facts available at the time and the extraordinary constructions of Western propaganda systems, see Chomsky and Herman, *Political Economy of Human Rights*, II, 6. The most serious scholarly analysis is Michael Vickery, *Cambodia* (South End, 1984), widely and favorably reviewed abroad but ignored in the U.S. because its conclusions lack ideological serviceability. See Herman and Chomsky, *Political Economy of the Mass Media*, chapter 6, on the rather comical efforts to sanitize the unacceptable factual record of Western response to this and other major atrocities.

17. Gleijeses, *op. cit.*

18. See p. 14-15.

19. February 1966; cited by Gareth Porter, *A Peace Denied*, 36, from congressional hearings.

20. *CSM*, July 10, 1987.

21. *New Republic*, April 6, 1987; Kondracke is quoting General Paul Gorman, with his hearty "Amen."

22. Lane, *ibid.*; Rielly, "America's State of Mind," *Foreign Policy*, Spring 1987; Oakes, "The Wrong Risk in Nicaragua," *NYT*, Feb. 10, 1987; Morley, "Beyond the Reach Of Our Good Intentions," *NYT Book Review*, April 12, 1987.

23. *Foreign Affairs*, Jan. 1967; secret memorandum of Feb. 7, 1965, *Pentagon Papers*, Senator Gravel Edition, III, 309 (Beacon press, 1972).

24. David Shipler, "Anxiety Pervades Washington's Korea Policy," *NYT*, June 21, 1987. On the record in recent years, see Tim Shorrock, "The struggle for democracy in South Korea in the 1980s and the rise of anti-Americanism," *Third World Quarterly*, Oct. 1986.

25. Wm. Roger Louis, *Imperialism at Bay* (New York, 1978), 550; Christopher Thorne, *The Issue of War* (New York, 1985), 225, 211.

26. Watt, *Foreign Affairs*, Winter 1983; see *TTT*, 187, for further quotes and comment. *Toronto Globe & Mail*, editorials, March 5, 18, 28, 1986. Editorial, "Elephant and the gnat," *Observer* (London), Aug. 23, 1987.

27. See chapter 5, note 72, for one remarkable example. For some examples of British and Canadian subordination to the principles of the U.S. culture of terrorism, see *TTT*, 144-5.

28. AP, *International Herald Tribune*, May 6, 1987. *Newsweek*, May 12, 1986.

29. For comparison, see *TTT*, 3.5, and my chapter in Walker, *Reagan vs. the Sandinistas*.

30. IADB Report No. DES-13, *Nicaragua*, January 1983, cited by Dianna Melrose, *Nicaragua: The Threat of a Good Example?* (Oxfam, London, 1985); Booth, *op. cit.*; Burns, *At War in Nicaragua*, 6-7; *Excelsior* (Mexico), May 13, 1987; translated in *Central America News Update*, June 7, 1987.

31. Michael Conroy, in Walker, *Reagan vs. The Sandinistas*.

32. *Wall Street Journal*, Aug. 4, 1987.

33. Mexican officials report that U.S. pressures connected to the trade embargo played a role in their decision to halt oil sales to Nicaragua; see Larry Rohter, *NYT*, June 20, 1987.

34. Quotations are from Philip Abelson, editor, *Science*, Feb. 20, 1987, reporting the data presented in this study.

35. UPI, "IMF sees global economic gains, says US deficits must be checked," *BG*, Sept. 27, 1987, citing the IMF World Economic Outlook released that day.

36. Keith Schneider, "New Product on Farms in Midwest: Hunger," *NYT*, Sept. 29, 1987, quoting Dr. Cornelia Flora of Kansas State University and

Joanne Komenda, who coordinates a church food pantry network for Nebraska farmers.

37. Frederick Clairmonte (senior researcher at UNCTAD) and John Cavanagh (Institute for Policy Studies in Washington), *The National Reporter*, Spring 1987. On capital flight, see David Felix, "How to resolve Latin America's debt crisis," *Challenge*, Nov./Dec. 1985.

38. Ambrose Evans-Pritchard, *Spectator*, May 16, 1987.

39. On North's role, and the NSC takeover of the operation after Congress had barred such covert actions, see *TTT*, 130-1.

40. Bill Nigut, *Chicago Media Critic*, April 1987, citing *NYT*, August 8,9, 1985 and other reports in the press, and *Times* editor Warren Hoge. Cited in *Propaganda Analysis Review*, Summer 1987; *Extra!* (FAIR), July 1987.

41. See Philip Taubman, "Nicaragua Rebels Reported To Have New Flow of Arms," *NYT*, Jan. 13, 1985, p. 1; Israeli supply of arms to the contras had been reported in a front-page story by Taubman on July 21, 1983. On the Israeli role, see *TTT*, 133. For more recent and comprehensive analysis of Israel's role as a mercenary state in the service of U.S. international terrorism, and its own interests in support for terrorist states, see Benjamin Beit-Hallahmi, *The Israeli Connection* (Pantheon, 1987) and Jane Hunter, *Israel's Foreign Policy* (South End, 1987).

42. Robert Parry and Brian Barger, AP, April 14, 1986.

43. See Chomsky and Herman, *Political Economy of Human Rights*, II, and earlier references cited there; also Herman and Chomsky, *Political Economy of the Mass Media,* chapter 6.

44. *WP*, Jan. 12, 1982; cited with discussion by William Minter, *King Solomon's Mines Revisited* (Basic Books, 1986), 318.

45. Alfonso Chardy, "Reagan weighs Nicaragua options," *MH*, March 9, 1986.

46. David Ignatius, *WP Weekly*, Dec. 22, 1986.

47. "The official who headed the United States humanitarian aid program for the rebels in Nicaragua said today that he twice ordered his planes to shuttle weapons for the contras in Central America at the direction of Elliott Abrams"; AP, *NYT*, Aug. 15, 1987, a brief item that passed without comment. In his congressional testimony after the public hearings ended, the head of the CIA's Central American task force, Alan Fiers, testified that he had arranged for military equipment to be shipped to the contras on planes designated for "humanitarian aid"; Adam Pertman, *BG*, Aug. 26, 1987. That such trickery would take place was, of course, always obvious. See *TTT*, p. 74.

48. Haynes Johnson, *WP Weekly*, Aug. 24, 1987.

4

The Limits of Scandal

It is important to understand what does, and what does not, constitute the "scandal" that erupted in late 1986. The major scandal in the eyes of elite opinion is that the Reagan administration was caught dealing with Iran, a terrorist state, in violation of its noble commitment to protect civilization from "the evil scourge of terrorism" (Ronald Reagan), a plague spread by "depraved opponents of civilization itself" in "a return to barbarism in the modern age" (George Shultz). At the dissident extreme, George McGovern describes the "humiliating fiasco" that is the real scandal of 1986: "An administration that came to power announcing that henceforth counterterrorism would become the keystone of American foreign policy was discovered to have been secretly selling arms to the most terrorist government in the world," namely Iran[1]—undoubtedly a terrorist government, but one that cannot aspire to the achievements of the U.S. and its client states in this regard, a truism that cannot be perceived. A lesser scandal was that congressional directives were evaded and a "secret government" established that evaded congressional scrutiny and perhaps, if one can believe the testimony of witnesses of very limited credibility, even the scrutiny of cabinet members and the president. But the bounds of scandal are narrowly delimited.

Within these bounds, there was scandal enough. The contempt for democratic processes revealed day after day served as a vivid testimonial to the true nature of the form of "conservatism" that calls for executive power immune from any requirement of accountability to the public or its elected representatives. Oliver

North's performance was a particularly chilling illustration of the fanatic commitment of latter-day "conservatism" to state power and violence, and its fear and hatred of democracy, already exhibited with sufficient clarity—for those who chose to see—in Reaganite policies. Even the the *New York Times* and *Wall St. Journal* were able to scent the whiff of fascism in his incredible testimony.[2] And one can appreciate the disgust inspired by the seedy gang that was organized by the state executive to evade public scrutiny, or—as observed abroad—by such matters as North's payment of $1.5 million to arms dealer Monzer Alkassar, banned from Britain as an "undesirable alien" and under investigation by the FBI and the Drug Enforcement Agency.[3] Nevertheless, it is worthwhile to scrutinize closely the limits of scandal.

Adopting the narrowest perspective as a start, the congressional inquiry took considerable care not to learn too much that would be unpleasant. The trails of its inquiry constantly led back to the CIA, and the operations partially exposed were not unfamiliar to those who have paid attention to the clandestine operations undertaken by the state executive through this medium over many years, with their terrible human cost. According to contra leaders, CIA Central America task force chief Alan Fiers was the man "most involved in the day to day management of the contras," Dennis Volman reports, citing congressional and administration analysts who confirm "CIA management" of the program during the period when the Boland amendment explicitly blocked such operations. Fiers was the man who "directed field operations, the man who was plunged into the midst of wheeling and dealing among the various contra factions, the man who not only carries out but also made policy," enjoying particularly close relations with the leader of the FDN (the main contra military force), the right-wing businessman Adolfo Calero, "who had a longstanding relationship with the CIA which dated back to Nicaragua even before the Sandinistas took power." Contra sources indicate that Fiers wanted to keep Arturo Cruz—the official democrat for a U.S. audience—"on board" in order to obtain congressional support, and tried to influence him through his "most trusted US advisers," contra lobbyists Bruce Cameron and Robert Leiken. But his goal was to protect Calero and the "'Somocista' and oligarchic clique" that ran the FDN and to work with "the US and Nicaraguan ultra right" to block contra reform, according to contra and U.S. sources. U.S. sources "close to the situation" note that Fiers's CIA experience in Saudi Arabia for many years (probably as CIA station chief) was also valuable as Saudi Arabia became one of the main backers of the contras through the clandestine network, and "knowledgeable sources, both among the contras and in the US," believe that Fiers and the CIA generally "had more influence in organizing and running the overall contra operation" than North, whom Fiers "manipulated" into doing what he wanted. Former CIA operative Ralph McGehee commented that "the committees are back-pedaling as fast as they can away from looking seriously at the CIA" even though "at every juncture they turn up new evidence which says 'CIA'." He notes that the complex web of covert operations not only have the CIA stamp, but also would require the kind of coordination that only the agency could provide, and agrees with Volman's report.[4] Fiers and other top CIA officials testified in secret after the public hearings ended, in a perfunctory manner, according to committee staffers, but sufficiently so as to convince Senator William Cohen, vice chairman of the Senate Intelligence Committee, that CIA "counterterrorism chief" Duane Clarridge was "instrumental in the Iran-contra enterprises"[5]—that is, in fomenting terrorism.

It is, furthermore, highly unlikely that the CIA or its supervisors in the executive branch would have given free rein to an incompetent blowhard of the Oliver North variety, a conclusion that seems inescapable after his testimony. Virtually every operation in which North claims to have been engaged turns out to have been calamitous, including those of which he was most proud.[6] His incapacity to tell the truth approaches the pathological. His teary tale about the threats from Abu Nidal that led him to accept a gift from General Secord appears to be fraudulent; there is no evidence of a meaningful threat, and the Pentagon reports that North made no request for protection during the period in question.[7] As for his story about leaks from Congress which impelled him to lie to them, *Newsweek* revealed that North himself was the source of the major leak he identified (with regard to the Achille Lauro), while the others, in connection with the attack on Libya, turned out to derive from the executive branch, as Senator Inouye documented in response. In an ode to North published by *U.S. News & World Report* during the wave of Olliemania, Marine Corps historian General Victor Krulak is quoted as dismissing his much-heralded exploits in Vietnam as "romanticized," a "Sunday-supplement tale" that "never happened."[8] Surely all of this must have been apparent to CIA

director Casey, apparently a canny operative, whom North claims
was his mentor and adviser.

But the committee carefully steered away from the obvious
CIA connections. That they would do so was evident from the
start, when they selected as senior investigator none other than
Thomas Polgar, an active member of the Association of Former
Intelligence Officers that lobbies Congress on behalf of the CIA,
whose many years in the agency include service in Indochina,
where he worked closely with such CIA figures as Theodore
Shackley, who was involved in arms sales to Iran. This rather
striking case of conflict of interest was of no concern to the media,
which also managed to overlook Polgar's tribute to Eugene
Hasenfus and the CIA in the *Miami Herald*.[9] The committee also
steered clear of the ample evidence of CIA-contra drug
connections, some of it revealed during the course of their
inquiry.[10] There was also no attempt to unravel the longstanding
connections of the figures involved in the Iran-contra operations
with convicted arms smuggler and ex-CIA agent Edwin Wilson,
who was "intimately involved in the creation of the contra
network" and the Iran affair and was close to General Richard
Secord and his associate former CIA official Thomas Clines, but
was not even interviewed by committee investigators or the
special prosecutor's office in the course of the hearings. Nor did
the committee pursue other clandestine operations of those who
testified or their contacts who did not, ever since Cuba and
Vietnam days, for the light that these operations would inevitably
shed on the matters at hand.[11]

Also avoided was the Israeli connection, though it plainly
loomed large. Commenting on the failure of the congressional
inquiry to pursue Israel's role, Senator John Tower, chairman of
Reagan's Iran-contra review board, observed that "If you think
Congress is going to pick up that hot potato, you're going to be
waiting a long time."[12] And in fact the ample evidence on the
matter "passed with little show of interest by the committee" or
Senator Inouye, who received extensive funding by PACs linked to
the Israeli lobby, columnists Evans and Novak observe. Visiting
Israel after the scandals erupted, Senator Inouye, described by
Prime Minister Shamir as "one of Israel's greatest friends in the
U.S.," denounced the media for turning the Iran-contra affair "into
a scandal of monumental scale and as a result [harming] the
credibility and integrity of my nation." Though the Israeli
connection was already obvious, he expressed his view that

nothing revealed should cause U.S.-Israeli relations to be "weakened or damaged"[13]—or, for that matter, to be explored in any depth.

In short, the investigating committees sought to narrow the investigation, evading crucial but unwelcome areas, and keeping to questions of procedure or "management style" of limited significance. Primary among them was what was constantly posed as the central issue, namely, whether President Reagan knew, or remembered, what the cabal was doing, or had authorized the operations. On this matter, Reagan's denials are doubted by a majority of the population and many commentators, but they appear to me credible. Largely a creation of the Public Relations industry, Reagan may well have been kept uninformed of matters that he did not have to address at press conferences. The matter is of little consequence in the real world, though significant in the world of imagery and illusion in which ideologists must labor to maintain the pretense that the public determines policy guidelines by voting for the chief executive.

But this narrow perspective on the limits of scandal is extremely misleading, since it leaves out topics of far greater significance, topics that are not on the agenda of legitimate concerns established by the state and adopted by the media, but that provide much insight into the culture of terrorism. Putting accepted conventions aside, let us turn to some of these.

What the U.S. has done in "the fledgling democracies" of Central America during the 1980s is not a scandal, and it has always been unthinkable that it would be the topic of any inquiry, either by Congress or the media. Rather, these achievements are considered a demonstration of our traditional benevolence and our use of power solely "in the service of certain values" such as freedom and democracy that we hold "to be not only good but self-evidently good."[14]

In the case of Nicaragua, the blatant illegality of the U.S. attack is not a scandal, not a factor inhibiting U.S. international terrorism. In June 1986, the International Court of Justice determined that U.S. actions constitute "an unlawful use of force" and violations of treaties. It ruled that "These violations cannot be justified either by collective self-defence [the U.S. claim]...nor by any right of the United States to take counter-measures involving the use of force in the event of intervention by Nicaragua in El Salvador, since no such right exists under the applicable international law." The Court found no credible evidence of

Nicaraguan support for guerrillas in El Salvador since early 1981, noting further that Nicaragua could not be charged with a higher responsibility to halt arms flow than El Salvador, Honduras and the United States, which claimed to be unable to do so despite the "extensive resources deployed by the United States." The Court also observed that El Salvador had not charged "armed attack" until August 1984, four months after Nicaragua had brought its claim to the Court.[15]

The World Court decision was simply ignored. The U.S. Senate expressed its commitment to international law by voting in favor of Reagan's $100 million military aid package two weeks after the Court had called upon the U.S. to terminate its unlawful use of force, eliciting no relevant comment. The Democrat-controlled House had signified its concerns for world order by voting the same way on the eve of the expected Court decision. The Court was dismissed as a "hostile forum" with a traditional "anti-Western bias"[16]—this same "hostile forum" had ruled in favor of the U.S. against Iran in 1980, but that was deemed irrelevant. Contra lobbyist Robert Leiken "blamed the court, which he said suffers from the 'increasing perception' of having close ties to the Soviet Union"[17]; the Soviet judge had withdrawn from the case, and the general conception is laughable, but natural within the curious current amalgam of Maoism and contemporary neoliberalism-neoconservatism. Even rational commentary held that the U.S. should disregard the Court's decision, because, as international law specialist Thomas Franck put it, the United States must maintain "the freedom to protect freedom"—as in Nicaragua. The United States then vetoed a UN Security Council Resolution (11-1, 3 abstentions) calling on all states to observe international law, and along with two client states (El Salvador and Israel), voted against a General Assembly resolution (passed 94-3) calling for compliance with the World Court ruling.[18] The General Assembly vote received no mention in the Newspaper of Record; its UN correspondent, the same day, preferred to report on overly high salaries at the UN. The Security Council vote merited a brief note, though not, for example, the 124-1 vote in the General Assembly the day before, the U.S. alone in opposition as usual, calling for a South Atlantic "zone of peace."[19]

The World Court decision, and the disdainful rejection of it, is not part of the scandal. It arouses no call for a congressional inquiry, and has been dispatched quickly to the memory hole, along with the condemnation of U.S. measures in the GATT

Council that monitors international trade and other similar irrelevancies. None of this impugns the reputation of George Shultz, with his ringing declarations that "I can assure you that in this Administration our actions will be governed by the rule of law."[20] And rightly, on the principle that the law is what the U.S. government says it is, a natural principle in a terrorist culture.

From these events, we perceive with great clarity the self-image of American elites: the United States is a lawless and violent state and must remain so, independently of such nonsense as international law, the World Court, the United Nations, or other international institutions. World opinion will inhibit the terrorist commanders in Washington only if it becomes articulate and sufficiently disruptive so as to impose costs that they are unwilling to face, just as domestic public opinion is of no account until it reaches a level of dissidence that threatens the interests of the powerful at home. Meanwhile starry-eyed ideologues pay their tributes in awed and reverential tones to our unique commitment to the rule of law: "There is no other country so involved in talking about fundamental law, its limits and flexibility."[21] Arguably true, so long as we recognize that the operative word is "talking."

U.S. international terrorism is "scandalous" only if it infringes upon the prerogatives of the powerful or carries a potential cost to elite interests. Congress does represent various power blocs; therefore, violation of explicit congressional directives is scandalous, at least after it can no longer be easily suppressed, in contrast to the framework of customary international law and "solemn treaty obligations," which are an irrelevance. Similarly, during the Watergate farce, largely a damage control operation by Congress and the media,[22] there was much outrage over the break-in at the Democratic Party headquarters, but not over the far more serious crimes of the Nixon and earlier administrations, exposed at exactly the same time, including the use of the national political police to undermine the Socialist Workers Party by repeated burglaries and other illegal acts from the early 1960s—not to speak of other FBI operations designed to foment violence in the ghettoes, undermine the civil rights movement and other forms of popular action, etc. The Democratic Party represents domestic power, the Socialist Workers Party—a legal political party—does not; hence the predictable difference in response to the major scandal concerning the SWP and the minor thuggery involving the Democrats. Nixon's "enemies list" was a scandal, but not the FBI involvement in the assassination of Fred Hampton by the Chicago police, exposed at the same time; it is scandalous to call powerful people bad names in private, but not to assassinate a Black Panther organizer. The Cambodia bombings were not part of the Watergate indictment. The issue arose in the congressional inquiry, but the crime alleged was the failure to notify Congress, not the bombing of Cambodia with tens of thousands of peasants killed. The exposures during the Watergate period constitute a "crucial experiment," conveniently arranged for us by history. The lesson taught by the Watergate affair is stark and simple: people with power will defend themselves, not surprisingly. Domestic repression and murderous aggression are legitimate, but not violation of the prerogatives of domestic power. Much the same is true in the present case. We learn a good deal about ourselves from the fact that these two incidents of submissiveness to power are regarded as a brilliant demonstration of the courage and integrity of the media and the fundamental soundness of our institutions and their exceptional performance under stress.

It is understandable, then, that the successful use of terrorism is not considered a scandal. On the contrary, it is welcomed and applauded, including large-scale state terrorism in the Middle East-Mediterranean region sponsored or carried out directly by the United States,[23] the successful terrorist operations in El Salvador and Guatemala, far greater in scale, and the increasing misery and repression in Honduras as the U.S. involvement deepens there. The attack against Nicaragua, given renewed authorization by Congress just as the World Court decision was announced, is regarded as perhaps a mistake, but it is not a scandal that shakes the foundations of the Republic. All of this makes perfect sense, when one understands the principles of the culture of terrorism.

Notes Chapter Four

1. Reagan, statement on discussions with Prime Minister Shimon Peres of Israel (*NYT*, Oct. 18, 1985), immediately after the Israeli bombing of Tunis, condemned as "an act of armed aggression" by the UN Security Council, with the U.S. abstaining. Shultz, "Terrorism and the Modern World," address before the Park Avenue Synagogue in New York, *Current Policy*, no. 629, Oct. 25, 1984, State Department, Washington D.C.; there is not a word here about U.S. or Israeli terrorism, though they dwarf the examples to which Shultz restricted attention in accordance with the Orwellian principle that the term "terrorism" refers to terrorist acts by *them*, not *us*; on the contrary, the Israeli and U.S. records on terrorism are lauded. For more on these topics, including Shultz's remarkable hypocrisy on this score, see my *Pirates and Emperors: International Terrorism in the Real World* (Claremont, New York, 1986; expanded edition, Black Rose, Montreal, 1987); on Shultz, p. 95, citing astonishing comments in the same speech. McGovern, "The Constitution, Foreign Policy and the U.S. National Interest," talk at a conference sponsored by the American-Arab Affairs Council, March 5-6, 1987, *American-Arab Affairs*, Spring 1987.

2. See editorial, *NYT*, July 15, 1987; Albert Hunt, Washington Bureau Chief, *WSJ*, July 15, 1987.

3. David Blundy, *Sunday Telegraph* (London), July 12, 1987.

4. *Volman, CSM*, June 8, 1987; McGehee cited by Jack Colhoun, *Guardian* (New York), July 1, 1987.

5. Jeff McConnell, *BG*, Aug. 19; Adam Pertman, *BG*, Aug 20, 1987, paraphrasing Cohen's comments.

6. See Murray Kempton, *Newsday* (*New York Review*, Aug. 13, 1987), on the fiasco that North presented as his proudest exploit. On his incompetence generally, see Joe Conason and Murray Waas, *Village Voice*, July 21, 1987.

7. Thomas Palmer, *BG*, July 19, 1987.

8. *Newsweek*, July 27, 1987; *U.S. News & World Report, The Story of Lieutenant Colonel Oliver North*, 1987.

9. Vince Bielski and Dennis Bernstein, *In These Times*, June 10, 1987; Polgar, "Decent Men outside the Law," *MH*, Dec. 14, 1986, cited by Bielski and Bernstein, who also review Polgar's careful avoidance of all crucial evidence during his cursory investigation for the committee of possible CIA involvement in the terrorist bombing at La Penca targeting Edén Pastora, among other evasions. Polgar's son is the legislative aide of Sen. Warren Rudman, vice-chair of the Senate panel, they note.

10. On the evasion of this topic, see Murray Waas, *BG*, Aug. 5, 1987; he also notes that a report by the House Select Committee on Narcotics Abuse and Control was misrepresented in the *Washington Post* and in a memo of the House Iran-contra committee, inaccurately exculpating the contras. On evidence of the CIA-contra-drug connection unearthed during the Iran-contra hearings, see Knut Royce, *Newsday* (*BG, LAT*), June 29, 1987, reporting secret Senate testimony on funding of the contras by the Colombian cocaine cartel through former CIA operative Felix Rodriguez, who helped oversee contra supply from the Ilopango military airbase in El Salvador. Also Dennis Volman, *CSM*, July 15, 16, Keith Schneider, *NYT*, July 16, 1987, and David Blundy, *Sunday Telegraph* (London), July 26, 1987, on testimony before the Kerry subcommittee of the Senate Foreign Relations Committee by a convicted drug smuggler who provided detailed evidence on complicity on the part of the CIA and other U.S. authorities. For earlier reports, after the scandals erupted, see Stephen Kurkjian, *BG*, Dec. 7, 1986; Vince Bielski and Dennis Bernstein, *In These Times*, Dec. 10, 1986, and subsequent reports by these authors. Also Rod Nordland, *Newsweek*, Jan. 26, 1987; CBS TV, "West 57th St.," March 31, 1987; Jonathan Kwitny, *WSJ*, April 22, 1987; Knut Royce, *Newsday*, April 6, 1987; and Joel Brinkley, *NYT*, Jan. 20, 1987, on drug smuggling by American flight crews ferrying arms to the contras.

11. Joe Conason and James Ridgeway, *Village Voice*, June 23, 1987. Congressional investigators finally interviewed Wilson after the hearings; AP, *BG*, Aug. 15, 1987.

12. Peter Grier, *CSM*, Aug. 11; Godfrey Sperling, *CSM*, Aug. 25, 1987. The *New York Times* report on Tower's reaction to the inquiry omitted this topic.

13. Rowland Evans and Robert Novak, *WP*, July 17, 1987; *Jerusalem Post*, Dec. 4, 1986.

14. Krauthammer, *op. cit.* See chapter 13. Also pp. 92, 99, 123.

15. International Court of Justice Year 1986, 27 June 1986, General List No. 70, pars. 251, 252, 157, 158, 233.

16. Editorial, *NYT*, July 1, 1987; Krauthammer, *op. cit.* The *Times* also falsified the Court's decision, claiming that it had accepted "collective defense" as "a possible justification for America's retaliation" for "prior attacks against El Salvador from Nicaragua"; the Court had explicitly rejected such justification, ruling that it had no basis in law, even if the U.S. could establish its factual allegations (also dismissed). Compare the editorial reaction in the *Los Angeles Times*, June 29, 1986, on the weakening of "the rule of law" resulting from the resort by the U.S. government to "brute force rather than the legal instruments of redress to confront a crisis of the region"; cited by Burns, *At War in Nicaragua*, 138.

17. Jonathan Karp, *WP, June 28, 1986.*

18. Franck, *NYT*, July 17; *NYT*, Oct. 29; *BG*, Nov. 4, 1986.

19. *NYT*, Nov. 4; *BG*, Oct. 28, 1986.

20. "Terrorism in the Modern World."

21. A. M. Rosenthal, *NYT*, Sept. 11, 1987.

22. See my "Watergate: A Skeptical View," *New York Review*, Sept. 20, 1973; editorial, *More*, December 1975; and introduction to N. Blackstock, ed., *COINTELPRO* (Vintage, 1976).

23. See my *Pirates and Emperors*, for a review.

5

The Culture of Terrorism

We learn more about our moral and intellectual culture by a closer look at the debate, or lack of it, over Central America. Its basic determinants we have already noted. Early concerns over El Salvador abated when successful terror reduced the danger that the U.S. might be drawn into a war that could be costly to itself. Guatemala was never a topic of much concern because the U.S. role was disguised by the use of client states and it appeared that domestic military forces were adequate to the task of violent repression. And hundreds of thousands of peasants starving in Honduras fall well below the threshold of attention. With regard to Nicaragua, concern remains high, again because of the fear that state terrorism might fail, with potential costs for the United States.

The controversy over support for the U.S. proxy army reflects these priorities. "Contra leaders and their backers in Washington," the media explain, "are acutely aware that the future of the entire project could turn on how much military success the contras can have" before the next congressional vote on aid. They understand very well that the purpose of U.S. aid "is to permit people who are fighting on our side to use more violence," in the words of Assistant Secretary of State Elliott Abrams.[1] Accordingly, the contra leadership does not approach Congress with the plea that they can win popular support through the appeal of their political program and organizing achievements in Nicaragua; rather they insist that with U.S. military aid and CIA direction they can kill enough people and cause enough destruction to "soft targets" to make a difference. In adopting this public stance, they register their understanding that the debate within elite circles is largely tactical, and that in a terrorist cultural climate, nothing counts except the success of violence.

This perception is well-supported in editorial and other commentary, which regularly stays within this framework of assumptions, warning—to select a typical example—that the contras "have some distance to go before convincing the American people that they are capable either of forcing the Sandinistas to the bargaining table or of scoring a military victory," and "may well be deprived" of further funding "unless Congress becomes convinced that they are up to the job." In the light of the inconvenient—hence irrelevant—diplomatic record to which we return, we may dismiss the reference to "forcing the Sandinistas to the bargaining table" as mere parroting of state propaganda, designed to cover up the real issue: "scoring a military victory." Syndicated columnist Smith Hempstone fears that "it will be difficult for Reagan to wangle a two-year financial commitment for the contras," though "a major contra military victory" before the next funding request "would help enormously."[2] Such commentary, virtually exceptionless, amounts to an acknowledgement that the contra leadership comprehends the mentality of U.S. elites quite well: in these circles, the overriding criterion is the success of violence. If it succeeds only after reaching the level of Pol Pot-style atrocities as in El Salvador and Guatemala, that is a proof of our heartfelt commitment to democracy and human rights; if it appears that violence may fail, as in Nicaragua, that shows that Nicaragua may be "beyond the reach of our good intentions."

In accordance with the guiding principle of "change of course," it is permissible to concede that events of the past reflected more unsavory features of our "national purpose," but now everything has changed, though in reality nothing has changed and our traditional victims will relive past horrors, suffering as well the burden of our uplifting rhetoric and self-congratulatory posturing as we keep them in their proper place. It is doubtful that any crime, however grotesque, might fail to be absorbed with equanimity into this remarkable system of intellectual self-defense.

Similar concerns over the effectiveness of violence were voiced internally during the Vietnam war. Thus William Bundy urged in June 1965 that "our air actions against the South should be carried on a maximum effective rate," including B-52 bombardment, though there was one—and only one—problem: "we look silly and arouse criticism if these [B-52 raids] do not show significant results." Meanwhile, B-52 raids in the densely populated Mekong Delta were showing "significant results" in demolishing the civilian society, presumably relieving these doubts.[3]

We therefore should feel no surprise when we learn that the U.S. command is proud of its success in directing its terrorist proxy forces to attack "soft targets" such as the "precise military targets" identified by the *New York Times*. Other "soft targets" include the health centers, medical workers and schools "targeted" by the contra forces with some success as noted, and civilian farms, which, as contra leader Adolfo Calero has explained, are legitimate targets.[4] State Department spokesman Charles Redman, at a July 1, 1986 press briefing, confirmed U.S. support for this strategy, explaining that cooperative farms "often have a dual military-economic purpose" and their inhabitants "are armed and receive regular military training." Citing Redman's statement, Americas Watch observes that it

> would do credit to George Orwell's Ministry of Truth. It would be interesting to know, however, whether [the State Department] considers how its theory that a cooperative has a "dual military-economic purpose" and, therefore, is a legitimate target for attack, might be applied, for example, to an unfortified Israeli kibbutz where attackers kill and injure children, burn houses and kidnap civilians. Is it now U.S. policy that such an attack would be legitimate?[5]

More important for assessing the nature of a terrorist culture is that the principles expressed by the State Department are generally accepted, even by critics of government policy. The media derisively dismiss atrocity mongering by Sandinista apologists who ignore the possibility that civilians assassinated by the contras might have been armed or accompanied by armed militia; the murder of agricultural workers in Israeli collectives, armed for self-defense, or rocket attacks on these defended outposts, is treated somewhat differently. *New Republic* editor Michael Kinsley, a liberal dove by the standards of American discourse, writes that the State Department defense of "bloody contra attacks on government-sponsored farm cooperatives" has merit, because "in a Marxist society geared up for war, there are no clear lines separating officials, soldiers and civilians"—a justification that could be offered with ease by Abu Nidal.[6] The attacks on other "soft targets" are also appropriate as a means "to undermine morale and confidence in the government," Kinsley continues, "a perfectly legitimate goal if you believe in the cause"—as he does, in essentials—"but impossible to achieve without vast civilian suffering." A "sensible policy," then, must "meet the test of cost-benefit analysis," an analysis of "the amount of blood and misery that will be poured in, and the likelihood that democracy will emerge at the other end."[7] In El Salvador and Guatemala, "cost-benefit analysis" apparently reveals that the policies were sensible: 150,000 corpses, well over 1 million refugees, unknown numbers tortured, raped and starved "poured in," and "at the other end," the kind of "democracy" that passes muster by the standards of liberal American opinion.

Kinsley's colleague, *New Republic* editor Morton Kondracke, offers his basis for cost-benefit analysis with refreshing clarity. "The *contra* movement seems to have done its part to earn refunding," he concludes, because, according to Reagan administration officials, the contras "have overrun several garrisons and cooperatives," which "contra leaders claim...are not civilian and agricultural" but rather "militarized"—as are Israeli kibbutzim. The success of violence is the crucial factor, and since it is adequate by his standards, the contras merit further support, particularly because contra military commander Enrique Bermúdez assures him of the popular support for his forces within Nicaragua—in the cooperatives burned to the ground by his intrepid warriors, for example.[8]

Departing from these impressive sources, we might inquire into the military victories that inspire Kondracke's admiration. The "most important military action we have carried out in the northern part of the country" according to contra spokesman Bosco Matamoros, duly reported as such by the *Times*, turned out to be slightly different as their correspondent later discovered on the scene: just another attack on "one of the most isolated villages in Nicaragua's northern mountains" in which the attackers never came close to "either the town's dirt airstrip or the small collection of shacks that serves as local headquarters for the Nicaraguan Army," but did succeed in burning down most of the houses in a nearby grain cooperative, stealing cattle from "distraught" peasants who report that "we came down here from the mountains to escape the contras" and cannot return "because they'll kill us," and killing three children and a pregnant woman with 18 other civilian casualties by shooting machine guns into houses as they ran by in this major military victory.[9] Kondracke concedes that this military victory, with children killed "after *contras* threw grenades into houses"—the only victory he cites—will apparently not help his favorites in "attracting popular support"; so we are left with "overrunning cooperatives" as a sufficient basis for renewing support for the proxy army.

Other "military victories" prove to be similar on investigation. "In their April report on military actions," the *London Times* notes, "the Nicaraguan rebels listed as one of their main achievements the destruction of a "Sandinistan Army garrison at La Victoria."[10] But when journalists visited this village in south-central Nicaragua, "they were able to find little evidence to substantiate the Contras' account." Rather, they found that in La Victoria, "formed two years ago by peasants fleeing from Contra raids in the North," there was no military garrison but rather a settlement of 45 families attacked by heavily armed contras who "came in shouting, 'Here come the sons of Reagan'." The sons of Reagan succeeded in overrunning the cooperative defended by untrained militia armed only with rifles, including a 13-year old boy who was killed, destroying many houses, killing, and burning crops. The CIA "has been frustrated in its attempts to stop American supported anti-Sandinista rebels attacking poorly defended state farms and cooperatives and killing innocent civilians, according to Western diplomatic sources with access to U.S. intelligence," the report continues (accepting this very dubious CIA claim as true), and has so far been unable "to change the image of the Contras from that of a ruthless horde to one of an effective military force with legitimate, populist aspirations"—the latter obviously being a proper task for the CIA.

But the contra "image" is adequate for the enlightened editor of a journal that seethes with endless rage over PLO terrorism, because "under U.S. influence the *contras* are promising democracy, just as under U.S. influence El Salvador is creating it," one of these arguments being as compelling as the other.[11]

Across the spectrum, it is recognized that success in the exercise of violence is the condition that the proxy army must satisfy to merit continued support, though it would be helpful if *we* could modify their "image." There are few qualms and no awareness of what is implied by those open commitments, as one should expect in a terrorist culture.

Similar assumptions prevail elsewhere. U.S. international terrorism has by no means been confined to Central America. As noted earlier, the worst single act of international terrorism in 1986 was the U.S. bombing of Libya, killing some 100 people according to Western reports. The pretext was fraudulent, as was known but concealed by the media at the time though the point is now tacitly conceded—without, however, any capacity to draw the obvious conclusions. At the time, the most extreme critics of Reagan were enthusiastic, arguing that it is quite proper to kill "innocent civilians, or murderous states would never fear retribution" (Anthony Lewis).[12] And though it is now conceded that the pretext was a fraud, respected commentators such as the 1987 Pulitzer Prize winner Charles Krauthammer continue to laud this "self-enforcement action" by the United States, which must play its role as global "enforcer," he blandly asserts. He goes on to denounce the United Nations for daring to condemn the attack as a violation of international law. The UN even stooped to the level of "condemning Western retaliatory actions such as the raid on Libya" without mentioning "the provocation"—conceded to have been a fabrication, a matter of no account. These are simply further signs of the commitment of the UN "to undermine the legitimacy of Western ideas, institutions, and interests" and to carry out other "mischief" that should, he urges, impel us to eliminate this institution, now useless since it no longer follows American orders.[13]

Within disciplined Western intellectual circles, few could comprehend that on the principle Anthony Lewis enunciates, innumerable people around the world are entitled to bomb Washington causing tens of thousands of casualties in retribution for the acts of the terrorist commanders who operate there with impunity.[14] It is the hallmark of a terrorist culture that observations such as these may never be expressed, and must be incomprehensible when voiced far from the mainstream, where elementary rationality and minimal honesty are not excluded as intolerable affronts to decency.

We learn more about the nature of a terrorist culture by a closer look at the current interpretations of the consequences of the Reagan Doctrine in Central America—taking care not to forget that these policies merely extend, to a higher peak of savagery, the Carter administration programs, which have ample precedent in U.S. history. Since the successful slaughters in El Salvador and Guatemala have been removed from elite concern and—largely—public awareness, let us turn to the attack against Nicaragua, still an issue because of the potential costs to us.

Documents circulated internally in the White House concede frankly that the contra armies organized by the U.S. government are a "proxy force" for which the U.S. must somehow construct a "political base" within Nicaragua, this task obviously being beyond the capacity of the "democratic resistance." Meeting at a sumptuous country club in Costa Rica with "catered buffet and open bar," the "collection of successful businessmen, bankers and attorneys" who make up the contra civilian leadership established by the United States as a classical Communist-style "front organization" explain the difficult problem they face: "to diffuse an impression of the contras as principally a military force with a vague, and largely conservative, political program" and to project a progressive image that might have some appeal within Nicaragua. The problems probably explain why their "exile Assembly" was largely ignored by the press; unreported, for example, was their conception of "democracy," to which we return. A further reason is that the "moderate" elements imposed for domestic propaganda purposes by the U.S. government (Arturo Cruz and Alfonso Robelo) "drew relatively cool receptions" and "a tepid response," while mention of the only civilian leader with real power, Adolfo Calero, elicited "thunderous applause."[15]

Calero was not permitted to enter Costa Rica. An avowed proponent of terrorism as just noted, he is the ultra-right civilian leader of the major military force of the contras, the FDN, based on the Somozist National Guard and commanded by National Guard Colonel Enrique Bermúdez. A secret 1982 Pentagon intelligence report described its basic elements as a "terrorist" organization headed by former National Guard officers. Before taking on the role of civilian figurehead, the most respected contra leader, Arturo Cruz, recognized that the proxy army had committed "damnable atrocities" against civilians and that their victory might lead "to a possible mass execution of the flower of our youth." After joining as their spokesman with a handsome CIA subsidy, he explained that they cannot be dissuaded from atrocities without "demoralizing the fighters."[16] Nothing has changed since, including the irrelevance of U.S.-backed atrocities to elite opinion. The horrifying record of contra atrocities compiled by human rights groups, priests in Nicaragua, and others, continues until the time of writing. Two investigators cite a high-ranking State Department official who describes the U.S. stance with regard to the atrocities of their proxy army as one of "intentional ignorance." The same has largely been true of the media and

Congress. To select examples virtually at random, U.S. journalists reported the killing of four civilians and abduction of nine others from an agricultural cooperative at San José del Pueblo; I located no report in the press. A report released by Michigan Congressman David Bonior and Bishop Thomas Gumbleton of Detroit detailing contra murders, rapes, kidnapping and other atrocities in late 1986 appears to have passed unnoticed. A book by a Spanish priest with extensive testimony from victims of contra atrocities also appears to have passed without notice. And so on, along familiar lines.[17] If these trivialities are brought up, they can be dismissed by the doctrine of "change of course."

Use of local collaborators and mercenaries to attack, suppress and control the domestic population is traditional practice. There are many examples. "Indian regiments were doing most of the work of conquering India for the English,"[18] who then relied on native mercenaries to keep the population under control. In the Congo Free State of King Leopold, who succeeded in reducing the population from 20 million to 10 million in two decades with Nazi-style atrocities, a native army of 20,000 men, given "a completely free hand to loot and rape," was instrumental in implementing the conversion of the country into a Belgian slave labor camp. In South Africa, the white regimes were able "to find African chiefs as allies and to make use of African levies pressed into military service," and black police and troops have conducted many of the worst atrocities until today.[19] The Nazis in occupied Europe also relied on local forces to carry out their murderous chores. The same was true of the French and later the U.S. in Indochina, and of imperial powers generally. In southern Lebanon, Israel employs local recruits to carry out torture, assassination, massacres and general intimidation. From the earliest days of the American colonies, indigenous elements were organized for terrorist operations, in the conquest of the continent and of the Philippines, and the attack on Indochina, including the Hmong tribesmen, recruited by the CIA for a murderous "secret war" conducted by many of the same people now engaged in the private phase of the U.S. war against Nicaragua,[20] then abandoned after their usefulness had come to an end.

The same practices have long been routine in the Caribbean and Central America. Official U.S. policy at the highest levels has been to rely on indigenous military forces to suppress the domestic population, a matter to which we return. Quite regularly peasants are organized for the task, as in the case of the terrorist

ORDEN in El Salvador, or Somoza's National Guard in Nicaragua, recruited by Somoza "from the poor peasants of the region" for his earliest operations in 1926 and later consisting largely of "usually illiterate, poverty-stricken *campesinos*."[21] The same has been true in Haiti, where the Duvalier dynasty formed the dreaded Tontons Macoutes from similar elements—a force that still carries out its grim work, still granted "a licence to bully, extort and kill" for "a once-only payment of $15." In one July 1987 massacre, hundreds were cut to pieces with machetes by sharecroppers whipped into a frenzy by landowners to kill "Communist priests," employing a device that is often effective in rallying impoverished and frightened peasants, and incidentally destroying a Church-initiated effort to organize the poor in an area of vast inequality; shortly after, a respected anti-Communist political leader and two aides were "hacked to death by a frenzied peasant mob after the victims were accused of being Communists."[22]

The enormous economic and propaganda resources of the dominant (often foreign) society combined with a depressed economy, ethnic rivalries, religious controls, exploitation of fear and ignorance, a mounting cycle of violence and other factors facilitate such efforts.

Apologists for U.S. terror and repression appeal to the fact that its agents are mobilized locally to justify the actions as "defensive" or even "populist." Nazis, the Belgian Monarch, South African racists, the U.S.-backed dictators of the Caribbean and Central America, and other torturers and mass murderers might have advanced similar arguments, with comparable justice. The sudden enthusiasm among U.S. elites for "tough peasants"—namely, those recruited for U.S. terrorist operations—is a noteworthy cultural phenomenon.

We read constantly in the U.S. media that the contra foot soldiers are peasants, as are soldiers generally in the Third World, including the soldiers press-ganged for service in the Salvadoran army and those who filled the ranks of Somoza's National Guard, often recruited in the areas where contras supplied by U.S. air drops operate today. The ranching country of central Nicaragua was a "traditional recruiting ground for the brutal National Guard that sustained the dictatorship" of Somoza, and with its moderately well-to-do private farmers, is the main center of contra support today.[23] Jorge Castañeda writes that the neglect of the Sandinistas for the "poor and backward peasantry of the northern reaches" in the first years after the fall of Somoza "when linked with ties the Somoza National Guard had in remote, poverty-stricken areas—traditional recruiting grounds for most Latin American armies—made this sector of the population ideal for *contra* enrollment" before it was "neutralized" by land reform and resettlement from areas of conflict, thus reducing the "meager popular support" for the contras in scattered and generally remote regions.[24] It comes as no surprise that "among the contras membership in the National Guard appears to hold little or no stigma," or that many joined the contras "because they were either members of the National Guard or had relatives who were," while others describe their service in the U.S.-trained elite battalions that have wreaked havoc in the Salvadoran countryside.[25] The Miskito areas were an early recruiting ground for the contras, but no longer, it appears, as a result of Sandinista reforms and the moves towards autonomy, unusual if not unique in the hemisphere, hence a target for contra sabotage by kidnapping and terror.[26] In fact, "during the past year, the number of volunteers [throughout Nicaragua] dwindled to almost none, contra commanders acknowledge,"[27] despite the extraordinary level of support provided by the foreign master and the increasing harshness of daily life under wartime conditions in a country that was only barely beginning to recover from the ruinous conditions that were Somoza's legacy.

Americas Watch reports that contra terror continues to be the primary source of human rights abuses in Nicaragua, though they also condemn government practices. They know of no "systematic violations of the laws of war in the course of military operations by the government" and conclude that there are *two* "political prisoners in the sense in which that term is used in the United States," one since "released without charges" after having been arrested for draft evasion. Amnesty International currently has no "prisoners of conscience" in Nicaragua.[28]

As in the Miskito areas, peasants sometimes joined the contras on the basis of real grievances, though these do not begin to compare with the abuse suffered under the reign of U.S. client states or its proxy army attacking Nicaragua. As to whether these grievances would have been properly addressed, we can only speculate, since the U.S. intervened at once to exploit and exacerbate them, in fear that Sandinista reforms might prove successful. That they are being addressed is sometimes ruefully conceded in the U.S. press, with the customary twist. A *Wall St. Journal* article, headlined "Managua Tightens Grip on Former

Contra Strongholds," reports how the Sandinistas have proceeded to "build support by handing state farms over to landless peasants and offering foreign exchange incentives to cattlemen to boost meat production," and inaugurating new dairy projects, while in the Miskito areas, "the government is repairing and painting schools and medical clinics and bringing movie projectors for the first time to Indian villages"[29]—thus undercutting the U.S. goal of saving the people from oppression.

Edén Pastora, the darling of contra supporters when he was leading the southern front attacking Nicaragua from Costa Rica with CIA and South African support, lost his status as a "great Central American patriot"[30] and disappeared from view after he was removed by the CIA for failure to follow orders. But he has not remained silent. He comments that

> in Nicaragua, the "contras" are referred to as "the guardsmen," which is not altogether wrong, because the former Somozist guardsmen force peasant youths to join their ranks and take them away to camps in Honduras... Instead of building up their morale to make them idealist guerrillas, they depersonalize and demoralize them. The peasants are turned into guardsmen, into a repressive and killing machine. The guardsmen murder prisoners of war and continue to say "yes, sir." The "contras" will never be able to enter Managua.

He describes contra chief Adolfo Calero as "a loyal soldier of the CIA, a pawn whose only merit is having been a Coca Cola salesman." He informed the French press agency that the "fascist contras" would "not respect their mothers" if they regained power. "The contras," he says, "are the ones that serve as instruments of Washington's policies against Nicaragua. They hold their meetings in the U.S. and receive thousands of dollars for putting themselves at the service of imperialism."[31]

Pastora is also interviewed in the national U.S. media, with such comments omitted, however.[32]

According to U.S. mercenaries serving with the contras, including Adolfo Calero's security chief Joseph Adams, Pastora is a prime target of "widespread assassination plots" involving "the most senior *contra* leaders," who also "maintain a list of Managua civilians—including members of the clergy as well as Sandinista politicians—who would be marked for assassination when FDN forces entered the Nicaraguan capital," to establish "democracy."[33]

Pastora's views on the contras are echoed by others in the region, rarely heard here, and without affecting their status as the "democratic resistance." A coffee-grower in Honduras describes the contras as "moneyed commanders and the commanded poor, turned into the dogs of war," a "gang" without a "true ideology and with profound internal inequalities," who recruit by force and promise pay "with the victory" while the money "goes into the biggest pockets."[34] An editorial in the right-wing Honduran journal *El Tiempo*, whose owner Chaim Rosenthal has called upon the U.S. to invade Nicaragua to overthrow the Sandinistas, states that "We know what is the cause of the terrorism that is flowering more rapidly than we had expected [within Honduras]: the presence of the contras with the complicity of the civilian and military authorities," describing popular discontent with the contras as a "powder keg" waiting to explode."[35] A retired senior officer of the Israeli army, an arms merchant in Central America for 4 years, describes the contras as "an invention of the media and some people from the psychological warfare department in the Pentagon" who will fight as long as "the Americans give us a lot of money...to play soldier for them and bullshit about democracy." Their commanders "sit in the jungle with a finger deep up their ass and think how to squeeze more dollars from the idiot gringos in Washington, just as the generals of South Vietnam did back then," while American journalists are led through Honduran jungles and told they are in Nicaragua—among other less complimentary remarks based on his observation of the media at work in Honduras.[36]

The most important currently available source of direct information about "the new contras," refurbished by official U.S. aid, is an account by Rod Nordland, an experienced correspondent with a distinguished record of important work, who spent a month in April-May 1987 with a contra unit in northern Nicaragua and then traversed the same area with Sandinista troops.[37] He found the comparison striking.

As they departed from their Honduran bases, contra "morale seemed high, their new backpacks burst with up-to-date matériel, the skies droned with the motors of C-47 cargo planes dropping ammo to them, courtesy of the CIA" along with supply helicopters ferrying military supplies "in Red Cross disguise" (as shown in an accompanying photo, yet another violation of the laws of war in the familiar sleazy style of the Reagan administration; this violation of international law, a device also employed in Carter's rescue operation for commanders of Somoza's National Guard, was denounced by the Red Cross in Geneva in a response to the *Newsweek* photo that received little notice here[38]). They were equipped with U.S. aerial reconnaissance maps showing the Sandinista base that was their assigned target "in such detail that the location of every latrine was noted" and were decoding messages on their portable computers.

In short, typical guerrillas.

But the contras soon degenerated into the same kind of "ruthless horde" described by the *London Times* reporter cited earlier, stealing food and cattle from terrified peasants, some of whom were "strong-armed" into serving as guides "and, worse, to walk on their point (the first man in the column) to make sure we weren't falling into a trap." The contras excelled at robbing the local peasants who were "paralyzed by our arrival, except one terrified woman who ground cornmeal for us so assiduously that she ignored her baby crying for attention," and whom they terrorized by their behavior as marauding bandits with their "skulls and crossbones tattooed on their arms," boasting names "like 'Exterminator' and 'Dragon'." They were "great at retreating; attacks, they never quite managed." They also never managed to impart any political message, nor did they appear to consider this as part of their task, even though "the independent-minded campesinos of the mountains are natural enemies of the Sandinistas," having been "hurt badly by the failing economy" and having received no benefits from the revolution. Nordland describes how the contras proceeded "to cement [the] loyalty" of a peasant who was bitterly anti-Sandinista for these reasons:

> We ate his chickens, beans, tortillas, bananas, plantains, cassava, grapefruits and agreed with him that it was a pity other contras had already eaten the eligible pigs. We slept in his yard, despite standing orders to camp away from homes lest civilians are killed in an attack. We sent him out to scout the hills for Sandinistas at night, and before dawn we walked him out on the point... Small wonder that, taken aside, neither he nor his wife would speak against the Sandinista troops who come through. The compas speak softly, they said, and gave political talks, but normally ask only for coffee... In the battle for hearts and minds, the contras are still the losers

even in the remote areas where they have potential support. They are still more "the losers" among the families whose children are kidnapped and forced into the contra army, including the family of one 14-year-old boy Nordland met with the contras, whom he later interviewed: "His family had been given a plot of land by the Sandinistas after their victory. 'How could they want to destroy the revolution,' [his mother] wondered, 'when it has helped us and so many other people'."

Nordland also interviewed a "relatively big landholder" whom he expected to be anti-Sandinista and who told him: "Mister, if the war just drags on like this, soon it will degenerate into banditry." Nordland's final conclusion: "Mister, it already has."

Returning to the same region with Sandinista troops who quickly swept the contras from the area in a counteroffensive that was "the biggest of the war—and the shortest," Nordland found a very different picture. Unlike the contras, who carefully avoid military targets, "concentrating on more lightly armed civilian militias and undefended targets" (when they are not simply marauding), the Sandinistas, whose conduct "made a striking contrast with the contras," "found contras and fought after only two days," and continued to do so. "Their discipline held firm after many months" in the remote mountains, though they were mostly "draftees on two-year tours of duty." "Where it had taken a mere three weeks for the contras we accompanied in the same mountains to turn into an unruly scourge, Sandinista troops on the march never even stopped at a peasant's house, except with permission from an officer—and then only to wait outside for drinking water... When they did requisition food, the campesinos told us, they always paid." Peasants also agreed that only the contras "impress campesinos as guides or make them walk in front of the troops."

An accompanying story quotes a March 1986 memorandum by Robert Owen, who described himself in congressional testimony as "the eyes and ears" of Oliver North. He had "few kind words for the Nicaraguan contras." For many of their leaders, Owen concluded, the war "has become a business"; "There are few of the so-called leaders of this movement who really care about the boys in the field." The commander of the Costa Rican-based southern front, Fernando Chamorro, "drinks a fair amount and may surround himself with people who are in the war not only to fight, but to make money." Another contra leader "had potential involvement with drug running and the sales of goods provided by" the U.S. government. More money to the contras "will be like pouring money into a sinkhole."

Nevertheless, the cost to the U.S. is limited, and the "ruthless horde" recruited for their services have been able, in part at least, to perform their assigned task of preventing Sandinista reforms and ensuring that "theirs must become a revolution of misery, a frightful object lesson to the people of the region" (Piero Gleijeses).

Arturo Cruz was the indispensable symbol of contra democracy—until he resigned from the leadership in 1987 accompanied by denunciations from Secretary of State George Shultz because his resignation "resulted from a failure to get his own way rather than a concern over democratic reforms in the movement." Jeane Kirkpatrick also discovered that the hero had feet of clay after his unconscionable dereliction. He was "a man of mercurial temperament" who "had lived outside Nicaragua for 20 years before he returned to work for the Sandinistas in July 1979" and "it seemed to many Nicaraguans that he was never comfortable working in the framework of Nicaraguan politics." He is "a technocrat" and "not a political man," a person who "seemed to evoke more intense admiration among North Americans than Nicaraguans," Kirkpatrick explained. At the same time, the congressional Iran-contra committee released a document showing that Oliver North's payments to Cruz began out of concern that Congress might disclose that he was on the CIA payroll, in particular, during the time when he was a candidate for President in the 1984 elections in Nicaragua.[39] Reports that Cruz was on the CIA payroll had been dismissed as a canard by contra supporters, and neither these comments on Cruz's newly-discovered weaknesses nor others reminded the reader that during the 1984 elections, Cruz was presented by the U.S. government, the media and the journals of opinion as the only hope for democracy in Nicaragua, with largely fabricated accounts alleging that the Sandinistas blocked his campaign by violence and other means because of his great popularity in Nicaragua, suddenly dissipated now that he is failing to perform his duties under U.S. orders.

Cruz describes the contra movement as "very ill."[40] Its main problem is that "it was artificially formed too soon by the US" which "used as its core a group which the Nicaraguan people had rejected—the Somocista National Guard." Its civilian leadership is "a mere 'clique' of businessmen and old-line politicians who were incapable of articulating a coherent political message." After a new contra directorate was formed at U.S. initiative in May 1987, "the senior US official who has worked with the contras for many years says, 'Unity will be the merest façade, kept together—at least until the US elections—by the ringmaster, CIA'"; the leaders are "opportunists," lacking "political or moral principles, or any real sensitivity to the Nicaraguan poor," a "liberal contra official" adds,

referring to the new democratic hopeful, Alfredo César.[41] "The
contras suffer from political anemia," Philip Bennett reports, and
"continue to neglect military objectives while raiding poorly
guarded symbols of the Sandinista revolution such as farm
cooperatives, often killing innocent civilians." Trips to the war
zone reveal that "roaming contra units rarely impart an explicit
political message." "Some contra leaders point to the difficulty in
devising a political formula to match the concrete promises of land
and social services espoused by the Marxist insurgency in El
Salvador."[42] A "leading US intellectual" who supports the
contras—and presumably qualifies as a "leading intellectual" for
this reason—complains that they cannot "figure out a social
program that would appeal to people, and then put it into some
kind of context," and have no interest in a political program or a
grass-roots structure. Another problem, this leading thinker
explains, is that it is hard to arouse Nicaraguans against the
government

> because of the social services they are provided with. Thus, the
> Sandinistas have been able to keep the opposition at the level of
> mere grumbling. How does one oppose such a regime? I don't
> think the contras have any idea.[43]

In fact, they and their backers, including this "leading intellectual," have a very good idea: you oppose such a regime by random
terror and the resources that can be mobilized by a violent superpower, in accordance with William Casey's insight that "It takes
relatively few people and little support to disrupt the internal peace
and economic stability of a small country."[44]

With his departure from the directorate formed by the U.S.
government to mislead Congress and the media, Cruz will
presumably forfeit his $7,000 monthly (tax-free) paycheck and
perhaps the "several million dollars from a private aid network
over the last three years, money that has never been publicly
accounted for," though Alfonso Robelo, the wealthy businessman
who stayed on to provide a facade of "democracy," will
presumably continue to receive the $10,000 per month provided
for his services.[45]

At the "exile Assembly," Cruz—at the time still playing his
assigned role and thus a heroic defender of democracy—told the
delegates that "all the conditions [for victory] are present, except
only that we have failed until now to define clearly and
consistently our own political positions,"[46] a minor defect.
Meanwhile senior U.S. officials bewail the fact that "the contras

can demonstrate no major political gains" and "have almost no support systems" within Nicaragua. They do not understand why the proxy army attacking Nicaragua from foreign bases is "not as effective as the leftist rebels in El Salvador," who have always fought within their own country, receive virtually no known outside aid, and face a military force far better equipped than the army defending Nicaragua from terrorist attack, with nearly 80 helicopters, 11 A37 bombers and 12 C47 gunships, and direct participation of the U.S. Air Force and other U.S. military forces in surveillance, coordination of bombing, and ground operations.[47]

Contra commanders complain of "the lack of airplanes and pilots" for their "rudimentary air force" and the lack of "small boats for river patrol." The problem they face is that they need dozens of flights per month to keep their troops functioning within Nicaragua, this "aerial resupply network" being the "key to the contras' ability to keep large numbers of fighters in the field."[48] "The air operation is the key to the war," according to a Western diplomat in Managua who monitors the rebels (presumably a U.S. Embassy official, probably CIA): "Without it, the contras couldn't make it."[49] According to Nicaraguan and Western estimates, U.S.-run supply flights reached the level of 30-40 flights monthly, delivering hundreds of tons of equipment, from April 1987, in an effort to ensure that the much-heralded Spring Offensive would be sufficiently violent to impress Congress.[50] The CIA "has equipped the rebels with a computer center that intercepts and decodes hundreds of Sandinista messages a day," information that is dispatched "via portable computers with special encoders to rebel units in the field."[51] In addition, extensive U.S. surveillance provides the proxy army with up-to-the-minute intelligence on Nicaraguan army deployment,[52] while the government must cope somehow with CIA commando operations, the constant threat of invasion, and other conditions that are also unimaginable in the case of an authentic guerrilla force. British journalists who travelled with the contras report that they are often "better equipped than the Sandinistas," describing their high-quality "state of the art" weapons and communication systems, and also explaining the basis for recruitment: "Sandinista price freezes on agricultural products mean that many peasants make less money now than they did under former dictator Anastasio Somoza"[53]—a result of the effort to maintain subsistence levels under wartime conditions for the poor who are left to starve in U.S. domains, in accordance with the approved "Central American mode."

Meanwhile contra supporters assure us that it was "the abuses
and horrors of the commandantes" that "led to what has to be seen
as a civil war—not, as the Sandinistas claim, the U.S. aggression
against Nicaragua."[54]

Despite the resources flowing in lavish abundance and the
direct U.S. participation, it doesn't work. Even journalists
impressed with their achievements agree that "without continued
airlifts and renewed American support, it is virtually impossible
that the contras can survive as an effective guerrilla force," thus
tacitly conceding that they are not "a guerrilla force" in any
meaningful sense of the term. U.S. officials fear that these
incomprehensible failures are "going to have long-term costs for
us," the same correspondent reports.[55]

The failures of the proxy army are particularly dramatic in
comparison with neighboring El Salvador. Close by areas where
thousands of government troops carry out ground sweeps,
guerrillas "nonchalantly held a town meeting" in a village just four
miles from a government military base that they had "devastated,"
carrying out "a frank, if highly political, discussion of the basic
needs and social issues affecting the majority of Salvadorans,"
with their audience plainly interested and supportive. Meanwhile,
government "Army patrols continue to enter areas of conflict as a
raiding force, rather than a governing presence with a political
vision that appeals to the peasantry," according to military
analysts; "both American officials and members of his own party
say Mr. Duarte has failed to administer effective social programs,
despite ample American aid," and "his ruling Christian
Democratic party, they say, has become a corrupt political machine
in a land where most Salvadoran peasants cannot find work, clean
water or health care." U.S. economic aid supports "the businesses
of the rich," whose "wealth...is safe because taxes are collected
irregularly and dollars can be quietly tucked away in Miami bank
accounts" and whose sons "are safe because there is no draft and
the army press gangs do not pick up young men in affluent
neighborhoods, one expression of the class character of the war."
Little U.S. aid "appears to reach the impoverished majority of
Salvadorans who live in the urban slums and the countryside,"
where U.S. aid officials rarely travel. "The poor are press-ganged
into military service" and "political power remains in the hands of
the urban elite," while "most Salvadorans are afraid of policemen
and soldiers, and few of the poor would dream of seeking legal

redress against a landlord because virtually no judge would favor a poor man."[56]

The armed forces, who "once applied scorched-earth tactics" and "supervised death squads on the ground and bombed from the sky," can now "afford to be more lenient" in areas where they have established control, the *Wall St. Journal* reports; "but as long as the left is a *political* threat, the army doesn't dare let go of the leash entirely" (my emphasis). A Catholic priest describes the rebuilt village of El Barillo, devastated by government terror, as now "a concentration camp." Villagers say that they are "afraid to talk" to an American journalist. They are "under the boot," an international human-rights worker observes. "The army fears that El Barillo's relatively efficient organization is a sign of continuing leftist influence," since nothing of the sort could be expected under government rule.[57]

"Democracy," American style.

These comparisons reveal, once again, the true "symmetry" between El Salvador and Nicaragua. It is not, as the ideological system contends, that in each country there are guerrillas fighting the central government in a reflection of the global "East-West conflict." Rather, in each country the U.S. has organized and directs a terrorist force that must use violence to achieve the ends of the foreign master and the local elites that rely on external power, unable to enter into a political struggle since they have nothing to offer the population beyond a renewal of misery and subordination. We can begin to speak of "symmetry," of "the East-West conflict," and of "U.S. security concerns," when the Soviet Union organizes a mercenary force to attack El Salvador from Nicaraguan bases and to terrorize the population, supplying them with sophisticated modern equipment in daily air drops, while the KGB runs sabotage programs in El Salvador with its own "assets" and forces a state of mobilization there by a constant and credible threat to invade outright, constructs a permanent Soviet military base in Nicaragua, runs military exercises there involving tens of thousands of Soviet troops, maintains threatening naval forces off the coast, floods the Salvadoran airwaves with hostile propaganda, conducts regular overflights to gather intelligence on Salvadoran army operations to be dispatched to "the sons of Gorbachev" marauding in the countryside, coordinates military attacks by its proxy forces in El Salvador, and so on. Then the conventional picture will be more than an object of ridicule. As of now, it hardly has the merits of complaints in *Pravda* about U.S. aggression in Poland, a pitiful victim of the East-West conflict.

Furthermore, the real world pattern is traditional, adequately explained in the documentary record of secret planning and even public commentary, and a predictable consequence of the roots of intervention within domestic U.S. society. Such facts cannot be perceived within educated circles if they hope to retain respectability. There, we can at most only contemplate "the mystery" of "why is it that the United States so often supports dictators," leaving it to "political scientists, philosophers and wise men to answer the question," which is too deep for ordinary mortals to comprehend.[58] And we may ponder the question of why Nicaragua remains "beyond the reach of our good intentions."

We might observe that business circles abroad seem to have little difficulty in penetrating the mystery that so troubles Americans. Discussing U.S. support for Ferdinand Marcos, which elicited the thoughts just quoted, the London *Economist* observes simply that "For many years Mr Marcos was good for American business and America's bases."[59] Hardly a profound insight, but sufficient to dissolve the mystery in this and numerous other cases.

Contra supporters, some of whom describe themselves as liberals or democratic socialists, find it natural that the U.S. should create a "proxy force" and attempt to construct a political base for it, because this reflects their conception of how the lower orders are to be managed. Correspondingly, they are enthusiastic about "the attractive new civilian leaders of the *contras*,"[60] who essentially share this conception. One of the few independent U.S. journalists accurately observes that the official contra leadership

> represent Nicaragua's old business and land-owning classes, the kind of Third Worlder that American officials and businessmen like to deal with. That is why they were picked in Washington to head the contras. What Cruz, Robelo and Calero all reflect is the plantation mentality that infected Nicaraguan political life during the many decades of U.S. manipulation and intervention. They share the assumption that Nicaragua really belongs to the United States, and that it is valid for would-be leaders to turn to Washington to find shortcuts to political legitimacy.[61]

The same is true of those who praise them here as virtuous democrats while applauding or averting their gaze from the social and political system imposed and defended by the United States in El Salvador, a system similar in character to what it hopes to restore in Nicaragua.

An American academic specialist on Latin America observes that the contra civilian leadership "tends to be—or was prior to 1979—economically affluent, representative of a tiny elite or a small middle class," men who were "alienated" by the revolution "because it challenged their privileges," creating "a topsy-turvy world in which their own welfare was being considered the equal of the formerly dispossessed." "Almost all the contra leaders are on the CIA payroll. Each of the seven members of the FDN directorate receives an annual salary of $84,000, tax free, compliments of Uncle Sam." Alfonso Robelo was a wealthy cotton grower and cooking-oil processor, formerly "president of the Superior Council of Private Initiative, the umbrella organization for most of organized private initiative." Arturo Cruz, who spent one year in Nicaragua from 1960 to 1985, "worked as an international civil servant and for the Inter-American Development bank." Adolfo Calero managed Coca-Cola of Nicaragua and had long-standing CIA connections. Aristides Sánchez was a wealthy landowner and close associate of Somoza. Most of those who finally opposed Somoza did so for the same reasons that led similar elements to oppose Trujillo, Marcos and other U.S.-backed dictators and state terrorists: he was robbing them, not merely the poor. It is hardly surprising that "they have never issued a detailed program of their social, economic, and political goals." Edgar Chamorro, who left in disgust after two years service as the contra spokesman selected by the CIA, states that they offer Nicaragua "nothing but a return to the past"; the contras "are being used as instruments of U.S. foreign policy by the CIA and the Reagan administration...and by the old Somozista gang to get back the money and power they lost in 1979."[62] Before joining the U.S.-directed civilian front for the contras, Arturo Cruz had described leading elements among them as "civic cadavers," noting that "most of these persons in positions of military authority within the FDN are ex-members of the National Guard, who unconditionally supported Somoza until the end against the will of the Nicaraguan people"—in fact, 46 out of 48 of the *contra commandantes* as of mid-1984. In October 1985, Cruz expressed his continuing unhappiness that the contras "are almost totally controlled by right-wingers, many of them followers of" Somoza, views that he reiterated after resigning from the CIA civilian front.[63]

The device of historical amnesia and tunnel vision cultivated in intellectual circles protects the press and other commentators from perceiving that the curious technical problem of inspiring "our friends" and constructing a political base for them has always bedevilled U.S. planners conducting their exercises of international terrorism, described with such euphemisms as "covert action," "low intensity warfare," "counterinsurgency," "pacification," or "containing Nicaragua." Throughout the Indochina wars, government experts struggled with the same problem: the U.S. is militarily strong but politically weak, as regularly discussed in captured Vietnamese documents as well as U.S. government analyses. Secretary of Defense McNamara pondered "the discouraging truth" that "we have not found the formula, the catalyst, for training and inspiring [our Vietnamese] into effective action"; all we can do is kill, he added. President Eisenhower attributed the high morale of the "Communist forces" in comparison with "the democratic forces" to the "sense of dedication" mysteriously produced by "the Communist philosophy." General Maxwell Taylor bemoaned the "national attribute" that "limits the development of a truly national spirit" among the South Vietnamese while speculating about "the ability of the Viet Cong continuously to rebuild their units and to make good their losses," "one of the mysteries of this guerrilla war" for which "we still find no plausible explanation"; the apparent contradiction with regard to the "national attributes" of the South Vietnamese is readily resolved when we recognize that the Viet Cong are by definition not South Vietnamese, since we are massacring their families and destroying their homes (in South Vietnam). In his Ten Point Program for Success in 1965, U.S. Ambassador Lodge proposed as Point One: "Saturate the minds of the people with some socially conscious and attractive ideology, which is susceptible of being carried out"[64]—the same perceptive advice now offered by Arturo Cruz and the "leading US intellectual" cited earlier. Somehow, it couldn't be done, so it was necessary to saturate the countryside with bombs along with general terror.

The U.S. propaganda services were no less baffled. John Mecklin, who was responsible for their operations in South Vietnam in the early 1960s, described the Vietnamese peasant as a man whose "vocabulary is limited to a few hundred words," whose "power of reason...develops only slightly beyond the level of an American six-year old," whose "mind is untrained and therefore atrophies." How, then, could they comprehend the benevolence of our intent while we were forcing them into concentration camps and slaughtering their families, or our sophisticated measures of "nation building"? But oddly, the political and military tactics of the Viet Cong, making use of techniques that were "skillfully entwined in the life and character of the Vietnamese peasant," "confounded not only the U.S. Mission but also the aristocratic leaders of the [U.S.-imposed] Diem regime." Their forces "were developed to a surprisingly sophisticated degree...with jungle arms factories, radio nets, clandestine hospitals, propaganda printing presses,... V.C. cameramen filming the action" in ambushes, and other such exploits. To the U.S.-organized military forces, the Viet Cong—South Vietnamese peasants with "atrophied minds"—seemed to be "eight feet tall."[65] What could be the explanation for this curious paradox?

Much the same was true in Laos, where the U.S. subverted the elected coalition government in 1958 because it was dominated by the left and later conducted one of the most intensive bombings in history to demolish the civil society of northern Laos as the sole means of blocking social reform and popular organization in this primitive peasant society; and in Cambodia shortly after, at an even higher level of slaughter. U.S. reporters were no less baffled over the familiar pattern than the American command. In his final summary report from Phnom Penh as the direct U.S. bombing ended, Sydney Schanberg raised "the key unanswered question: How have the insurgents—without any planes of their own, and without the extensive artillery support the Government troops have, with only small arms and mobile weapons...—been able not just to match the Government forces, which are more than twice their size, but to push the Government forces back and sustain the offensive for six months without any significant lull?" Exactly the question now raised by his *Times* colleagues with regard to El Salvador and Nicaragua. "Since the insurgents are not superhuman," Schanberg muses, "there must be other explanations for their success." Perhaps they are so "determined and capable" because they "are less fatalistic than the Khmers on this side" and "believe they can change their environment" (U.S. Embassy official). In this regard, "the enemy"—from the peasant society of inner Cambodia—are quite different from those who Schanberg calls "the Cambodian villager," who "usually has no politics" and "is not interested in taking sides, only to be left alone to farm and fish and feed his family and once in a while to celebrate on a Buddhist holiday."[66] Just as in Vietnam and Laos, and now in Central America.

Over and over again, we discover that "our side" is unable to develop popular support or to survive political competition, unless, of course, popular organizations have been demolished and the ideological system, the military, production, commerce and finance—in short, the entire decision-making apparatus, the means of life, and the means of violence—are firmly in the hands of approved elements. This inability has always been incomprehensible in an intellectual culture committed to the rule of force, and to "reform" dictated from above in the interests of the foreign master. The current bafflement over the failures of the proxy army despite its extraordinary advantages, and the endurance of the Salvadoran guerrillas who lack anything remotely comparable, is a familiar refrain.

The constant perplexity over these paradoxes is not difficult to resolve, but the solution is unacceptable, therefore impossible to perceive, even when presented by respected mainstream figures. The bitterly anti-Communist French military historian and Vietnam specialist Bernard Fall explained the point lucidly during the early stages of U.S. aggression in Vietnam. He raised the question why the Americans, like the French and British before them, "must use top-notch elite forces, the cream of the crop of American, British, French, or Australian commando and special warfare schools" who are "armed with the very best that advanced technology can provide" to defeat local insurgents in Vietnam, Algeria and Malaya, "almost none of whom can lay claim to similar expert training and only in the rarest of cases to equality in fire power." "The answer is very simple," he wrote. "It takes all the technical proficiency our system can provide to make up for the woeful lack of popular support and political savvy of most of the regimes that the West has thus far sought to prop up,"[67] or the civilian fronts for the proxy armies it has mobilized. He might have added that it also takes all the eloquence that advocates of state terrorism can muster to disguise the facts, just as the stern commitment of a terrorist culture to ignorance and insulation from unpleasant reality is required if we are to miss the obvious point of the lesson. The very same problem, Fall warned, would soon be faced by the U.S. in South Vietnam, as it was; and in all of Indochina, in Central America today, and in other tortured lands tomorrow.

In Indochina, Australian journalist Denis Warner, also passionately anti-Communist, could perceive the source of the problem: "in hundreds of villages all over South-East Asia the only people working at the grass roots for an uplift in people's living standards are the Communists,"[68] while the U.S. is dedicated to restoring the old order of suffering and corruption. This perception being unacceptable, U.S. ideologists were compelled to provide a different answer: the war in South Vietnam was simply an expression of the East-West struggle, with the South Vietnamese its passive victims; and the sly Communist leaders in Moscow and Peking are more adept at manipulation than their innocent American counterparts, while "our Vietnamese" (and Laotians, and Cambodians) are "fatalistic" or "corrupt." Similarly today, it cannot be perceived that the situation in Central America has the same essential features as the U.S. attack against South Vietnam. Rather, it must be that the Salvadoran and Nicaraguan people are passive bystanders, victims of the East-West conflict, with the innocent Americans unable to match the trickery of the devious Communists of the Soviet bloc.

And so we are informed by "objective journalists," merely describing the facts. James LeMoyne explains that "creating a base of popular support appears essential to guerrillas"—a remarkable discovery of the 1980s—and "it is one of the fundamentals that Cuban trainers have emphasized to both Salvadoran rebel leaders and Sandinista commanders," who plainly could not have achieved this profound insight by themselves.[69] "The contras' American advisers," he continues, "appear to have been far less expert in the art of guerrilla war" and have not given adequate thought "to making democracy, with its emphasis on individual choice, into a doctrine of revolutionary war." Thus "the Nicaraguan contras need to study the Salvadoran rebels' success in organizing popular support," just as Americans in Vietnam tried to ape the methods of their South Vietnamese enemy.

LeMoyne, however, goes a step beyond his predecessors in the Indochina Agitprop system. The contras, he explains, face problems beyond those confronting the guerrillas in El Salvador, namely, the repressive apparatus of the Sandinistas which has "hindered the contras" and impeded their efforts to construct a political base. "The rebels face similar restrictions in El Salvador," he notes, "but they are less consistently applied there." The physical elimination of the independent media by violence, the murderous attack that destroyed the national university, the outright murder of the political opposition by the security forces, the assassination of the Archbishop who attempted to defend the "popular organizations" that were effectively demolished by U.S.-organized terror, the slaughter of trade union activists, journalists, human rights workers, priests and nuns, students and teachers, and tens of thousands of peasants, the scorched-earth tactics that devastated the countryside and created hundreds of thousands of refugees, the torture and mutilation and savage terror that traumatized the society—all of this is slight in comparison to Sandinista repression, in the eyes of the *New York Times* Central America correspondent. In the same issue of the *Times*, LeMoyne denounces Salman Rushdie for "writing a great deal of admiring drivel at the knees of various Sandinista commanders" which makes it "easy to consign his brief book to the bonfire where accepted truths belong," as he is "swallowed by an exotic revolution whose darker sides he barely manages to glimpse"—in contrast to this tough-minded journalist, who is not fooled by the "Communists" and surveys the Soviet-American conflict in Central America with clear-eyed objectivity and no failure to "glimpse the darker side" of the U.S. operations in defense of democracy.[70]

These are persistent themes of the reporting from Central America by the leading *Times* correspondent in the region—which, it should be noted, is of high quality by general media standards. We return to further examples.

As noted earlier, it is a truth, whatever the facts may be, that Nicaragua is a Stalinist prison camp while El Salvador is struggling towards democracy with U.S. assistance. A review of the U.S. ideological system shows that this required picture has been presented with dedication and skill.[71]

According to the official view, Nicaragua is a Hitlerian state in its internal practices and its threat of foreign adventures. "There is no comparison between South Africa and Nicaragua," President Reagan explained in a press conference. "In South Africa you're talking about a country, yes, we disagree, and find repugnant some of the practices of their government but they're not seeking to impose their government on other surrounding countries" in the manner of the Nicaraguan aggressors[72]; one finds no South African troops in Namibia in violation of international law, for example, and no South African moves to destabilize Botswana, Lesotho, Angola, Mozambique, and other states of the region.

The U.S. government view is expressed in a joint State Department-Defense Department document entitled "The Challenge to Democracy in Central America," distributed in celebration of International Human Rights Day on December 10, 1986:

> In the American continent, there is no regime more barbaric and bloody, no regime that violates human rights in a manner more constant and permanent, than the Sandinista regime.

Commenting, Americas Watch observes that civilian noncombatant deaths attributable to government forces in Nicaragua over seven years, in the course of an attack of mounting intensity by the United States and its proxy army, might possibly reach 300, most of them Miskito Indians in 1981-2; in comparison some 40-50,000 Salvadoran civilians were "murdered by government forces and death squads allied to them" during the same years, along with "a similar number" during Somoza's last year, "mostly in indiscriminate attacks on the civilian population by the National Guard," and still higher numbers in Guatemala[73]—all of these atrocities supported or directly organized by the United States, contrary to much illusion.

Furthermore, those responsible, in Washington as in Central America, remain in power today, apart from the Somozist National Guard and wealthy business elites that the U.S. government is laboring to reinstall in accordance with its conception of "democracy." When Morton Kondracke visits El Salvador to rejoice in its march towards democracy, he is greeted by President Duarte, who presided over most of the slaughter, and his defense minister General Vides Casanova, who supervised it in accordance with his principle that "the armed forces are prepared to kill 200,000-300,000, if that's what it takes to stop a Communist takeover." Kondracke concludes that the Reagan administration deserves credit for the wonderful achievements of the 1980s, having "handled El Salvador better than the Democrats managed Nicaragua." His fellow-editors assure us that "the depredations...of the *commandantes*" in Nicaragua are "greater and more systematic depredations by far than Somoza's," including the slaughter of some 40-50,000 people by the Somoza regime after years of torture, killing, robbery and enrichment of the "democrats" while the population starved.[74]

The editors of the *Washington Post* conclude that Duarte "has worked hard, governing in a democratic manner, starting to tame the criminal right and to subordinate the armed forces, prosecuting a war and a social revolution, and cushioning as best he can the

cruel economic effects of war, backwardness and social change."
In the real world, the "criminal right" are elements of the security
forces whom Duarte lauds for their "valiant services" in their
murderous assault against the population while laboring to ensure
that Congress provides them with the necessary means,[75] the rule
of the armed forces remains absolute as demonstrated by their
complete immunity from prosecution for past or present atrocities,
and Duarte's constructive policies are a figment of the editors'
imagination, as they can learn from the occasional news reports
they publish. But Duarte is doing the job for which he was
commissioned, and therefore, they continue, "the United States
has a firm obligation to support an imperfect but striving
democracy in El Salvador," where, they assure us, the guerrillas
could not possibly remain a "major presence" were it not for the
"Sandinista government in nearby Nicaragua," evidence as always
being an irrelevant annoyance when the state has spoken.

Duarte's popularity in the United States is not matched in El
Salvador, where a 1986 poll by his Christian Democratic Party
indicates that less than one-fourth of the country's voters would
support him in new elections; what the figures would be if the left
were not excluded and the population not traumatized by terror,
no one can judge, though we may recall Duarte's admission that
"the masses were with the guerrillas" when he joined the
government and the onslaught of terror began in full fury.[76] And
while the remarkable democratic achievements under his
government are praised with enthusiasm in the Free Press, the
population of El Salvador perceives something rather different.
Public opinion polls conducted by the Institute of Public Opinion
of the Central America University in El Salvador in
January-February 1987 reveal that 10% of the population "believe
that there is a process of democracy and freedom in the country at
present" while 18% think the situation has deteriorated and 28%
believe "that there have been improvements, but that repression
continues"; the remainder, almost half the population, "think that
nothing has changed." A majority believe that Duarte's new
economic policies will harm the poor, while few think the rich
will be harmed (63%, 9%, respectively), and a substantial
plurality say that the agrarian reform "might have helped" but the
Duarte government's "promises were lies" (41%, as compared to
22% who see advantages in the reform).[77]

Duarte is also less than a hero in South America. Throughout
his

recent trip to the emerging democracies of South America, he was shunned by moderates and plagued by angry crowds. As he attempted to address the Argentinian Congress, over half the representatives filed out of the chamber. In Uruguay, he was denied permission to address the General Assembly and denounced by the Christian Democratic Party for his "obvious alignment with the Reagan administration." Similar displays of opposition were evident in stopovers from Brazil to Peru.[78]

"Arriving in Uruguay, Argentina and Brazil, Duarte received unwarm welcomes," the Costa Rican journal *Mesoamerica* reports. A labor union official declared that "the working class of Uruguay condemns his arrival to the country because he does not represent democracy" but rather "heads a regime characterized by notorious violations of human rights" and "he facilitates Reagan's penetration into Nicaragua." "Duarte's daughter broke into tears in Brazil amidst boos and hisses by angry crowds waving signs saying 'Duarte is a murderer, a genocide'" and "the strong objection to Duarte's presence in Brazil forced him to change or cancel some public ceremonies planned." "The greatest embarrassment endured by Duarte came when the Brazilian Congress was summoned to pay tribute to the visitor and a ridiculously low number of representatives turned out: 30 of the 479 representatives and seven of the 69 senators!"[79]

In Uruguay, Argentina and Brazil, where there is a good deal of experience with such matters, they know a killer when they see one.

Duarte's popularity in the U.S. is reminiscent of Anwar Sadat, also a great hero in the United States, considerably less so in Egypt as American reporters discovered to their surprise when they travelled to Cairo to cover the memorial after his assassination. Duarte remains indispensable to the military because of his ability to ensure the flow of funds from Congress, and business circles have offered him ambiguous support for similar reasons. The general population has little choice. As long as he remains an outstanding democrat within the U.S. ideological system, fulfilling his assigned role, his prospects are reasonably secure.

Contra lobbyist Bruce Cameron charges the "liberal-left" with a double standard because it regards human rights violations by the Sandinistas as "less serious" than in El Salvador, while democratic socialist Ronald Radosh explains that "The need for pressure against the [Sandinista] regime" and "U.S. protection to the democratic resistance" is "more necessary than ever"; "The Sandinistas should be pressured to do no less than the Duarte government did in El Salvador," he adds.[80] Again we see how easy it is to tolerate, indeed not even to perceive the most gruesome atrocities as long as they are committed by "our side." If such statements at first seem shocking, we should bear in mind that Radosh's insight is perceptive. Suppose that the Sandinistas were to adopt the methods of the Duarte government, as Radosh advocates, resorting to physical destruction of the independent media and murder of the political opposition along with savage terror and mass slaughter of the population generally to destroy popular movements and to restore the old order under the control of the military and privileged civilian sectors dedicated to enriching themselves and serving the foreign master, while the pack animals die of disease and malnutrition and semi-slave labor and pesticide poisoning in the approved manner. Under these conditions, the U.S. would be pleased to support their "imperfect but striving democracy," to the polite applause or indifference of American intellectuals who assure us of their profound dedication to the cause of the suffering poor of Central America. The general reaction here to what is taking place in the "fledgling democracies" shows that this judgment is painfully accurate.

In such ways as these the educated classes serve their function in a terrorist culture.

Notes Chapter Five

1. Stephen Kinzer, *NYT*, May 10, 1987; Robert Pear, *NYT*, Nov. 25, 1985.

2. Editorial, *CSM*, May 6, 1987; Hempstone, *BG*, Aug. 21, 1987.

3. For references, see my *For Reasons of State* (Pantheon, 1973), 71, 158.

4. See *TTT*, 11.

5. Americas Watch, *Human Rights in Nicaragua, 1986*, February 1987, 144-5.

6. That Nicaragua is a "Marxist society," whatever that is supposed to mean, is a dogma of the propaganda system standing alongside of the "fact" that there were no elections, etc., requiring no evidence, untroubled by the policies of preserving the private economy and the conclusion of observers concerned with fact that Marxist-Leninists "are a minority" of the Sandinista leadership and that "above all, the two Ortega brothers—the President and the defense minister—are now more powerful than the rest of the leadership combined, and they belong to a rather common breed of third world authoritarian leaders who are not Marxist-Leninist" (Gleijeses, *op. cit.*). The phrase "Marxist," as noted earlier, is merely a term of generalized abuse in U.S. political rhetoric, lacking any further content.

7. Michael Kinsley, *WSJ*, March 26, 1987.

8. *New Republic*, August 10, 1987.

9. Stephen Kinzer, *NYT*, July 19, 1987. Correspondent Larry Boyd reported from the scene that at least 10 civilians were killed by the attackers who reached the edge of town and largely destroyed a nearby cooperative; Pacifica radio, July 20, 1987.

10. *Times* (London), May 26, 1987.

11. Kondracke, *New Republic*, Aug. 10, 1987.

12. *NYT*, April 21, 1986. On the events, the fraud and the background, see *Pirates and Emperors*, chapter 3, and my article "International terrorism: What is the remedy?," *Third World Affairs*, Jan. 1988.

13. "Let it Sink," *New Republic*, Aug. 24, 1987, a remarkable collage of fabrications and hysterical abuse that merits closer analysis.

14. Lewis was writing on the assumption that the bombing of Libya, with 100 killed, was a response to a bombing in Berlin in which one American GI had been killed, so that a ratio of 100 to one is apparently praiseworthy. Nicaragua, then, should be entitled to bomb U.S. cities killing 1 million people (by accident), or perhaps many more, if we consider relative population size. Apart from this, there was no credible evidence then, nor is there now, of Libyan involvement in the disco bombing in Berlin.

15. Bruce Cameron and Penn Kemble, *From a Proxy Force to a National Liberation Movement*, ms., Feb. 1986. Philip Bennett, *BG*, Nov. 25, 29, 1986.

16. See *TTT*, 12f. Cruz has since dropped out; see below.

17. July 16, 1982 DIA "Weekly Intelligence Summary," leaked in 1984 (Council on Hemispheric Affairs, "Misleading the Public," April 3, 1986); *Report of Donald T. Fox, Esq. and Prof. Michael J. Glennon to the International Human Rights Law Group and the Washington Office on Latin America*, April 1985; AP, Nov. 30, 1986; AP, Feb. 26, 1987; Teófilo Cabestrero, *Blood of the Innocent: Victims of the Contras' War in Nicaragua* (Orbis Books (New York), Catholic Institute of International Affairs (London), 1985). See *TTT* for examples and sources—far from complete—on contra atrocities, and a brief comparison of the U.S and foreign media.

18. V. G. Kiernan, *The Lords of Human Kind* (Columbia, 1986), 42.

19. Chinweizu, *The West and the Rest of Us*, 59ff. (citing E. D. Morel, *The Black Man's Burden* (Monthly Review press, 1969), 116ff.); Minter, *King Solomon's Mines Revisited*, 32; Kurt Campbell, "The Warriors of Apartheid," *BG* Magazine, March 1, 1987.

20. See "The Road from Laos to Nicaragua," *Economist*, March 7, 1987. Fox Butterfield writes that General Richard Secord was "secretly attached to the C.I.A. mission in Laos running the clandestine war against the North Vietnamese"—in reality, against the peasants of northern Laos, though the well-documented facts are inadmissible; *NYT*, Dec. 6, 1986.

21. Bernard Diederich, *Somoza* (Dutton, 1981), 12, 311.

22. Stephen Downer, *Daily Telegraph* (London), July 20, 1987, who estimates the number of the Tontons Macoutes at about 300,000; Joseph Treaster, *NYT*, Aug. 10, 1987. On the July 1987 massacre, see AP, *BG*, July 26; Pamela Constable, *BG*, July 27, 28; Reuters, *NYT*, July 26; AP, *NYT*, July 28, 1987. An investigating commission estimated the number killed at more than 200, citing dire poverty and unequal land distribution as factors that "spurred the massacre." The majority of the population barely survive while the "local bourgeoisie, in certain cases very rich,...controls agricultural production, public transport, commerce and political power," also monopolizing state land, the commission reported. Reuters, *BG*, Aug. 30, 1987.

23. Paul Ellman, *Manchester Guardian Weekly*, Jan. 25, 1987; Aryeh Neier, *New York Review*, April 9, 1987. Clifford Krauss describes the province in question (Chontales) as unique in Nicaragua, noting that under Somoza, "large parts of Chontales were controlled by right-wing ranchers who rented small plots to peasant cattlemen" and that Somoza had distributed land in the province, which was not part of the anti-Somoza struggle; the Sandinistas were unable "to supply the credit and supplies the peasants used to get from the old landowners," leading to resentment fueled by the conservative church hierarchy; *WSJ*, Aug. 3, 1987. Much the same is

reported in nearby Nueva Guinea, where the Sandinistas forcibly removed 6000 peasants in 1987 from a largely inaccéssible region where peasants had been given land by Somoza and where Edén Pastora's ARDE, in sharp contrast to the CIA-backed FDN, had carried out several years of organizing, according to James LeMoyne ("All Things Considered," NPR, July 9; see his *NYT* stories of June 17, June 28, 1987, reporting rights abuses by Sandinista soldiers in the region).

24. *LAT*, Feb. 22, 1987; *Le Monde diplomatique*, May 1987. We should add that the resettlement was in large measure forced, not voluntary. See the regular Americas Watch reports for judicious appraisals.

25. James LeMoyne, *NYT*, March 5, March 3, 1987.

26. Bertrand de la Grange, *Le Monde*, Feb. 20 (*MGW*, March 1, 1987); Frederick Kempe and Clifford Krauss, *WSJ*, March 2, 1987, deploring the failure of the U.S. to consider "Miskito politics" while "the Sandinistas have done much to improve their treatment of the Indians." For background, see Martin Diskin et al., *Peace and Autonomy on the Atlantic Coast of Nicaragua*, Latin American Studies Association (LASA), Sept. 1986. On forced recruitment by contras in this area and other terror, intensified after the congressional approval of military aid in June 1986, and their "brutal mistreatment of refugees," alongside of improvement in government practice, see Americas Watch, *Human Rights in Nicaragua 1986*, Feb. 1987; they conclude that "Many Miskitos on the Rio Coco now consider [the Miskito contra force] KISAN, not the Nicaraguan government, to be the greater threat to their safety and livelihoods." They also report that earlier flights of Miskitos to Honduras were "much more involuntary than we first reported," and that KISAN is now forcibly preventing the return of refugees, of whom thousands returned voluntarily in 1986. The media commonly refer to the CIA-supported rebels as "the Miskitos," implying that they represent the entire Indian population, with no further qualification; e.g., Neil Lewis, *NYT*, Sept. 25, 1987.

27. Julia Preston, *WP weekly*, Sept. 21, 1987.

28. *Human Rights in Nicaragua 1986*. An Appendix reviews fraudulent claims concerning political prisoners by the State Department, an analysis that applies as well to irresponsible allegations by the International League for Human Rights and its consultant, contra lobbyist Robert Leiken. For further analysis of falsifications in the report by the International League and earlier articles by its then-program director Nina Shea, see David MacMichael, letter, *NYT*, Dec. 23, 1985; editorial, *Nation*, Sept. 6, 1986; Alexander Cockburn, *Nation*, Sept. 13, 1986. The League had no objection to Leiken's congressional testimony lobbying for contra aid, citing the forthcoming report. One wonders what the reaction would be to a report on Israel by an international human rights group advised by a Libyan lobbyist for Abu Nidal who led them through Israel (to which, of course, the group would never be admitted, in distinction from "totalitarian" Nicaragua). On the remarkable record of the International League in protecting Israel from exposure for human rights abuses, see

Towards a New Cold War, 450, and my *Peace in the Middle East?* (Pantheon, 1974), 197; and material quoted in *Palestine Human Rights Bulletin*, no 2, pp. 1-5, Aug. 30, 1977, from my correspondence with League Chairman Roger Baldwin on their double standards.

29. Clifford Krauss and Frederick Kempe, *WSJ*, Feb. 6, 1987.

30. *J. of Contemporary Studies*, Spring/Summer, 1985; see *TTT*, 131, on some of the astonishing claims of this weird right-wing research center with respect to Pastora, then their hero.

31. "Pastora Comments on CIA, Contras' Struggle," *El Siglo* (Panama), Feb. 9, 1987 (FBIS VI, Central America, 10 Feb. 1987, p. 19); AFP, April 7, 1987, reprinted in *Central America News Update*, April 26, 1987; "Pastora: I would like to meet with the Nicaraguan Government," *Excelsior* (Mexico), reprinted in *Central American NewsPak* (Central America Resource Center), July 6-19, 1987.

32. See the lengthy but largely vacuous report of a discussion with Pastora by James LeMoyne, *NYT*, July 4, 1987.

33. Allan Nairn, *Progressive*, March 1987.

34. *Excelsior* (Mexico), April 2, 1987, reprinted in *Central America News Update*, April 27.

35. Cited by Burns, *At War in Nicaragua*, 74; Rosenthal, who also owns a bank and an insurance company, quoted in an interview in Israel, *Davar*, June 1, 1987.

36. Eli Teicher, *Ma'ariv* (Tel Aviv), March 20, 1987.

37. Rod Nordland, "The New Contras?," *Newsweek*, June 1, 1987. His picture shows how little has changed since the period described by Christopher Dickey, *With the Contras* (Simon & Schuster, 1985) or by the interviews presented in a 1984 German publication: Dieter Eich and Carlos Rincón, *The Contras: Interviews with Anti-Sandinistas* (English translation, Synthesis, 1985).

38. UPI, "Red Cross rips contras for use of emblem," *BG*, June 18, 1987, 125 words; no mention in the *New York Times*. The London *Economist* observes in this connection that "misuse of the Red Cross symbol in times or zones of conflict is a war crime, and punishable as such," under the Geneva conventions; Aug. 29, 1987. On the evacuation of National Guard commanders by a DC-8 jet "disguised with Red Cross insignia," see Peter Kornbluh, in Walker, *Reagan vs. the Sandinistas*.

39. Knight-Ridder Service, *BG*, March 18, 1987, paraphrasing Shultz's House testimony; Kirkpatrick, *BG*, March 15, 1987, syndicated column. Stephen Engelberg, *NYT*, July 15, 1987. Cruz rather evasively denied the charge that he was on the CIA payroll while posing as a presidential candidate and withdrawing under U.S. pressure to discredit the elections, and lobbying Congress as an "independent democrat." See *TTT*, 138.

40. AP, March 15, 1987. On his assessment of his contra colleagues before agreeing to serve as front man to mislead the American public, see pp. 78, 95.

41. Dennis Volman, *CSM*, March 11, 1987, paraphrasing Cruz's remarks in a 7-hour interview; Volman, *CSM*, May 22, 1987.

42. *BG*, April 5, 1987.

43. Dennis Volman, *CSM*, May 18, 1987.

44. *WP*, May 8, 1983, cited by Peter Kornbluh in Walker, *Reagan vs. the Sandinistas*.

45. James LeMoyne, *NYT*, Feb. 21, 1987; AP, March 22, 1987, citing the *Washington Post*.

46. *MH*, Nov. 25, 1986.

47. James LeMoyne, *NYT*, Dec. 15, 1986; on current Salvadoran military strength, see William Branigan, *WP*, March 23, 1987. Assessments of Nicaraguan military strength in the U.S. press are often fanciful constructions, including reservists and militia to support the tales of a massive military machine. According to Paul Knox of Canada's leading journal, the *Globe and Mail* (Toronto), reporting from Managua, "Diplomats here put the number of regular soldiers in the armed forces at about 33,000." The Salvadoran military lists 38,650 Army, 1,290 Navy, 2,700 Air Force (*USA Today*, April 2, 1987).

48. LeMoyne, *NYT*, Dec. 15, 1986; Peter Grier, *CSM*, June 23, 1987, the latter a low-keyed account of the absurdity of the earlier pretense by "contra supporters" in the U.S. that they lacked "the most basic fighting tools." On contra reliance on U.S. air supply, see Marjorie Miller, *LAT*, March 1, 1987, Peter Ford, *CSM*, April 10, 1987. See also Nordland, *op. cit.*, on the scale of the U.S. supply to the proxy army.

49. LeMoyne, *NYT*, June 28, 1987.

50. "Contra supply flights reach new levels," *Dallas Morning News*, June 23, 1987.

51. LeMoyne, *NYT*, June 28, 1987.

52. Apart from regular overflights, with Nicaraguan protests naturally ignored, the Navy has experimented with Israeli-designed pilotless remote-controlled drones launched from the U.S. battleship Iowa in the Caribbean, used earlier by Israel in Lebanon; *International Defense Review* (Geneva), March 1987; cited by AP, March 17, 1987.

53. Richard Evans, *Observer* (London), July 12, 1987; Mike Davies, *Daily Telegraph* (London), July 12, 1987.

54. Ronald Radosh, *Tikkun*, 1.2, 1986.

55. James LeMoyne, *NYT*, Aug. 22, 1987; Dec. 15, 1986.

56. James LeMoyne, *NYT*, April 5, April 7, 1987; Feb. 16, 1987.

57. Clifford Krauss, *WSJ*, anonymous staff reporter, *WSJ*, April 9, 1987.

58. Christopher Lehmann-Haupt, *NYT*, May 14, 1987, reviewing Ray Bonner, *Waltzing with a Dictator* (Times Books, 1987). Lehmann-Haupt is particularly amazed that "contrary to official assertions at the time, the United States Embassy in Manila knew that President Marcos was about to declare martial law in 1972 and did not act to stop him." How is such a

departure from American traditions conceivable? On the reasons for U.S. support for the Marcos coup, and the enthusiastic response to the coup by the U.S. government and foreign investors, see Chomsky and Herman, *Political Economy of Human Rights*, I, 230ff., and Stephen Shalom, *The United States and the Philippines* (ISHI, 1981), chapter 7.

59. Sept. 5, 1987.

60. Fred Barnes, *New Republic*, Aug. 31, 1987.

61. Randolph Ryan, *BG*, Feb. 28, 1987.

62. Burns, *At War in Nicaragua*, 65ff.; on Robelo, Shirley Christian, *Nicaragua* (Vintage, 1986), 51. Burns adds that he was "once a Somoza vice-president."

63. See p. 89; for further references, see *TTT*, 13.

64. For references from the *Pentagon Papers*, see *For Reasons of State*, 95ff.

65. Mecklin, *Mission in Torment* (Doubleday, 1965), 76ff.

66. *NYT*, Aug. 12, 1973. On the myth of the happy peasant in the "gentle land" and the fanciful constructions about Buddhism, see Vickery, *Cambodia*, chapter 1.

67. Fall, *Street Without Joy* (Stackpole books, 1967), 373, revised edition of a book written in the early 1960s.

68. Warner, *The Last Confucian* (Macmillan, 1963), p. 312.

69. LeMoyne, "Teaching the Contras Leftist Rebels' Methods," March 8, 1987. In the style of "objective" journalism, LeMoyne does not present his conclusions as his own, but attributes them to "former Salvadoran rebels and American officials."

70. *Ibid.*; "Three Weeks in Managua," *NYT Book Review*, March 8, 1987, a tirade masquerading as a review of Rushdie's *The Jaguar Smile*. See Alexander Cockburn, *Nation*, April 4, 1987, for appropriate commentary.

71. See also my article and Jack Spence's in Walker, *Reagan vs. the Sandinistas* and my introduction to Morris Morley and James Petras, *The Reagan Administration and Nicaragua* (Pamphlet Series, Institute for Media Analysis, New York, 1987); also Marc Cooper, "Whitewashing Duarte: U.S. Reporting on El Salvador," NACLA *Report on the Americas*, Jan/March 1986.

72. Reagan, press conference of Aug. 13, 1986; cited in Burns, *At War in Nicaragua*, 147. Reagan is not alone in this interesting assessment. While his Central America policy is widely condemned in Europe, by 87% of West German opinion for example (*Central America Report*, Guatemala, July 31, 1987), his view of the world is shared in client states, even on the left. In Israel, for example, Kibbutz Beit Alpha (the oldest Kibbutz in the leftmost branch of the Kibbutz movement, associated with the dovish Mapam Party) manufactures armored cars for the internal security forces in South Africa. But its secretary, who sees "no problem" in supplying South Africa or the Israeli army with armored cars to control African and

Arab demonstrators, nevertheless says that they have some standards: "our decision is not to market to Chile or Nicaragua or any totalitarian state." Aryeh Kiezel, "In South Africa demonstrations are broken up with armored cars from the kibbutz," *Yediot Ahronot*, Aug. 18, 1987, a critical report in this right-wing mass circulation journal.

73. Americas Watch, *Human Rights in Nicaragua*. The colossal scale of Reagan administration lying documented in this and other Americas Watch reports, and elsewhere, will surprise even the most cynical. It is considered perfectly normal by media commentators, who feign outrage that a presidential candidate should have failed to identify the source of a quote in a campaign speech, thus demeaning this august office.

74. *New Republic*, Aug. 10, 24, 1987; Sept. 29, 1986. The "depredations of the *commandantes*" that account for this judgment, apart from the failure to maintain the rule of privileged elites linked to U.S. power ("democrats"), include crucially the unwillingness to accord Israel the loyalty required by this Stalinist-style journal—the term is appropriate—as a criterion for its approval. Specifically, the failure to reestablish the links with Israel established by Somoza cost Israel a substantial market for arms, provided through Somoza's final slaughter; see Beit-Hallahmi, *The Israeli Connection*, 91f.

75. See *TTT*, 106, and 109ff. for more on Duarte and his role.

76. Joy Hackel, *St. Louis Post-Dispatch*, July 25, 1986. See *NYT*, Feb. 21, 1981.

77. *Central America Bulletin* (Berkeley), June, 1987, citing press reports in El Salvador; the responses on the agrarian reform were from a similar poll conducted in late December 1986. Figures rounded throughout.

78. Hackel, *op. cit.*

79. *Mesoamerica*, San José, June 1986.

80. Cameron, letter, *Nation*, April 5, 1986; Radosh, *WSJ*, Dec. 19, 1986. Both of them claim to be critical of atrocities in El Salvador, but this pose is fraudulent, plainly so in Radosh's case, as exhibited by his recommendation of the Duarte method for establishing "democracy." Neither advocates that we organize a "proxy force" to attack El Salvador to put an end to atrocities that are vastly worse than anything chargeable to the Sandinistas; the same is true of the terrorists they support, as documented regularly by Americas Watch and other serious human rights investigators. Cameron received $66,000 to lobby Democrats in favor of contra aid, the source apparently being Carl Channell, now facing a jail sentence for his part in the illegal propaganda operations of the Reagan administration. See Peter Kornbluh, *Village Voice*, Oct. 13, 1987.

6

Damage Control

The partial exposure of Washington's international terror network in late 1986 necessitated a project of damage control to ensure that nothing significant would be perceived or learned, not a simple matter in the light of what we have done in Central America in the past decade. This project relies upon the pretense that the foreign policy of the Reagan administration is foolish, incompetent, out of control. Sophisticated observers shake their heads in dismay and despair over "All the President's Midgets."[1] The same was true during the Watergate farce. The reaction merits skepticism. This is the characteristic response when the outlines of operative U.S. policy begin to appear through the veil of doctrine. The instinctive reaction is to narrow the focus of inquiry to conceal the systematic nature of the criminality now being partially exposed. All problems must be blamed on the failings of incompetent individuals, not traced to their institutional roots (after all, even the most magnificent system may contain a bad apple or an overzealous patriot). And crucially, the nobility of U.S. intentions must be protected from any challenge.

In conformity with these overriding principles, as we have seen, many crucial issues are simply off the agenda: the historical and documentary record that reveals the general and largely invariant guidelines for U.S. policies; the institutional setting within which policy develops; the recent application of these policies in Guatemala and El Salvador; the normal conditions of life within the Caribbean and Central American domains of long-term U.S. influence and control and what these teach us about the goals and character of U.S. government policy over many

113

years; and similar matters elsewhere that might yield a degree of understanding of the origins and nature of the problems that must now be addressed. Such matters are not fit topics for reporting, commentary and debate. Rather, the agenda must conform to elite requirements, generally set by state propaganda, though debate is permissible insofar as dominant elites disagree on tactical and procedural matters. Within these limits, basic doctrines are beyond question and controversy, for example, the firm commitment of U.S. policymakers to democracy, economic development and human rights. Contemporary events must be reported and discussed in these terms, and historical memory must be shaped so that these doctrines are not called into question, or even considered controversial.

The project of damage control is much facilitated by the technique of historical amnesia and tunnel vision. This allows us to avoid what might otherwise be embarrassing (and surely pertinent) questions. Among those that come to mind at once are these:

> What explains the sudden conversion of U.S. elite opinion to profound concern for human rights and democracy in Nicaragua precisely in July 1979, when the Somoza clan, our long-term allies, were driven from Managua, and the Carter administration failed in its effort to retain his hated National Guard, so that it would be in a position to restore the old order with new faces?

> What were the U.S. and Israel doing in Iran before they began the scandalous arms dealings with Iran in 1985, according to the chronology provided by the Tower commission and the congressional hearings—that is, when there were no hostages to rescue?

> Why was there great outrage over the suspension of the pro-contra journal *La Prensa* the day after Congress issued what U.S. government officials described as a virtual declaration of war against Nicaragua, but total silence when Israel, at the same time, permanently closed two Jerusalem newspapers on the grounds that "although we offer them freedom of expression,...it is forbidden to permit them to exploit this freedom in order to harm the State of Israel" and as the High Court held, "It is inconceivable that the State of Israel should allow terrorist organizations which seek to destroy it to set up businesses in its territory, legitimate as they may be" (*La Prensa* was aided by a contra lobbying organization funded by the superpower attacking Nicaragua)?[2]

A crucial condition of respectable discourse is that such questions as these be suppressed.

Let us consider some features of the technique of damage control.

In Congress, a leading critic of Reagan policies, Rep. Michael Barnes, expresses his support for the "noble objective" of the Reagan administration: "to somehow 'democratize' Nicaragua." But the contras, he adds, "are not the instrument that will achieve that objective."[3] He sees the democratic process in operation among "our friends" in the region—Honduras, Guatemala and El Salvador, where no reasonable person could utter the word "democracy" without a shudder. And we must persevere in our commitment to bring democracy to Nicaragua, undeterred by contemplation of what is revealed by a record of U.S. intervention extending over 130 years.

Turning to the media, in the "ultraliberal" press, a critic of the Reagan administration writes in a news analysis that Lt.-Col. Oliver North, who was at the "vortex of scandal," "became increasingly committed to democracy in Central America, especially the cause of the contras."[4] Even before Col. North's testimony, which revealed his utter contempt for democracy with brutal clarity, what was the evidence that he cared about democracy—in Nicaragua or the United States—or even knew what the word means, or that the contra leadership or the U.S. government are interested in democracy, or ever have been? None is necessary, since we are dealing here with doctrinal truths.

It is an important feature of American culture that these doctrines serve as the presuppositions of discourse, entirely beyond the reach of discussion. It is a doctrinal truth, whatever the facts, that the Reagan Doctrine was "designed as a foreign policy tool to bring democracy to places where Soviet-sponsored regimes came to power in the 1970s," though there are questions as to whether we should aid "the resistance in Nicaragua" (Stephen Rosenfeld), that is, the proxy army attacking Nicaragua from its foreign bases, maintained in the field by supplies flown in daily thanks to the bounty of their superpower sponsor. We must support the "elected governments in the region," the editors of the New York Times demand, strengthing the "democratic regimes" in El Salvador, Honduras and Guatemala and their "elected presidents," and protecting them from the depredations of "the Sandinistas," not an "elected government" with an "elected president," and surely not "a democracy" such as our client states. The editors of the Washington Post agree. The Central American conflict pits "the Marxist regime" in Nicaragua against "the elected

government of El Salvador" and "the Nicaraguan resistance," and
we must help "friendly governments in the region cope with the
overflow of Sandinista power"—not the overflow of American
power in violation of international law, as determined by the
World Court with overwhelming UN endorsement—while
assigning to "Nicaragua's fellow Latins the burden of moving it
along a democratic path" as proposed in the Arias plan, which,
outside of the Free Press, treats the governments in Central
America on a par, with no mention of Nicaragua. "Admiral
Poindexter believed that the President's general policy was to help
the contras democratize Nicaragua," James Reston informs us *after*
listening to Poindexter's remarkable testimony; "Maybe the
tragedy began first with the corruption of language," he adds,
though surely without understanding why these words have a
certain merit.[5]

When the intellectual elite turn to their task of restoring the
faith, we descend to low comedy. In the *New York Times
Magazine*, *New Republic* literary editor Leon Wieseltier assures
us—with perhaps a touch of desperation—that "It would be hard
to exaggerate the purity of heart that the Reagan Administration
feels" as representatives of "a great and good power." "The pure
hearts dream of democracy in Nicaragua" and proceed with
"exaggerated humanitarianism," but they err in the atmosphere of
"intellectual righteousness of Mr. Reagan's Washington," soon to
be displayed, even more vividly than before, in the congressional
hearings. To recover from "the moral and intellectual intoxications
of the Reagan years," we must add a touch of "realism" to the
"lofty idealism" that has inspired the Reaganites as they exulted in
the slaughter of some 150,000 people in Central America,
enthusiastically supported Israeli massacres, and in general,
became apologists "for some of the worst horrors of our time" in
the words of international human rights monitors, and agents of
these horrors.[6] But in their dealings with Iran, Wieseltier
continues, the Reaganites "have made a mockery of one of the
administration's finest articles of faith, that terrorists and their
taskmasters not be appeased."[7] This is a common refrain, never
accompanied by the observation that if international terrorists are
to be shunned, then Washington must close down.

With regard to Nicaragua, Wieseltier urges that we replace the
"lofty idealism" of the Reaganites by a "realist anti-Communism."
Sober realism dictates that we act "to prevent the final integration
of the Sandinista state into the structure of Soviet domination and

to prevent the Sandinistas from interfering in the lives of their neighbors," goals that cannot "be accomplished without the tightening vise of the contras." Turning to the real world, we quickly discover that one consequence of Reaganite policies from the outset, predictable and predicted, was to compel the Sandinistas to rely on the USSR, abandoning their efforts at neutralism, so as to justify the attack launched against them for quite different reasons. This is, furthermore, a standard pattern of U.S. intervention, Guatemala in 1954 being one familiar case. As for the idea that the U.S. must prevent Nicaragua from interfering in the lives of its neighbors—something we would never do—it is worthy of note that the doctrinal truth remains unaffected by the absence of credible evidence of such interference, including the pathetic efforts of the most recent State Department propaganda.[8] The remainder continues in the same vein, in conformity with the norms of educated discourse.

The norms are not entirely exceptionless, as earlier references indicate,[9] and are quite different from those to be found in the professional Latin Americanist literature. But the uniformity is nevertheless striking and instructive, revealing features of the dominant intellectual culture that receive much less attention than they merit.

We might note that the effects of Reaganite programs in ensuring Nicaraguan dependence on the USSR, imperceptible to elite opinion, are obvious enough to the Nicaraguan opposition they profess to support. Opposition parliamentarian Mauricio Díaz, while expressing his objections to the new Constitution, nevertheless observes that

> This country has little alternative to tying itself more and more closely to the military and economic community of eastern Europe. The fruit of the US strategy will be if Nicaragua truly becomes, at some point, a part of the East-West confrontation. I am not opposed to support from the socialist countries. Certainly, if the Sandinistas were not getting arms from the Warsaw Pact, our country would be in the hands of the FDN, that is clear. And the FDN is not a democratic option. Eduardo Frei died hoping that Pinochet would give power back to the civilians. We know that something equivalent or worse would occur here in Nicaragua. We are against the FDN and we are against the counterrevolutionary option.[10]

The alleged commitment of the United States to bring democracy to Nicaragua, a crucial principle of damage control, is assumed with virtual unanimity by commentators, untroubled by the question of its curious timing and the demonstrable efforts of the U.S. to destroy meaningful democracy in Latin America and elsewhere, a fact that also cannot be perceived, indeed an idea that cannot be entertained. Editorials assure us that the "unchanging goal" of the administration is "democracy and free elections in Managua," though the "Reagan administration must take care that its efforts to bring democracy to Nicaragua are not at the expense of democracy already in place in neighboring Honduras."[11] In the news columns, we read that the U.S. "has been seeking a comprehensive regional treaty that will...compel the democratization of the countries, particularly Nicaragua," and that Congress sees diplomacy as "a fresh approach to the US policy of using the contras to press Nicaragua's leftist government into becoming more democratic."[12] In the case of official enemies, or even foreign states that are not simply U.S. clients, the proclamation of some alleged intention does not entail that it is the actual goal of policy, but when Washington pronounces its objectives, the claim becomes unchallengeable fact and no rational analysis is permissible, even thinkable.

Dozens of similar examples can be cited, and one will be hard put to find any deviation in the media from this mindless incantation of state propaganda even after the stark revelation of the disdain for democracy in Reaganite circles during the Iran-contra hearings—as if the factual record of the 1980s, or the historical record, did not suffice to allow a rational assessment of this passion for democracy.

In such cases as these, as in the call that the U.S. remain true to its vocation of "protecting freedom" and so on, we see illustrated the great advantages of adherence to the Party Line: no facts are necessary, history is as irrelevant as elementary rationality. The principles of the doctrinal system are Higher Truths, requiring no argument, susceptible to no challenge.

This rigorous adherence to doctrinal truths, repeated day after day, no doubt succeeds in its purpose of establishing state doctrine as sacrosanct. The perpetrators as well no doubt come to internalize what they say and to lose the ability to call it into question. The very absence of argument helps instill required beliefs, assigning them the status of background assumptions that it would be bizarre to question. Given the tacit elite consensus on fundamentals, and the subordination of the political and information systems to concentrated state and private power, closely linked, there is little danger that alternative conceptions will reach a large audience, and if by chance they do, they must bear a heavy burden of proof not required by the chanting of authorized slogans. The system works very well to constrain independent thought and keep it within approved limits, at least among articulate and political active segments of the population.

The contras are "the rebels" or "the resistance," or even "the democratic resistance" (Ronald Radosh) or the "Nicaraguan freedom fighters" (Mark Belnick, Counsel for the Senate Investigating Committee, questioning Elliott Abrams).[13] Elsewhere in Central America the "leftist insurgents" are "subversive groups," in the terminology of news reporting.[14] It is only in internal documents by their lobbyists that the contras are correctly described as a "proxy force" for which we must somehow construct a popular base.

As noted earlier, critics are concerned only that Reagan's "active promotion of democracy" may be too "aggressive." At the dissident extreme of the media, Tom Wicker criticizes the Reaganites on the grounds that the U.S. has no "obligation to install democracy by force in Nicaragua," and Sol Linowitz, another critic, urges that the U.S. and its Central American allies should not "desist from their goals of political reform" in Nicaragua—so that it can become a "democracy" like Honduras, El Salvador, and Guatemala, safely ruled by the military and the U.S.-linked oligarchy. He explains further that we should support the Arias plan, which "certainly does not mean abandoning the goal of advancing human rights and democratic politics in Nicaragua" in accordance with Reaganite humanitarian passions: "Indeed, the centerpiece of the Arias plan is democratic change in Nicaragua," the standard misrepresentation of the wording of the plan, to which we return, in the U.S. doctrinal system, and noteworthy again for the tacit assumption that "democratic change" is a lesser problem in the U.S.-backed terrorist states.[15] Editorials and commentators assure us that "Washington's overriding goals are the security of Nicaragua's Central American neighbors and the stability of democracies throughout Central America," and that Congress has supported "stepped-up military pressure" in the hope that it "may influence the Sandinistas to leave their neighbors alone and reestablish internal democratic freedoms."[16]

Examples are legion. The authors are aware—or could easily become so—that the Sandinistas have been requesting international supervision of the borders since 1981 so that the

Central American countries would "leave their neighbors alone," a proposal always rejected by the United States, which is committed to military intervention in the region as it has been for over a century. They might also learn—though not without some effort—that as of mid-1986, Nicaragua was the only Central American country to have accepted the Contadora treaty (rejected by U.S. clients), which would bar arms imports and remove foreign military advisors from the region, a fact virtually suppressed in the U.S. media[17]; and that in December 1986, Nicaragua once again requested that the UN send an independent fact-finding mission to the border after a conflict there, "in order to determine the causes of tension and recommend relevant measures to prevent a further worsening of the situation" (UN Ambassador Nora Astorga), a proposal rejected by Honduras with U.S. backing, as always, and also unreported.[18]

The authors of these typical commentaries could also easily learn, if they do not already know, the facts cited earlier concerning Nicaraguan trade with the Soviet bloc when Reagan announced the May 1985 embargo, also declaring a National Emergency in the face of the threat to our existence posed by Nicaragua, renewed yearly since[19]; but to consider these and similar facts would clearly be improper, inconsistent with the required image of an agent of the Kremlin conspiracy. It would also shed too much light on the real purpose of the embargo: to overcome this neutralist stance so as to justify the U.S. aggression undertaken for quite different reasons.

The authors also are capable of understanding that the predictable effects of isolation, embargo and terrorist attack are to reduce the possibilities of democracy and to increase domestic repression. They know, or can easily discover, that U.S. allies such as Israel enforce measures at least as harsh under far less onerous circumstances and that the United States too adopted such measures at home during World Wars I and II, though it was not under attack by a superpower; in fact, its national territory had not been threatened since the War of 1812.[20] One can only imagine what the internal policies would be if a terrorist army organized by the USSR were rampaging through Arizona and Montana with a base in Idaho, heavily supplied with air drops, with Canada serving as a major Soviet military base with massive permanent Soviet military maneuvers preparing for an invasion, Soviet fleets of unimaginable power cruising offshore and regular Soviet reconnaissance flights coordinating the terrorist attacks of their proxy armies, and U.S. air waves dominated by hostile radio and television from abroad. Would the U.S., under those circumstances, permit free travel by Russians who have published outrageous lies about the U.S. in the course of their lobbying and apologetics for the terrorist forces, and who are visiting with the open intention of digging up further information—or inventing it, if necessary—that can employed to gain support for the attack on the border states? Or would it permit the publication of a major journal of wealthy Communists who had managed to hoard American capital, funded by the Soviet Union, lining up in the terrorist crusade? Given the actual record under vastly less provocative conditions, the questions are hardly worth raising, though it should be noted that a realistic analogy is impossible to construct.

The authors could also easily discover that repressive policies were not only the predictable effects of the two-pronged U.S. war against Nicaragua, combining terrorist attack with barriers to trade and aid, but also the intended effects from its earliest days. In the World Court proceedings, former CIA analyst David MacMichael testified that the 1981 CIA program ratified by the administration had as its purpose: to use the proxy army to "provoke cross-border attacks by Nicaraguan forces and thus serve to demonstrate Nicaragua's aggressive nature," to pressure the Nicaraguan Government to "clamp down on civil liberties within Nicaragua itself, arresting its opposition, demonstrating its allegedly inherent totalitarian nature and thus increase domestic dissent within the country," and to undermine its shattered economy. We hardly need the testimony, since these predictable effects were surely the intended ones. But to understand such matters, it is necessary to escape the confines of the ideological system and to question the sanctity and nobility of U.S. intentions. That is excluded, as an intolerable departure from civilized norms.

A closer look at the substantive content of formal civil liberties is also excluded, though it is hardly an insignificant issue, even in states such as Costa Rica, which have an impressive democratic record (or in the U.S., for that matter). The Council on Hemispheric Affairs and the Newspaper Guild (AFL-CIO) discuss the topic in their regular surveys of the Latin American media.[21] They point out that in Costa Rica, where civil liberties "have been observed to a degree unmatched by any of the Spanish-speaking republics of Latin America," the population "in practice...often can obtain only one side of the story, since wealthy ultraconservatives control the major daily newspapers and broadcasting stations"; here the effective control over information is guaranteed by the "free market of ideas" as it functions in a society with concentration of resources in private hands, and therefore no limits on freedom of the press would be perceived from the Orwellian standpoint of U.S. ideology on the matter.

In El Salvador, which the Council lists as the worst violator of press freedoms after Chile and Paraguay, reporters continue to "work under the constant threat of harassment and death" with at least 20 journalists killed since the 1979 coup and a greater number "disappeared" or forced into exile. The "prevailing sense of insecurity...has profoundly affected moderate and right-wing journalists" while other publications "have been forced to close as a result of right-wing death-squad violence" and those that remain are largely "controlled by wealthy ultra-conservatives"; and, of course, "freedom of expression remained suspended [in 1985-6] under a state of emergency" that had been in effect since March 1980, but was virtually unmentionable in the U.S.[22] Similarly, "restrictions on press freedom in Honduras remain unofficial but pervasive, producing a system of self-censorship," because of government blacklists and general fear.

Others have made similar points. In the journal of the Committee to Protect Journalists, Alan Nairn writes that "The main method of censorship employed by the Guatemalan army [who effectively rule the country behind a democratic façade] is murder, directed primarily at the local press." He notes that "since 1978, about 47 Guatemalan journalists have been assassinated, many of them in quite spectacular fashion—radio broadcasters dragged out of the station while on the air, prominent newspaper journalists machine-gunned while they are driving downtown." The mass slaughter of civilians by the ruling generals

> had never been discussed in the Guatemalan press—radio, T.V. or newspapers. And that had been accomplished without a system of formal censorship. There is no ministry of censorship in Guatemala. It's simply an ad hoc system where journalists who dare to discuss such things are killed.

Writing on El Salvador in the same journal, Ruben Martinez concludes that the situation is improving in that terror has declined from the peak years of U.S.-sponsored atrocities, but "press freedom is still very limited for those who do not echo the official line." The two largest dailies are "extreme right-wing," and their editors laud the freedom of the press, observing that they can criticize the government as harshly as they like—"since current conditions do not inhibit the political right from speaking out," Martinez adds, meaning that they will not be assassinated or "disappeared" by the security forces or the terrorist squads associated with them. These journals do not even accept paid ads from left-of-center opposition groups, nor does a smaller one, close to Duarte's PDC. Another smaller journal, *El Mundo*, is "by far the most open of the dailies," accepting ads from opposition unions and human rights groups that call for freedom for political prisoners, an end to the war, and measures to deal with "the economic hardship of the working class." The "most daring source of information" is the small weekly news bulletin of the Catholic University of Central America (UCA), "limited in circulation" but willing to accept articles from opposition unions and political opposition groups. The most "significant sign of *apertura*" in the press is an editorial in *El Mundo* adapted from a UCA piece, in which the most extreme statement quoted is that the army "has succeeded only in not losing the war," a statement that "would have been impossible to make publicly in the terror-filled atmosphere of the early 1980s." Americas Watch also observes that state terror has sufficed to ensure that "since 1981 the Salvadoran press has either supported the government or criticized it from a right-wing perspective."[23]

These matters are never discussed as we laud our achievements in bringing "democracy" to El Salvador, just as heavy censorship and closing of journals, detention and expulsion of editors, even refusal to grant permission to publish, is off the agenda with regard to Israel. One will search the U.S. media in vain for impassioned demands that *La Crónica* and *El Independiente* be permitted to reopen in El Salvador, protected by an international military presence from the Duarte security forces, which continue to reign unchallenged. Indeed, who has even heard the names of these journals destroyed by state terror, their editors and staff murdered and mutilated by the security forces, driven from the country, or intimidated into silence, the physical plant demolished? In contrast, violations of press freedom in Nicaragua that evidently fall far short of murder and general terror evoke unbounded outrage.

These are crucial requirements for the operation of damage control.

The Reagan administration has assumed from the start that it could count on domestic hypocrites to feign indignation over the intended consequences of its terrorist acts, applying lofty civil libertarian standards that they do not for a moment accept (as is easily demonstrated by comparative analysis[24]) while blaming the travail of Nicaragua on "Communist mismanagement," "Sandinista paranoia" or their "inherently totalitarian nature." Everything has proceeded exactly as anyone familiar with American history and culture would have anticipated.

The concern of the editors of the *Christian Science Monitor* that we act to "reestablish internal democratic freedoms" in Nicaragua is widely echoed. Thus, the *New York Times* endorses the Arias plan because it calls for "restoring freedoms and holding elections in Nicaragua."[25]—there having been no elections according to *Times* doctrine. Such hopes for *restoration* of democratic freedoms in Nicaragua must be a reference to the Somoza period, if words have meaning, hence an appeal for a return to those happy days, when, in fact, there was little concern voiced over conditions in Nicaragua; "from 1969 to 1977 the networks spent a total of one hour on Nicaragua—all on the 1972 earthquake," while El Salvador was also ignored.[26] These interesting formulations are standard not only in editorials but also in what are called "news columns," where we read, for example, that the Arias plan calls for "the creation of a democratic system *in Nicaragua*" and that Guatemala "favors *re-establishment* of a democratic system" in Nicaragua.[27] The *Washington Post* also demands that we must turn "Nicaragua *back toward* democracy" and assures us that the U.S. "is working through the contras to *restore* democracy to Nicaragua"—as under Somoza, presumably; and Reagan is also laboring to "break the Sandinistas' Cuban and Soviet ties"—which, of course, the Reaganites relish and have desperately sought to strengthen in the traditional pattern discussed earlier.[28]

There is, in fact, a way to give some sense to the pretense that that the U.S. is concerned to bring democracy to Central America and that elite opinion truly feels concern over the lack of democracy in Nicaragua (under attack by a superpower). It is only necessary to understand that like most terms of political theology, the term "democracy" has two meanings: its dictionary meaning, and a technical sense devised for indoctrination exercises. In the technical sense of the term, as discussed earlier, "democracy" exists only when elements favorable to the interests of U.S. investors are guaranteed the capacity to rule the political system. At home, that means that the political and ideological systems must be under business control, a result achieved long ago. In the Third World, "democracy" requires that the media and political system be in the hands of local oligarchies or similar elements committed to the form of "development" favored by U.S. investors, that the public be marginalized (by violence, if necessary), and that the military, with its long-established links to the U.S. system of violence, be granted free rein.

We can therefore understand how, on the one hand, Ronald Radosh and others can describe the contras as the "democratic resistance," while on the other, Edgar Chamorro, the CIA-appointed contra spokesman "who knows the contras far better than anyone in Washington," can characterize them as "the most 'undemocratic force' in Central America, the combined product of the CIA, Somoza, and the Argentine military."[29] Both usages of the term "democracy" are appropriate, the first in the Orwellian sense of approved discourse, the second in the dictionary sense of the term. The Orwellian sense is required for damage control, standing alongside the term "people's democracy" flaunted by other commissars.

In the technical Orwellian sense of the term, the "fledgling democracies" of Central America much lauded by elite opinion are indeed "democracies." Similarly, the "collection of successful businessmen, bankers and attorneys" who met at a Costa Rican country club to propound a "progressive" political program under the watchful eyes of their masters are surely "democrats." The reason is that they can be counted on to oppose reform measures that would direct the resources of Nicaragua to the poor, and they insist upon domestic advantages that would guarantee something like the traditional system of rule—but with *them*, rather than the Somoza clan, in the driver's seat, subordinated, of course, to the Ruler of the Hemisphere, the "enforcer" in Charles Krauthammer's apt and admiring phrase, always on call to break the bones of anyone who gets out of line. Nicaragua, in contrast, is not a "democracy" for the sufficient reason that business- and landowner-based groups were not represented much beyond their numerical proportion in the pre-election system of governance, as Thomas Walker observes, and in the 1984 elections, privileged elites linked to U.S. state and business interests were not guaranteed the required advantages: domination of the media and the political system in addition to the power that flows from control over economic life—all of this a severe affront to "democracy." That is presumably why the "moderates" left the

pre-election junta[30] and why they refused under heavy U.S.
pressure to take part in the 1984 elections while the "leader"
chosen by the United States, Arturo Cruz, was funded by the
CIA—elections that did not take place according to the U.S.
doctrinal system because the right outcome was not guaranteed by
the distribution of power. Similarly, the "moderates" remain
admirable democrats despite their lack of a political program and
their insistence at the "exile Assembly" that in contrast to the
victorious Sandinistas in 1979, who gave business elements a
place within the ruling coalition, they will exclude the Sandinistas
totally from "any representation in the governing junta" after their
victory (Pedro Joaquín Chamorro, former editor of *La Prensa*, who
openly supported the contra attack on leaving for Costa Rica after
having tacitly supported it before).[31] That stand is entirely
consistent with "democracy" in the Orwellian sense of U.S. usage,
just as other measures to exclude "Communists" (another term of
Newspeak, referring to anyone who does not accept "democracy")
are considered legitimate, at home as well, including measures of
extreme violence in our dependencies. It is therefore unnecessary
to demonstrate the democratic credentials of the official
"democrats," or to consider any additional facts about Nicaragua.

On similar grounds, we can understand the perceptions of U.S.
government officials struggling to bring "democracy" to the Third
World, for example, the legendary General Edward Lansdale, who
was dedicated to these tasks for many years in Southeast Asia.
Explaining his progress in laying the basis for democracy in Laos
after the U.S. had succeeded in subverting the coalition
government established by a democratic election, he reported
proudly, in secret, that "There is also a local veteran's organization
and a grass-roots political organization in Laos, both of which are
subject to CIA direction and control and are capable of carrying
out propaganda, sabotage and harassment operations."[32] As in
Laos, so in Nicaragua: democracy under CIA control.

The same principles explain why the liberal press finds
nothing odd in running an article on the opening of Congress in
the Philippines, lauding "the return of full democracy" and
quoting Rep. Stephen Solarz, who says that this "marks the
transition of the Philippines from dictatorship to
democracy"—with a headline reading: "Aquino's decree bans
Communist Party," and a lead paragraph reporting that President
Aquino, in a presidential decree, stipulated penalties of
imprisonment for membership in the Communist Party, thus

reversing the policy of the Marcos dictatorship, which legalized the party in the mid-1970s.[33] One may imagine the response to similar moves in Nicaragua, outlawing the domestic political opposition.

On the same principles, we can explain State Department concerns that the government of Guatemala in the early 1950s was too democratic (in the dictionary sense of the term), treating the Communist Party "as an authentic domestic political party and not as part of the world-wide Soviet Communist conspiracy."[34] As a secret State Department intelligence report commented in 1955, a year after the successful destruction of Guatemalan democracy,

> Arévalo, faithful to his program, insisted upon the maintenance of an open political system; and neither the military, debilitated by internal rivalries, nor self-seeking politicans were able to circumscribe his policy. It was in this atmosphere of *laissez-faire* that the communists were able to expand their operations and appeal effectively to various sectors of the population...,[35]

so Guatemalan democracy obviously had to go. On the same essentially invariant principles, we can understand why democracy is untainted, and hence no critical commentary is heard, when the military retains tight control over communities in El Salvador where fear of leftist *political* contamination remains (see p. 93). If we proceed to less obvious cases, where more subtle questions arise, we can also understand how it can be that, in the cause of establishing democracy, U.S. occupation forces worked with considerable success to restrict democracy to limits acceptable to established privilege in Japan and Europe in the early post-World War II period, at the direction of the civilian leadership in Washington.

All becomes clear, once we have understood the norms of educated discourse.

Notes Chapter Six

1. David Broder, *WP Weekly*, Dec. 15, 1986.

2. See my chapter in Walker, *Reagan vs. the Sandinistas*, for further details. *La Prensa* support for the contras was barely concealed. In April 1986, for example, one of the owners, Jaime Chamorro, openly supported Reagan's request for aid to the contras, writing in the *Washington Post* that "Those Nicaraguans who are fighting for democracy [the standard code phrase for the proxy army] have the right to ask for help wherever they can get it"; *WP*, April 3. See *Right to Survive: Human Rights in Nicaragua* (Catholic Institute for International Relations, London, 1987), for discussion of the *La Prensa* case, and analysis of the human rights situation in Nicaragua in a more general context; an interesting review by Alita Paine and Juan Mendez of Americas Watch describes the study as "carefully researched and fair," discussing questions that remain ambiguous (*The Tablet* (London), Sept. 19, 1987). "While *La Prensa*'s opposition to Somoza is often cited to confirm the newspaper's democratic credentials, shortly after conservative Pedro Joaquín Chamorro, Jr. took editorial control in 1980, 80 percent of the staff resigned and founded the independent, pro-Sandinista paper *El Nuevo Diario*" (COHA's *Washington Report on the Hemisphere*, July 23, 1986), a fact invariably suppressed here. One of those who left was editor Xavier Chamorro, now editor of *El Nuevo Diario*, which could claim to be the authentic successor to the journal that courageously opposed Somoza. The fact that the new *La Prensa* lacks democratic credentials, however, is in no way relevant to its suspension by the government or the earlier censorship, acts that should be deplored by those who honestly hold truly libertarian standards, a group so small in the U.S. or elsewhere as to be virtually undetectable.

3. Council on Hemispheric Affairs *Washington Report on the Hemisphere*, interview, Nov. 12, 1986. The liberal Washington Office on Latin America describes Barnes as "the most consistently visible and active opponent of Reagan administration policies in Latin America"; *Update*, Nov./Dec. 1986.

4. Ben Bradlee, Jr., *BG*, Dec. 7, 1986.

5. Rosenfeld, "Doctrine that Cost Too Much" (the standard liberal complaint), *WP-MGW*, July 26; Editorial, *NYT*, Aug. 19, 1987; editorial, *WP*, June 16; Reston, *NYT*, July 19, 1987.

6. See *TTT*, chapter 1.5.

7. "What Went Wrong?," *NYT Magazine*, Dec. 7, 1986. To fully appreciate these comments we must bear in mind that their author has been a prominent advocate of U.S. and Israeli international terrorism.

8. See *TTT*, chapter 3.5.4; Morley and Petras, *The Reagan Administration and Nicaragua* and my introduction; CIA analyst David MacMichael's testimony at the World Court (the Court considered and dismissed these charges with some derision), UN Official Document A/40/907, S/17639, 19 Nov. 1985.

9. See particularly the series of judicious appraisals in *Dissent* by Abraham Brumberg, former editor of the State Department journal *Problems of Communism*.

10. *Envío*, Managua, Nov. 1986, a series of interviews with opposition leaders. Within the U.S. doctrinal system, Díaz's democratic credentials are tarnished by the fact that his branch of the Social Christian Party refused to bend to U.S. pressure and boycott the 1984 elections, thus interfering with the U.S. effort to discredit them and eliminate them from history.

11. Editorials, *CSM*, May 6, 20, 1987.

12. Bernard Gwertzman, *NYT*, Jan. 8, 1987.

13. June 2, 1987; *NYT*, June 3.

14. Richard Halloran, "Latin Guerrillas Joining Forces, U.S. Officers Say," *NYT*, March 3, 1987.

15. Wicker, *NYT*, July 11, 1986; Linowitz, *NYT*, May 30, 1986, July 3, 1987.

16. Editorial, *CSM*, Nov. 24, 1986.

17. Nicaragua declared its readiness to sign the Contadora Group's draft treaty on June 21, 1986; "North-South Monitor," *Third World Quarterly* (London), Oct. 1986. The rejection of the treaty by the U.S. client states (*London Guardian*, June 13, 1986) was not reported by the national press. The Nicaraguan acceptance of the treaty received oblique mention in two small items in the *New York Times*, under the headings "Nicaragua Makes Offer to Limit Some Weapons," "U.S. Condemns Offer by Nicaragua on Treaty" (June 22, 23), focusing on Reagan administration rejection of the move as "propagandistic." Both items appeared in the "Around the World" roundup of marginal news. The *Washington Post* ignored the acceptance. On the terms of the treaty, see *Contadora Primer*, *International Policy Report*, Sept.-Nov., 1986.

18. AP, Dec. 10, 1986. The *New York Times* was able to spare 45 words to report the Nicaraguan request for a Security Council session, Dec. 10. It was not reported in the *Washington Post*.

19. See p. 28, and *TTT*, 144.

20. On these measures in the U.S. and its leading client state, and the general hypocrisy of the current pretense of civil libertarian concern on the part of those who favor—or even most of those who oppose—the

terrorist attack against Nicaragua, see *TTT*, 3.6 and my chapter in Walker, *Reagan vs. the Sandinistas*.

21. See *Survey of Press Freedom in Latin America, 1985-6*; also press release, Jan. 4, 1987.

22. See my chapter in Walker, *Reagan vs. the Sandinistas*, for a record.

23. *CPJ Update*, Oct./Nov. 1986; July/Aug. 1987. Americas Watch, *The Continuing Terror*, Sept. 1985. See also Herman and Brodhead, *Demonstration Elections*; Jack Spence, in Walker, *Reagan vs. the Sandinistas*. To understand control over information in the region, one must also take into account the extensive foreign (including U.S.) broadcasting operations that dominate access to information within much of Nicaragua; on this matter, see Howard Frederick's chapter in Walker, *Reagan vs. the Sandinistas*.

24. See references of note 20.

25. Editorial, *NYT*, Feb. 28, 1987.

26. Jack Spence, in Walker, *Reagan vs. the Sandinistas*.

27. Elaine Sciolino, *NYT*, May 14, 1987; my emphasis.

28. Editorials, *WP Weekly*, March 31, 1986, *WP*, Jan. 9, 1987; my emphasis.

29. Burns, *At War in Nicaragua*, 62, citing Chamorro in May 1986, after his departure from the contra ranks.

30. Walker, *Nicaragua*, 45, 88, 104.

31. AP, Nov. 24, 1986.

32. *Pentagon Papers*, Gravel edition, II, 647.

33. UPI, *BG*, July 27, 1987.

34. Cited by F. Parkinson, *Latin America, The Cold War, & The World Powers* (London, 1974), 40.

35. "Communism in Guatemala," Department of State-Office of Intelligence Research, July 1, 1955; cited by Gordon Bowen, "U.S. Policy Toward Guatemala," *Armed Forces & Society*, Winter 1984.

7

The Perils of Diplomacy

In its interactions with the Third World, the United States faces the recurring problem already discussed: while militarily strong, it is politically weak. One consequence is the regular need to resort to violence to demolish "popular organizations." Another is the constant effort to evade diplomatic settlement. These facts being unacceptable, the ideological institutions have the task of portraying them as the opposite of what they are. In particular, the diplomatic record must be recast in such a way as to justify further resort to violence rather than political settlement on the principle that the enemy cannot be trusted, whoever it happens to be (typically receiving the technical designation "Communist," meaning Enemy of the State).

The conclusion that "Communists cannot be trusted" is fair enough, as long as we add the missing phrase: "Nor can anyone else, particularly, the United States." The classic demonstration of Communist iniquity is Soviet behavior violating the Yalta and Potsdam agreements, but even this case, which the ideological system selects as its strongest grounds, merely illustrates the truism just expressed. In a careful analysis based on the now fairly rich documentary record, Melvyn Leffler concludes that "In fact, the Soviet pattern of adherence [to Yalta, Potsdam, and other wartime agreements] was not qualitatively different from the American pattern."[1] Turning elsewhere, we find ample evidence to illustrate how political weakness impels U.S. planners to evade peaceful settlement of disputes and to violate agreements and treaties.

The record in Indochina is instructive in this regard. The United States was aware, from the late 1940s, that in supporting the French effort to reconquer Indochina and taking over directly when France abandoned the task, it was confronting the major nationalist forces in the region. U.S. efforts to construct a "political base" for the clients it imposed were a complete failure. As a result of political weakness, the United States was compelled to overturn the Geneva agreements of 1954 at once, to subvert the elected government of Laos in 1958, to escalate the war against South Vietnam in the early sixties while desperately evading the political settlement sought on all sides, and to expand the war to all of Indochina. Finally, when unable to avoid signing an agreement theoretically terminating hostilities in Paris in 1973, the U.S. proceeded at once, for the same reasons, to undermine it in a last effort to achieve by force what it had abandoned on paper.[2]

The factual record evidently lacks ideological serviceability, so it has been replaced by a mythical reconstruction crafted to satisfy doctrinal requirements. Whatever the facts, the record must show that it is the Communist enemy that cannot be trusted. The importance of this task of sanitizing history has been heightened by the understanding that U.S. was bound to face the same basic problem elsewhere, and would have to respond in essentially the same ways: in Central America in the current period, for example, where political weakness necessitates resort to violence and evasion of diplomacy, along with a concomitant and unceasing commitment to damage control to prevent awareness of the facts.

The principle that the Communist enemy cannot be trusted to live up to agreements coexists, though uneasily, with a second doctrine: *we* seek negotiations and political settlement, while *they* refuse, and must be driven to the negotiating table by force. The question might arise, then, why we should use force to drive them to negotiations if they will violate them anyway. But there is no need to solve the paradox, since the questions are academic: in circumstances of U.S. political weakness, as in Indochina and Central America, the U.S. is not pursuing a diplomatic settlement but rather using force to eliminate this threat, and for the same reason, U.S. adherence to agreements is an unlikely prospect. These remarks are obvious, well-supported by the historical and documentary record, and, being unacceptable for a general audience, beyond the limits of respectable discourse.

Let us now consider how these problems are dealt with through "historical engineering."

Recall that hawks and doves alike debate contra aid on the assumption that its major purpose is the "noble objective" of "democratizing Nicaragua," and argue that a secondary purpose has been to compel the Sandinistas to agree to negotiations. The opposition of "the left wing of the Democratic Party" to contra aid is "insufficient," Ronald Radosh explains, because "it does not present any incentive that could force the Sandinistas to the bargaining table."[3] Liberal critics of contra aid often adopt the same premises while questioning the efficacy of this instrument to achieve the desired end: compelling the "Marxist-Leninist regime" in Managua to accept a political settlement.

A slight difficulty with this doctrine has already been discussed. Nicaragua had been pursuing the path of diplomacy since the conflict erupted, while the U.S. sought throughout to overcome the danger of peaceful settlement, whether the issue is monitoring of borders, removal of foreign advisers and guarantees against foreign bases, direct negotiations, appeal to the International Court of Justice and the United Nations, or, repeatedly, the Contadora proposals. Furthermore, U.S.-organized terror had the predictable effect, and surely the conscious purpose, of restricting the possibility of internal freedom. Had the Japanese fascists attained our level of hypocrisy, they might have justified Pearl Harbor on the grounds that it was necessary to compel the United States to overcome its vicious internal racism and begin serious moves towards true democracy, and argued that they must continue the attack because of the harsh measures that the U.S. instituted, demonstrating its totalitarian nature, including martial law and suspension of elementary rights in its Hawaiian colony, dispatch of the Japanese-American population to concentration camps, and measures of internal control and repression[4]; we may imagine how such an argument would have been received. Hence there are a few problems with the standard version.

Though not all partisans of U.S. state terrorism would go to the extremes of Ronald Radosh in the remarks just quoted, still some historical engineering is plainly in order, including a sanitized version of the diplomatic record. We have seen how this result is achieved in most cases: simply by ignoring or suppressing the facts, rejecting the World Court as an irrelevant "hostile forum," and so on. Let us have a closer look at how it is done in the case of the Contadora efforts over more than four years.

Reviewing the record, the *Times* has only this to say:

One treaty was eventually accepted by Nicaragua, which then rejected revisions demanded by the United States and Central American states. In 1986, talks stalled on a new plan.[5]

Let us inspect the factual record that lies behind this version of history, which places the onus for failure on Nicaragua for foot-dragging and rejection of U.S. proposals, and on some unspecified problem of 1986.[6]

Until September 1984, the Contadora draft treaty was supported with enthusiasm by the U.S. government. Secretary of State George Shultz described it as "an important step forward" while bitterly condemning the Sandinista Marxists for having "rejected key elements of the draft"; we return to Shultz's interesting conception of diplomacy, as he expresses it. In June 1984, Reagan informed Congress that aid to the contras must continue so as to pressure the Sandinistas; otherwise, "a regional settlement based on the Contadora principles will continue to elude us." U.S. diplomats denounced Nicaragua for "blocking a settlement" that the U.S. supported. "In mid-September [1984], at a meeting of the European Economic Community in San José, Costa Rica, Secretary of State George Shultz sent a telegram to every foreign minister present urging that 'no economic aid be given to Nicaragua because of its refusal to sign the Contadora Peace agreement'."[7]

In September 1984, Nicaragua accepted the Contadora draft without reservations, becoming the first Central America state to do so; this is the "one treaty...*eventually* accepted by Nicaragua." This unanticipated action, a slight embarrassment to Mr. Shultz since it was announced just before his telegram arrived in San José, caused virtual hysteria in Washington. Senior government officials demanded actions "to punish Mr. Ortega and the Sandinistas for accepting the Contadora proposal," the *New York Times* reported, apparently without irony. The U.S. then pressured its allies to reject the treaty, suddenly found to be unsatisfactory now that it could be implemented. A leaked National Security Council document exults in the success of these pressures, which "trumped the latest Nicaraguan/Mexican efforts" to achieve a diplomatic settlement.

The mysterious "stalling" of the 1986 agreement—namely, the rejection of the treaty by U.S. clients (unreported) and Nicaragua's willingness to accept it (barely noted)—we have already discussed. Recall that these events were followed at once by a congressional vote of aid to the contras, to compel the Sandinistas to accept a diplomatic settlement, there being no limit to tolerable absurdity in a good cause.

News columns blame Nicaragua for blocking the plan it accepted in 1986 to the annoyance of the United States. Thus, Bernard Gwertzman reported that the purpose of a Contadora mission to Central America is "to persuade Nicaragua and the other countries to sign" their document[8]—referring to a renewed effort to persuade U.S. allies to join Nicaragua in accepting the Contadora treaty. Crucially, the press must identify Nicaragua as the source of all tension and conflict, since it is an official enemy.

We might compare the *Times* version of these events with that of Costa Rica, presented in a report from San José, Costa Rica, in a leading Mexican newspaper:

> The US tried by all means available to prevent the signing of the Contadora Group Act for Peace in Central America in 1985 and 1986. The US also strongly pressured Costa Rica, in alliance with Honduras and El Salvador, to block the negotiating process, according to statements made here today by a high official of the previous [Monge] Costa Rican government.

> Gerardo Trejos Salas, Vice Foreign Affairs Minister from the middle of 1985 to May 1986, said, "As a first-hand witness, I can affirm that, at least during the time that I was Vice Foreign Affairs Minister in the Monge government, Washington tried by all means available to block the signing of the Contadora Peace Act."

Trejos presented further details of U.S. pressures on its allies to block "the peace process begun in January 1983."[9]

Plainly not a useful version of what—in fact—happened in these years, therefore not one available to readers of the U.S. press.

In 1987, Costa Rican president Oscar Arias advanced a new peace plan. The response to it illustrates further the exigencies of damage control.

This plan, supported by Congress but opposed by the Reagan administration,[10] offers the best chance "to persuade Nicaragua to permit a more democratic society and rein in its revolutionary army," Democratic Senator Terry Sanford announced[11]—implying, again if words have meaning, that Nicaragua's "revolutionary army" is illegitimately rampaging in Nicaragua when it seeks to defend the country from U.S. attack. The "political guts" of the Arias plan, Stephen Rosenfeld comments, is that "Nicaragua's ambivalent fellow Latins" are "to oversee Sandinista delivery on political assurances made to them in the treaty process," and Nicaragua "shares blame" for the failure of this plan (for which it indicated approval, while the Reagan administration rejected it) because the "Managua Marxists...refused to countenance discussion of its own internal democratization, and threw sand in everyone's eyes." The central feature of the plan, the *New York Times* observed approvingly, is that "Nicaragua would 'democratize' and the United States would stop aid to the contras," but the Sandinistas "have long refused to accept an election process that jeopardized their power"[12]—in contrast to El Salvador, where "the masses," who "were with the guerrillas" when the terror began according to Duarte (see p. 102, above), were permitted to choose within a narrow center-right spectrum controlled by the military and oligarchy after the murder of the political opposition and the intimidation or outright destruction of its popular base by terror.

The reaction was similar throughout, including the doves.

The Arias plan made no mention of Nicaragua. It called for moves towards democracy throughout the region while insisting upon "the right of all nations to freely choose their own economic, political and social system."[13]

Little attention was given to the fact that as part of its efforts to sabotage the Arias plan, the Reagan administration made it clear that "if the administration felt its views and interests were not reflected in the regional arrangements it would continue to fund the Nicaraguan contra rebels despite agreements reached by the [Central American] leaders," so Reagan "peace emissary" Philip Habib informed "high-ranking senators and their aides."[14] Within Central America, there is no difficulty in understanding that the U.S. and its allies were disturbed over the Arias plan, and why this should be so: "Neither Salvadoran President José Napoleón Duarte or the US administration is comfortable at the prospect of an amnesty and cease-fire arrangement with the FMLN [guerrillas], as called for by the Arias plan."[15] A careful search through the small print reveals that the national media in the U.S. are also aware of this fundamental problem with the Arias plan, and the reason why no plan calling for internal freedom and democracy can possibly be implemented except in some formal sense within the U.S.-established terrorist state:

> Salvadoran and Guatemalan officials are reportedly concerned because the plan would require their governments to declare an amnesty for guerrillas, an immediate cease-fire in their battle against rebel groups and permission for the rebels to form political parties and have access to the press.[16]

Meaningful steps in this direction are inconceivable as long as the state terrorists continue to rule El Salvador and Guatemala. While the opposition in Nicaragua has suffered severe harassment during the U.S. war against Nicaragua, it can at least function without fear of being slaughtered. But as the record of the 1980s clearly shows, this is not likely to be the case in El Salvador and Guatemala as long as the United States remains in command and the security forces it has established or supported maintain unchallenged power. As for Honduras, the provisions for democracy will continue to have little meaning until some basis for popular participation in the political system is established. And as history shows, any moves towards these ends would call forth stern U.S. retribution, in defense of "democracy."

There are, to be sure, crucial respects in which the Arias plan was directed to Nicaragua rather than to the "fledgling democracies" preferred in the United States, and these should be clearly understood. In the states that conform to U.S. requirements, democratic principles can be adopted at a purely formal level with few meaningful consequences. Control over resources by the military, the oligarchy, and business and professional elites guarantees effective dominance of the political system and the media as long as popular organizations are suppressed, and for that, resort to terror will normally suffice. Willingness to undertake the task of wielding the rod serves as a qualifying condition for receipt of U.S. aid,[17] and as recent history demonstrates, the successful use of terror, as in Duarte's El Salvador, will mobilize the support of enlightened opinion in the United States. If the terror becomes too ugly to be suppressed, it can be attributed to unknown sources, to death squads that cannot be controlled by "the moderate center" that we support, or to Marxist guerrillas. And when its goals have been achieved, we can point to the reduction of terror as proof that our support for "the moderate center" is the right course. "Free elections" can be conducted once the required conditions are established by state terror, to the applause of articulate U.S. opinion, hawk and dove alike. There need be no concern over "freedom of press" or "free access" to the political system, given the threat or application of terror to ensure that the media do not stray from approved bounds and that unwanted political alternatives, which can be designated as "Communist," are eliminated. All of this is entirely acceptable in a terrorist culture, not only with regard to Central America, where it has been the norm under U.S. influence for many years.

In contrast, it is hazardous for Nicaragua to agree to the conditions of the Arias plan, or any other. If it lives up to them, the fact will be suppressed or converted by the U.S. propaganda system into a proof of their totalitarian nature, exactly as was accomplished in the case of the 1984 elections by the U.S. government disinformation system with the media meekly doing their duty.[18] Furthermore, there is little reason to suppose that the U.S. will adhere to any formal agreement that is reached, so that subversion, economic pressures and the other measures available to a terrorist superpower are likely to continue, perhaps eliciting a Nicaraguan reaction that will violate the formal agreements and thus call forth still greater U.S. terror in retribution. A small and weak country facing a violent superpower that can operate with few constraints has quite limited options.

The extraordinary imbalance of forces and the subordination of the intellectual culture to the demands of power guarantee in other ways as well that the Arias plan, or any other like it, will target Nicaragua primarily. It has been critically important for the United States to "trump" any Contadora effort, because the Contadora nations, while subordinated to U.S. power, nevertheless constitute an element in world affairs with sufficient independence to be able to resist U.S. demands, to a limited but intolerable degree. If a peace agreement can be confined to the Central American states, the U.S. ability to dominate the process is considerably enhanced, because of its influence over the participants. In El Salvador, the government would collapse, as would the system of military and class privilege that it was instituted to protect, if it deviated too sharply from U.S. orders. Guatemala, another terrorist state, while not a mere creation of the U.S. government, is still highly dependent on it to preserve its own system of military and class domination. Honduras is barely more than a fiefdom, where the military and the wealthy can maintain their ability to rob the poor as long as they merit the support of the United States. Costa Rica, with a democratic tradition of 40 years, is a business-dominated society with a collapsing economy, unable to maintain the social welfare programs that underlie domestic tranquility or its relatively open internal order without substantial U.S. support. In short, these governments are highly dependent on the United States, and are dominated internally by elements that would naturally be hostile to any forces in the region that might undertake social reform in the interests of the poor majority. When the Reagan administration was weakened by the partial exposures of its clandestine terror network, the countries of Central America gained a margin of maneuver, and were able to move towards a settlement that might diminish the danger of expanding regional conflict. But the U.S. can safely count on them to focus attention on Nicaragua, in accordance with the elite consensus within the United States, when the time comes to evaluate the process of "internal democratization" or other aspects of adherence to any diplomatic settlement. There will be no question of sanctions against El Salvador, Guatemala or Honduras for their failure to adhere to such an agreement.

We can hardly doubt that articulate opinion within the United States will adopt state doctrine on these matters. The failure of democratic reforms in the terrorist client states—indeed, the impossibility of such reforms without dismantling the security apparatus that bars any meaningful popular participation in the political system—will pass unnoticed, not tarnishing the success of "democracy." As we shall see directly, the explicit refusal of Guatemala to accept the terms of the August Central American agreement that it signed was considered too insignificant even to report, and the meaningless gestures made by El Salvador in this direction barely received mention, just as heightened repression there after the agreements were signed was disregarded. The same pattern will surely persist. The U.S. government has determined that El Salvador is a "fledgling democracy," as it is, by the Orwellian standards of U.S. discourse; this fact suffices for intellectual opinion, in the case of Guatemala and Honduras as well.

Or consider the crucial matter of freedom of expression. As we have seen, freedom of expression, while important, has limited consequences in Honduras or even Costa Rica, while in El Salvador and Guatemala, formal freedoms can easily be granted, with the understanding that as in the past, attempts to use such freedom will lead to mutilation, torture, disappearance or execution. In Nicaragua, however, the situation is radically different, for reasons already discussed. Radio and television in much of the country are dominated, even in wartime, by foreign broadcasting. In the early 1980s, *La Prensa*, which has little relation except in name to the journal that opposed Somoza, was the only significant opposition journal in the region; indeed in the hemisphere, if by "opposition journal" we mean one that takes a stand in opposition to the basic structure of the socioeconomic

order and is open to critics of it, and if by "significant" we mean
that resources are available to reach beyond narrow segments of
the population. If true internal freedom were permitted in
Nicaragua, as surely it should be, then the resources of the terrorist
superpower, of the international business community, and of
domestic economic privilege would ensure that the media are
dominated by right-wing elements linked to U.S. interests, merely
by the workings of the "free market of ideas" under existing
conditions. Again, Nicaragua must bear a burden from which other
states, which conform to the requirements of U.S. power and
privilege, are entirely exempt. None of this implies that the burden
should not be borne; only that we should not succumb to the
system of delusion carefully erected in our own business-run
partial democracy.

For such reasons as these, it is correct that any peace
agreement among the Central American states will be largely
restricted to Nicaragua, and only its adherence to an agreement, as
determined by hostile power, will be a topic of concern.

Returning to the diplomatic maneuvers of 1987, in its
continuing efforts to sabotage the Arias plan, the Reagan
administration pressured Salvadoran president Duarte to block a
scheduled June meeting of Central American presidents in
Guatemala. A Guatemalan official reported that Reagan emissary
Philip Habib, performing his usual role, was responsible for
Duarte's request for postponement of the meeting, and that Duarte
"personally told Guatemala's president the reason he asked for the
postponement was because of US pressure."[19] Another meeting
was scheduled for August 6, after preliminary discussions with the
Contadora countries as intermediary; their intervention produced
a version of the Arias plan for the presidential summit on August
6. The Reagan administration had assumed that it would succeed
in blocking the Arias plan. Testifying before Congress on July 9,
Philip Habib refused to consider the possibility, raised in
questioning, that the plan might be approved by the Central
American nations, answering simply that "It can't happen."[20]

In a last-ditch effort to undermine the Central American
efforts, the Reagan administration produced its own "peace plan"
on August 5, with the obvious intent of sabotaging the scheduled
August 6 meeting of the Central American presidents and laying
the basis for renewed contra aid. The Reagan plan, proposed
jointly with Democratic House Speaker Jim Wright, was radically
different from the Arias plan. As noted earlier (18f.), it imposed no

conditions on U.S. allies and called for dismantling the political system in Nicaragua including the scheduled 1990 elections, and unilateral disarmament for Nicaragua, in return for a meaningless "pledge" that the U.S. would stop running the proxy army. The tactic worked in the United States, where the plan was taken quite seriously, but backfired dramatically in Central America. The presidents meeting in Guatemala signed an agreement modelled on the Arias plan, which "differs significantly" from the Reagan proposal, as elements of the media perceived.[21] "The U.S. initiative provided the 'glue' to bring together the often-hostile Central Americans, said one Guatemalan diplomat" quoted in the *Wall St. Journal*: "I think it was an incredible tactical error on the part of the U.S.," he added,[22] undermining Washington's effort to block a political settlement. In Guatemala City, the *Central America Report* commented that the U.S. initiative "aroused the nationalistic instincts of the Costa Rican and Guatemalan delegations," which felt "insulted." President Cerezo of Guatemala stated that "Nobody should fall into the trap of giving too much importance" to the Reagan plan, and President Arias "scratched a Honduran proposal to include the Reagan plan in the agenda" of the presidents' meeting.[23]

In Europe, it was recognized at once that "Reagan's hasty and bungled proposal bodes ill for a change in US policy in the region," and that Central American countries "interpret it as a move to torpedo their own initiatives." Washington correspondent Alex Brummer of the London *Guardian* expressed his surprise that the Reagan proposal was "treated with extreme deference in the [U.S.] media" immediately after the Iran-contra revelations: "It is quite startling that the Reagan plan, which has been seen as nothing more than a spoiler elsewhere in the world, has been so well greeted in the US."[24] Startling it may be, but not surprising in a terrorist culture, nor in any way unusual.

When the Reagan-Wright plan was proposed, there were questions about its seriousness, but George Shultz rejected them forcefully, stating "this is not a ploy" but rather a proposal that is "reasonable, sensible," a further expression of the "refreshingly blunt candor" that entrances Congress and the media. A few days later, after the failure of this attempt to sabotage the Arias plan, administration officials made it clear that these assurances were lies. "White House officials concede," the press reported, "that they drafted the Wright-Reagan plan with a focus on domestic political aims"—namely, to lay a basis for renewed contra aid after the anticipated Nicaraguan rejection of this impossible proposal—"rather than diplomacy, and that the approach backfired" when the Central American countries, rejecting the Reagan proposal, approved a version of the despised Arias plan. White House officials confirmed that they offered the Reagan-Wright plan "because they thought prospects for getting more aid for the Nicaraguan rebels, or contras, from Congress would improve if the Sandinistas refused to negotiate"—meaning, if they rejected the Reagan-Wright plan as was anticipated; "Aides said they also believed the announcement of the plan would confuse the meeting of Central American Presidents...in Guatemala two days later and probably scuttle their attempt to agree on a peace plan of their own that most Administration officials considered unacceptable."[25]

Throughout these August 1987 events, the damage control operations proceeded, though considerable backtracking and some rather convoluted reasoning was necessary as the events developed. It was necessary to achieve several aims: (1) to ensure that the Central American plan is interpreted as essentially similar to the Reagan plan in focusing attention on "democratization" in Nicaragua alone; (2) to place the onus on Nicaragua for breakdown of the agreements, real or contrived; and (3) to craft a proper version of history. The approved version must be that U.S. pressures were the crucial factor in compelling the Sandinistas to agree to a political settlement—namely, one that they had tentatively approved while the Reagan administration sought in every way to undermine it; and generally, in compelling them to pursue the diplomatic options that they had been requesting for 6 years while the U.S. "trumped" these efforts at every turn. Given the unfortunate fact that the Central American presidents approved a diplomatic settlement that the Reagan administration desperately sought to sabotage, history must show that U.S. violence and the forthright Reagan-Wright plan were instrumental in bringing about this agreement. A difficult task, one might think, but not beyond the resources of the Free Press. It is instructive to pursue the process of historical engineering step by step through the first crucial weeks.

Stage one began when Washington announced the Reagan-Wright plan. As noted earlier, it was evidently impossible to perceive, even in the full glare of the Iran-contra hearings, that a Reagan pledge to cease aid to the contras in return for Nicaraguan demobilization is pure farce. Editorials interpreted the

Reagan-Wright plan as "a fresh opportunity" for Managua to show good faith, adding that "Congress and the White House deserve credit for their effort to move the process forward" (*Christian Science Monitor*). Welcoming the proposal, the *Times* editors stated that with this effort to undermine the Arias plan, "the White House has made clearer its backing for the regional peace effort promoted by Costa Rica's President, Oscar Arias"; they warned that Congress "has to be clear-eyed" and called on Washington "to keep the faith with all of Central America's democrats—including the internal opposition in Nicaragua—in opposing thuggery from every quarter, Sandinista or contra." "Every quarter" did not include Washington, in the "clear-eyed" vision of the editors.[26]

In the news columns, James LeMoyne stated that the Arias plan "shares the central intent of Mr. Reagan's plan, which is to demand internal political changes in Nicaragua," shading the facts in accord with Washington doctrine. He added that a "written interpretation" within the White House explained that Washington would not be required to cut off aid to the contras under the Reagan plan, "but would reduce it only in relation to the degree to which the Sandinistas permit the rebels to take part in Nicaraguan politics and society," as judged in Washington, thus granting the U.S. the right to continue the war after Nicaraguan demobilization and disarmament, a small fact that escaped notice. LeMoyne reported further that all Central American participants in the conference "were gratified" by Reagan's proposal, "except Nicaragua," which "offered a far more hostile assessment," risking isolation[27]; this claim was at once undermined when the Central American countries responded to the "incredible tactical error" of the Reagan administration by dismissing its proposal and endorsing, in effect, the "significantly different" Arias plan that Washington opposed, leaving Washington entirely isolated.

At the critical end of the spectrum, Tom Wicker expressed doubts about Reagan's plan, noting that he "has been at least as reluctant a negotiator as anyone in Managua," something of an understatement.[28] But "the United States has no historic or God-given mission to bring democracy to other nations," as Reagan is attempting to do according to state doctrine, taken as sacrosanct; and the threat of renewed aid to the contras if the Sandinistas do not accept Reagan's proposal "is unlikely to cause them to make the demanded reforms" when they were "unwilling to make them" under military pressure, the assumption being that the military pressure was not a factor in the suspension of internal rights but rather was an effort to restore them, a curious reading of the historical record. At the other extreme, former *Times* executive editor A. M. Rosenthal was euphoric, calling upon those who "would rather have the war continue than see if the Reagan administration can possibly end it" to abandon their cynical ways and "give peace a chance." He described the Reagan plan as "close to the plan that had been proposed by President Arias of Costa Rica..." (admittedly, "with some exceptions"). Though the Reagan plan "could lead to a Sandinista double-cross about political freedom," still this hope for a "decent solution" should "be taken with total seriousness."[29] Ronald Radosh was even more enthusiastic. The "Wright plan," as he called it, is "the first major effort to end the Nicaraguan civil war"—translating from Newspeak: the first *U.S. government* effort, designed to fail as was quickly conceded and thus to perpetuate the U.S. attack against Nicaragua. "The major provisions of the proposal match and build on those suggested" by President Arias, he added, a transparent falsehood. The Wright plan "builds on [the] understanding" of the Nicaraguan opposition "that it is not the contra war that has forced the Sandinistas to resist democratization"; rather, "most Nicaraguans" know, so he has determined by careful study of Nicaraguan opinion, that it was Sandinista policies, "not the United States, that led to an increased armed opposition." Other obiter dicta of a similar nature follow, always untroubled by fact.[30]

The Reagan effort having failed, the damage control operation had to shift to stage two. Noting that the peace plan signed by the Central American presidents was "significantly different" from the Reagan proposal and "closely follows" the Arias plan, James LeMoyne reported that its internal democratization provisions are "seen as particularly directed toward Nicaragua," as indeed they are in Washington, therefore in the Free Press; evidently LeMoyne had forgotten his earlier insight that El Salvador and Guatemala can hardly accept amnesty, cease-fire "and permission for the rebels to form political parties and have access to the press."[31] "These provisions, if carried out by Nicaragua, would be a major concession by Sandinista officials, who have sharply limited political organization and press freedom in recent years," LeMoyne continued, not mentioning the background, the state of civil liberties in the "fledgling democracies," or the fact that international observers of the Nicaraguan elections of 1984 compared them quite favorably with those in El Salvador; in fact, the extensive evidence on this matter has been effectively suppressed by the *New York Times*, as elsewhere in the U.S. media. Crucially, LeMoyne does not mention that "these provisions" can hardly be carried out in El Salvador and Guatemala without dismantling the U.S.-backed apparatus of state terrorists. But all of this is beside the point for the two usual reasons: atrocities conducted by "our side" are not atrocities, but rather errors in a noble cause; and since it all happened yesterday, we may appeal to the doctrine of "change of course" if anyone should be so obtuse as to remark on these irrelevancies.

Others can perceive some possible problems apart from the "Marxist-Leninist totalitarians" in Managua. Asking "what chances does the regional consensus have," the *Central America Report* in Guatemala City answers: "Much will depend on the ability to influence Honduras and El Salvador not to stray from the spirit of the agreement and the cooperation of the Democrats and liberals in Washington," who have the task of keeping White House terrorists under some sort of control. Furthermore, as Guatemalan Defense Minister Héctor Gramajo announced at once, the agreement "does not apply to our country." The rector of the Jesuit university in San Salvador commented a few weeks later that "Nicaragua will be the [country] most in compliance" with the peace plan and that others "may fail" to comply.[32]

Reactions in the U.S., however, followed a different course. Former *Times* chief editor A. M. Rosenthal denounced efforts to "destroy the contras, whose existence brought about the opportunity for negotiations," an audacious version of history, but the one required, and therefore True, though transparently false for familiar reasons already discussed. *Washington Post* editor David Ignatius held that peace prospects "seemed to improve slightly following President Reagan's proposal for a cease-fire and the adoption of a peace plan by leaders of five Central American countries." In the real world, peace prospects *declined* with Reagan's effort to undermine the negotiations in progress, and improved slightly after it was rejected, though U.S. opposition continued to make peace a remote prospect. For Ignatius, however, the problem for the future is not continuing U.S. opposition to a political settlement but rather establishing "a democratic Nicaragua"; that "is what the [contra] war has been all about," so Washington doctrine stipulates, thus again establishing the claim. A reconciliation in Nicaragua will be difficult, he adds, because "both sides have blood on their hands": namely, as he goes on to explain, many contra soldiers have been killed in battle and "the

Sandinistas have similar tales and totals." By the standards of the culture of terrorism, this is a fair accounting of the atrocities by "both sides."[33] One would perhaps find a similar accounting, with similar justice, in the literary productions of Abu Nidal.

The editors of the *Washington Post* noted "the hesitation in Mr. Reagan's embrace of the Arias plan," but urged that "he deserves some forbearance" for his courage in coming this far, "at no small cost to his standing with loyal constituents." But "the main burden rests on the Sandinistas," not the U.S. aggressors. The reason is that "Mr. Reagan has Congress keeping a wary eye on him," monitoring his every act with the hawk-eyed vigilance exhibited so dramatically in past years: "The Sandinistas should have the whole hemisphere's wary eyes on them." No eyes need be cast upon client states, since their good faith in creating the conditions for democracy and eliminating internal repression can be taken for granted; or perhaps they will be monitored by Shultz, Abrams, and the *Washington Post*.[34]

The *Wall St. Journal* described the discomfiture in Washington after a version of the Arias plan was accepted in Guatemala City. The Reagan-Wright plan, two *Journal* reporters observe, was conceded to have been a fraud (after it had failed), intended to lay the basis for renewed contra aid when the Sandinistas rejected it. But damage control requires that we identify the Reagan plan with the Arias plan that Washington sought to undermine. Thus they continue: White House officials "concede privately that they never expected the Sandinistas to call Mr. Reagan's bluff by participating in a peace plan that had the backing of other Central American countries." This statement makes sense only on the assumption, here intimated, that the Reagan plan was the plan approved in Guatemala City by the Sandinistas, "calling Mr. Reagan's bluff." It would make no sense to say that the Sandinistas "called Mr. Reagan's bluff" by signing a peace plan that he had vigorously opposed and struggled to undermine. In fact, the Central American countries rejected the Reagan effort to torpedo the negotiations and signed an agreement similar to the Arias plan, for which Nicaragua had indicated measured approval all along. The *Journal* also fails to note that accurately understood, the Reagan effort was simply a replay of 1984, when the Sandinistas did indeed "call Mr. Reagan's bluff" by accepting the Contadora proposals.[35]

The *Wall St. Journal* reports further that

to convey what it considers the proper degree of skepticism at today's session [of Latin American ambassadors convened by the

> State Department in Washington], the administration will give
> U.S. envoys a copy of the 1973 Paris Peace agreement that was
> negotiated to end the U.S. involvement in the Vietnam War. The
> agreement was subsequently ignored by North Vietnam.

This "Vietnam experience" is one factor in administration "skepticism" about the Central American agreement, the *Journal* continued. This interesting farce was extended the following day in the lead story by Neil Lewis in the *New York Times*, discussing the meeting in Washington led by Elliott Abrams. Along with the obligatory falsehood that the Central American agreement "is principally focused on Nicaragua," Lewis reports that copies of the 1973 Paris agreement were distributed to the envoys "as a case study of how an agreement with ambiguous provisions could be exploited and even ignored by a Communist government." Lewis then adds his own gloss: "In violation of the 1973 accord, North Vietnam overran South Vietnam and united the two parts of Vietnam under its banner in 1975.[36]

In these news reports, we see illustrated the utility of a carefully crafted historical record, designed by the loyal media to serve the needs of state power. It was not quite correct to say, as I did earlier, that the Paris peace agreements of 1973 have been forgotten. It is only the facts that have been forgotten, or to be more accurate, suppressed from the very day the agreements were announced; the version provided by the state authorities is well-remembered, and was immediately invoked as part of the effort to undermine the Central American peace plan.

In the unlikely event that the envoys gathered by the State Department had taken the trouble to read the Paris Peace agreement in conjunction with the simultaneous pronouncements of Henry Kissinger and the White House, they would have made the enlightening discovery that the U.S. government announced at once, in the clearest and most unequivocal terms, that it would violate every major provision of the agreement and continue to try to attain its aims by force.

The Paris agreements committed "the United States and all other countries [to] respect the independence, sovereignty, unity and territorial integrity of Vietnam as recognized by the 1954 Geneva agreements on Vietnam," identifying the 17th parallel separating North and South Vietnam as a "provisional...military demarcation line" pending reunification of Vietnam by "peaceful means" and "without foreign interference." In the South, the agreements recognized two parallel and equivalent "South

Vietnamese parties," the U.S.-backed GVN and the PRG, based on the NLF (National Liberation Front, "Viet Cong" in the terms of U.S. propaganda). These two parties were to achieve national reconciliation by peaceful means under conditions of full civil liberties while "Foreign countries shall not impose any political tendency or personality on the South Vietnamese people" and "the United States will not continue its military involvement or intervene in the internal affairs of South Vietnam." The two South Vietnamese parties will settle "The question of Vietnamese armed forces in South Vietnam...without foreign interference," and the U.S. is barred from introducing advisers, technicians, or war material into South Vietnam and must withdraw all such personnel within 60 days.

These are the essential terms of the Paris Accords. Turning to Washington, Kissinger and the White House announced before the ink was dry that they were rejecting the agreements they had signed in every critical respect, and they did so with complete clarity and forthrightness. Washington announced that it would maintain the right to provide "civilian technicians serving in certain of the military branches," and proceeded to keep or introduce 7,200 of them, including "retired" military men under the supervision of a U.S. Major-General, thus nullifying the provisions on U.S. personnel. More significantly, the U.S. announced that it would continue to regard the GVN as the "sole legitimate government in South Vietnam"—thus nullifying the central provision of the agreement—with "its constitutional structure and leadership intact and unchanged"; this "constitutional structure" happened to outlaw the second of the two parallel and equivalent parties along with "pro-communist neutralism" and any form of expression "aimed to spreading Communist policies, slogans and instructions," and the GVN, with U.S. backing, announced that such "illegal" activities would be suppressed by force, as they were, thereby nullifying what remained of the agreements.

In short, the U.S. announced at once that it intended to disregard every essential provision of the scrap of paper it had been compelled to sign in Paris after the Christmas B-52 bombings of Hanoi and Haiphong had failed to force North Vietnam to sue for peace on American terms. These terror bombings were undertaken in a final effort to compel Hanoi to abandon the October 1972 agreement that the United States had rejected after indicating its acceptance. The January 1973 Accords reinstated the essential provisions of the October agreements, in fact those of NLF proposals from over a decade earlier, which Washington had undermined by violence for the usual reasons of political weakness. But all of this was beside the point, given the instant announcement that Washington did not have the slightest intention of adhering to the agreements that it could no longer evade.

Had the envoys reviewed the record of what transpired next, they would have discovered that the U.S. government proceeded to implement its clearly stated intentions at once, in explicit violation of the clear and unambiguous terms of the Paris agreements it had just signed. In public and in congressional testimony, U.S. officials expressed the administration's pleasure in the early successes of the resort to violence by its South Vietnamese clients, with U.S. backing, to eliminate any possibility that the actual terms of the accords might be realized. The media, including the most outspoken doves, adopted the administration statement of intent as the actual terms of the agreement, thus guaranteeing that U.S. violations would proceed with impunity and that the inevitable response by the Vietnamese enemy would be interpreted as yet another proof of Communist iniquity.[37] This remarkable display of media servility laid the basis for the renewal of the war as U.S.-backed violence elicited the predictable response after the attempt of the hated enemy to observe the agreements proved hopeless, and also laid the basis for the interpretation of "the Vietnam experience" now conveniently invoked as the U.S. considers how best to undermine the unwanted peace plan proposed by the Central American states.

It would take little effort for journalists and others to convince themselves that these are the essential facts of the matter, but such independence of mind is next to inconceivable in a highly conformist intellectual culture.[38]

We may, incidentally, feel confident that the fanciful tales spun to conceal the meaning of the Central American agreement will be exploited in some future effort to justify the use of violence by the state managers.

Outside of the media, others too dedicated themselves to establishing the version of the Central American accord dictated by Washington. New York Mayor Edward Koch announced that "he had been asked by an independent committee made up of Americans to observe the implementing of the five-nation Central American peace plan," and would therefore lead a delegation *to*

Nicaragua to monitor its compliance with the accord. They will undoubtedly find violations, though nothing comparable to what an honest investigation would quickly reveal in the "fledgling democracies," which are beyond the scope of the narrowly and precisely focused libertarian concerns called into operation by the state authorities. The "independent committee" is not identified, apart from one member, Charles Robb, "a member of Freedom House, a nonprofit organization devoted to encouraging democracy around the world." Further inquiry suggests that Freedom House is sponsoring this effort to monitor *Nicaragua's* compliance with the accord, that being the only serious issue, as stipulated by the state. In the press, it is a "fact" that Freedom House is "devoted to encouraging democracy around the world"; it is so regarded by the state and elite opinion, so that no verification is necessary. Investigation would quickly show that the Freedom House conception of "democracy" conforms very well to official demands, as does their conception of the ways a Free Press should be mobilized in the service of state power.[39]

In a classic of state propaganda disguised as "news," James LeMoyne reviewed the Central American agreement, modifying it to correspond to the Reagan proposal that was rejected. Again adopting Washington doctrine, he states that though the treaty is "regional in scope," "there is no doubt that its main provisions are principally directed at Nicaragua and will affect Nicaragua more than any of the other nations that signed the accord"—true, of course, under the conditions of media obedience discussed earlier, but this is presumably not LeMoyne's point. The agreement, he continues, requires that the Sandinistas "agree to stop running the country like a one-party revolutionary socialist state" and replace their "Cuban-style Marxism" by "a kind of Mexican one-party state" (quoting an unnamed "diplomat"). Putting aside the accuracy of the characterization, observe how easily, with a mere stroke of the pen, we dismiss the problem of dismantling the reigning security systems that make any talk of "internal democracy" mere black humor in the U.S. client states.

Even with this convenient interpretation, LeMoyne's "news report" still perceives problems in the Central American plan. "One major issue the treaty does not cover is security concerns." One example is mentioned: "Soviet military aid" to Nicaragua, which apparently has no security concerns in the shadow of the "enforcer," just as U.S. military aid to its clients raises no security concerns for anyone in the region—peasants in the Salvadoran hills, for example. Another problem is that the Salvadoran guerrillas "have repeatedly refused" Duarte's "appeal that they give up their guns, form political parties and run in elections"—thus presenting themselves as a sacrificial offering to the security forces, who will gladly slaughter them as in the past, if the need arises, a prospect that is not a problem. LeMoyne quotes Salvadoran and Honduran officials along with Western diplomats (probably from the U.S. Embassy) and Costa Rican officials who are permitted to discourse on why "Nicaragua had agreed to the treaty." To provide appropriate balance, one Nicaraguan is also quoted: rebel leader Pedro Joaquín Chamorro, who vows to continue the fight until he perceives "an irreversible track to democracy in Nicaragua"—in his sense of democracy, which, as we have seen (p. 125), excludes the Sandinistas from participation.[40]

On the same day, Canada's counterpart to the *New York Times* also reviewed the Central American agreements. The article quotes "regional political analysts" on Reagan's "flagging prestige" as revealed by the fact that the Central American presidents "pointedly refused to discuss a proposal made by Mr. Reagan just before the summit." Observers and participants generally "left no doubt they saw the meeting as a rebuff to the United States and a milestone of independent decision in an area Washington has long considered its backyard." Latin American "officials speaking privately often express irritation over what they see as U.S. indifference and arrogance," and this case was no exception, with the conservative Guatemalan press joining in with the conclusion that "the summit had damaged Mr. Reagan's image."[41]

A few days later the contra leadership announced that they would maintain their military apparatus intact and reserve the right to continue to receive weapons until there was "a genuine guarantee of lasting freedom of expression and political organization" in Nicaragua, by their standards, and demanded direct negotations with the Sandinistas while remaining a foreign-supplied military force. Whatever one thinks of this decision, it amounts to a rejection of the regional peace treaty, which assigns no role to nongovernmental armed forces and calls for their dissolution. It was therefore reported under the headline "Nicaragua Rebels Pledge to Accept Latin Peace Plan," namely, the one they had just announced that they would reject.[42] As part of its pretense that the proxy army has the status of an indigenous force, Washington interprets the agreement as requiring negotiations between the Nicaraguan government and the contra civilian front established by the Reagan administration. This version goes well beyond the text, but if history is a guide, we may expect it to prevail.

The contra leaders proceeded to ask "President Reagan to seek Congressional approval for renewed military and non-lethal aid for the contras, but to hold the military aid in escrow unless the Nicaraguan Government fails to comply with terms of a peace plan now being negotiated," as determined in Washington and Miami. They reported that they had "enough money and matériel in the pipeline to sustain them during the five weeks after the authorization to fund them expires," until the proposed November cease-fire[43]; other reports indicate that their supplies would last well beyond, and there is little reason to doubt that the U.S. government will provide further military support, if it so chooses, in one or another way. Contra leader Pedro Joaquín Chamorro travelled to Montevideo, Uruguay, in early September at the invitation of CAUSA, a branch of Reverend Moon's Unification Church which, as reported by the Uruguayan media, "is a terrorist organization whose South American headquarters are apparently based in Montevideo." Chamorro "came to solicit his host's 'humanitarian and military' aid for [the] contra cause."[44]

Meanwhile killing of civilians continued. Immediately after the "acceptance" of the peace plan, an ambush of a civilian vehicle by the "sons of Reagan" in northern Jinotega province killed 5 employees of the Agrarian Reform Ministry, wounding two others, barely reported and eliciting no comment. The *New York Times* chose to ignore the story, preferring speculations by its Managua correspondent as to whether Nicaragua would live up to its promises. No articles appeared datelined Washington speculating on the likelihood that the U.S. would suddenly begin to adhere to agreements and international law, nor were there articles datelined New York speculating on the possibility that the world's greatest newspaper, in an equally startling reversal, would monitor Washington's ongoing behavior, thus accepting, for the first time in its history, the most elementary obligation of a free press. A formal protest by Foreign Minister Miguel D'Escoto to George Shultz was also ignored in the Newspaper of Record.[45]

The government of Nicaragua at once "endorsed the [Central American] proposal energetically," stating that "it was prepared to lift a state of emergency, restore full press and political freedoms and allow former rebel leaders to return to the country and engage in open political activity" if the U.S. ends contra aid, and went "beyond the letter of the peace agreement" by announcing "Nicaragua's intention to remove all foreign military advisers from the country," a matter not touched upon in the agreements. The government also arranged public meetings with the opposition and Cardinal Obando to form the National Reconciliation Commission called for in the agreement.[46]

The Guatemala agreement had specified that each of the five Central American countries should establish such a Commission to ensure compliance with democratization and other conditions. The Commission was to consist of a government official, a prominent private citizen, a Bishop, and an opposition figure, the latter two selected by the government from lists provided by the Church and the opposition parties. On August 25, Nicaragua became the first country to abide by this agreement, selecting Vice-President Sergio Ramírez, Gustavo Parajón (president of the Judicial and Human Rights Commission set up by Protestant churches), Cardinal Obando, and Mauricio Díaz of the Popular Social Christian Party, who "votes regularly against the Sandinista National Liberation Front in the National Assembly," and whose party "has criticized Sandinista policies on the economy, education, and relations with the Roman Catholic Church." Cardinal Obando, the most prominent and outspoken opponent of the Sandinistas, was named president of the Commission.[47]

It would be difficult to imagine a more forthcoming fulfilment of the agreement. Accordingly, the U.S. government at once denounced the Sandinistas for having "stacked the council in their favor," thus proving that they are "only paying lip service to the Latin American peace accord," a charge prominently displayed. The fate of the Commissions elsewhere remained undiscussed.[48]

Two weeks later, on Sept. 7, President Duarte established the Commission in El Salvador. The Commission contains no critics of the regime apart from the right-wing opposition. The "prominent citizen" selected was ex-President Alvaro Magaña, "the conservative banker the Salvadoran military proposed as president in 1982 when the U.S. vetoed death-squad leader Roberto D'Aubuisson," Chris Norton observes. Magaña was selected to be president of the Commission, and a conservative Bishop was named Commission secretary. The other members were the head of the rightist Arena Party and the secretary-general of the Christian Democratic Party. Norton continues:

> Diplomats interviewed here [in San Salvador] say that in contrast to Nicaragua's commission—to which the government named a principal opponent—the Salvadorean commission has no such figure. "They're all sympathizers of the right and the military," a Latin American ambassador says. "With this panel Duarte has closed the political spaces for dialogue."[49]

The signing of the agreement was also followed by a wave of repression to which we return, arousing no comment here.

The contrast to the appointment of the Nicaraguan Commission is striking in two respects: (1) while the Nicaraguan Commission was headed by the most outspoken critic of the regime and was broadly based, the Salvadoran Commission was restricted to the center-right and headed by the U.S. candidate for president; (2) while the appointment of the Nicaraguan Commission elicited an immediate outburst of abuse against the treacherous Sandinistas, Duarte's moves passed in silence, not suggesting that Duarte is failing to live up to the spirit of reconciliation and only paying lip service to the Central American accord.

The same comparison holds with regard to the other "fledgling democracies." The announcement by the Guatemalan military, the effective rulers, that Guatemala was not subject to the agreements appears to have passed with no notice. The same was true of the announcement by Honduras that "it considered itself exempt from a provision in the Arias peace plan to establish a National Reconciliation Commission," on the grounds that "there are no internal rifts or Nicaraguan contra camps in the country," and plainly no problems of internal democratization or free elections for such a Commission to pursue in accordance with its mandate.[50] Furthermore, Honduras has given no indication that it intends to live up to the terms of the agreements by dismantling the bases on its territory from which the contra armies operate and that are used to supply them by air drops, nor could it do so even if it chose, given the realities of force in the region as determined in Washington. Guatemala did proceed to establish a Commission on September 9, selecting the Vice-President, the leader of the Conservative Party, a Bishop, and as private sector delegate, the co-owner of the most rightist newspaper in the country, reputed to have been a personal friend of General Ríos Montt, perhaps the most extreme of the recent batch of mass murderers. The government did not appoint Guatemala City Archbishop Prospero Penados del Barrio, "a highly regarded and ardent critic of human rights violations."[51] The Commission of Reconciliation, then, will deal with problems arising within the spectrum from ultra-right to center-right, in the most violent country of the region, the one with the longest-running guerrilla struggle. All of this too appears to have passed without notice. As U.S. allies or outright clients, Guatemala, Honduras and El Salvador are exempt from the conditions of any agreement they might sign, which the U.S. government will ensure is "directed at Nicaragua" (James LeMoyne).

As always, the state establishes its priorities, the intellectual culture, with the rarest of exceptions, takes its cues and obeys.

In subsequent weeks, Nicaragua took a series of steps towards meeting the conditions of the agreements on internal freedoms, for example, permitting the pro-contra journal *La Prensa* to reopen. No detectable steps were taken elsewhere. Thus in El Salvador, no one suggested permitting *La Crónica* and *El Independiente* to open, and indeed, such a proposal would be absurd, since there is every reason to suppose that an attempt to create an independent press would, once again, call out the death squads run by the U.S.-backed security services, at least if it began to have any substantial outreach—in accordance with the usual interpretation of the "clear and present danger" concept of free speech, within U.S. dependencies. No steps were taken in either of the two U.S.-backed terror states to create conditions under which journalists would be permitted to speak their minds without fear of state terror. No openings were developed in Honduras or Costa Rica for dissident media, but then, the problem of free expression is handled here, as in the United States, by the exigencies of the market, where media corporations that deliver audiences to advertisers have the resources to control the information system, along with other means deriving from the distribution of wealth and effective power.

Discourse on these matters continued to pursue predictable lines. The optimists believe that "*even* the Nicaraguan government is willing to comply with the peace plan."[52] The pessimists are skeptical of the intentions of the Marxist-Leninist totalitarians. Like President Arias, liberal opinion in the United States wants to see a business-run capitalist democracy in Nicaragua, and has only limited concerns with the terror states since they meet the primary condition: they respect the rights of the privileged and are dedicated to the Fifth Freedom. Arias does note that "social injustice and exploitation of the many by the few" poses a problem

in Central America, but "obtaining democracy in Nicaragua is the
key to 'durable peace' in the region, Arias says."[53] Articulate
opinion within the United States agrees, across the very narrow
spectrum. Democracy already exists in the Orwellian sense in the
other signatory states, though further improvements would be
nice. If we could bring ourselves to attend to such trivialities, we
would be happier if fewer people were starving in Honduras or
surviving in military-run concentration camps in Guatemala; and
liberals, at least, hope that it may some day be possible to escape
the ever-present fear of torture and assassination in El Salvador.
But these are distinctly lesser problems, as long as wealth and
privilege are secured and U.S. domination is not threatened. The
framework of news reporting and discussion is therefore
understandable, and it is not difficult to predict its future course.

President Duarte welcomed the leaders of the U.S. proxy army
to San Salvador and consulted with them, eliciting no comment. A
similar public meeting between President Ortega and the civilian
leadership associated with the guerrillas in El Salvador might have
fared differently in the media. Similarly, President Ortega's
announcement "that, like 100 other leaders around the world, he
has accepted an invitation to sit in the stands at the 70th
celebration of the Russian revolution this November in Moscow,"
aroused predictable outrage at this further proof that he is merely
an agent of the USSR. Less was heard about the Honduran
delegation sent to Moscow in Sept. 1987 "to discuss the possibility
of opening more export markets in the Eastern European Bloc."[54]

President Reagan announced at once "that he would continue
to support the rebels, and may seek additional military aid to tide
over rebel soldiers until the Sandinistas had demonstrated good
faith by carrying out internal changes," as determined in
Washington, "a move that would kill the peace plan," Nicaragua
observed. To further underscore its rejection of the plan, the
Reagan administration announced that it "has decided that a
regional peace plan for Central America cannot work unless the
United States provides long-term support for the rebels in
Nicaragua, perhaps even months after a cease fire"; "We want to
try and work with [the Central American plan] and we are not
against it," a senior official stated while announcing this clear
intent to subvert the agreement: "If any of them think we are trying
to subvert the agreement it is crucial they understand we are not,"
he added.[55] The device is the familiar one: reject the peace
agreement while offering an interpretation diametrically opposed

to it in the expectation that it will be adopted within the ideological institutions, thus nullifying the actual agreements and placing on the enemy the onus for the eventual failure that the U.S. is working to ensure. In short, the model that was employed with perfection in January 1973, though it is difficult to imagine that that triumph will be fully reenacted.

The White House announced further that it continues to regard the Reagan-Wright plan as "the operative agreement," while characterizing the Guatemala plan as "more a preliminary agreement than a final peace treaty" (Elliott Abrams), and adding that the U.S. reserves the right to modify it in accord with its own goals. Democratic congressional leaders made it clear that they would permit the administration to continue to use contra aid funds appropriated for the year ending September 30 after that date, though the administration has no "legal authority" to do so,[56] thus doing what they can to ensure that the war will continue and that the Central American peace agreement will fail.

Pursuing its efforts to "trump" this latest attempt at a peaceful settlement, the Reagan administration sent point man George Shultz to the Senate on September 10 to announce a request for renewed aid to the contras. To make absolutely clear the administration intent to sabotage the Central American accord if possible, the new request called for a substantial *increase* over the preceding year, $270 million extending over 18 months, hence into the next administration; the request is calculated at a rate of $180 million per year, up from the current $100 million. Shultz announced, with his usual candor, that "This president will not stand idly by—this Secretary of State will not stand by—and permit countries as near to our borders as Nicaragua to become a place from which the Soviet Union and its allies can militarily threaten our friends or our country's national security." Therefore we must provide even more lavish funding than before to maintain the proxy army, which will collapse without extensive support from the Godfather, since unlike guerrilla forces, it has been able to establish no self-sustaining base within Nicaragua. An unstated feature of the Shultz proposal is to shift the spectrum of the discussion to the right and to lay a basis for blaming the cowards and Comsymps who refuse to go along for whatever problems arise in the subsequent period; and there are sure to be many, considering the terrible situation in the region, even if by some miracle the U.S. were to live up to a political agreement, violating well-established precedent.

Shultz informed the Senate "that peace negotiations under way in the region would not succeed unless the United States continued to support the rebels trying to topple the Soviet-backed Government of Nicaragua," the *New York Times* observed, failing to add that the accord signed by the Central American presidents calls upon "the Governments of the region, and the extra-regional governments which openly or covertly provide military, logistical, financial, propagandistic aid in manpower, armaments, munitions and equipment to irregular forces or insurrectionist movements to cease this aid, *as an indispensable element for achieving a stable and lasting peace in the region.*"[57]

In short, the Reagan administration request is in explicit violation of the indispensable condition for peace, formulated as a central feature of the accord. It could not be more clear and explicit that George Shultz is calling upon Congress to join him in ensuring that the political settlement will founder, so that the U.S. may proceed in the preferred course of violence. The familiar record replays.

One might also observe that the indispensable condition for peace need hardly have been written into the peace agreements. For the United States to organize attacks against Nicaragua from the Honduran bases it has established for its proxy army is already a violation of international law, and the World Court had already ordered the United States to desist from these illegal actions. The Central American agreements do not have a higher status than international law or the decisions of the World Court, for which the United States has already shown its utter contempt with the support of elite opinion; and these agreements, to which the United States is not a signatory, are not more binding on the United States than its solemn commitments to international law and the decisions of the World Court. Thus if the U.S. government chooses to observe the requirements of the Central American agreements, this will simply be a matter of expedience, resulting from the perceived cost of failing to do so, a fact that might be borne in mind by the domestic population in the United States, the only force that can impose these costs.

On September 17, Congress turned down the request for an immediate increase in military support for the proxy army, choosing instead to provide several million dollars in "humanitarian" aid—while acknowledging that there are substantial unspent funds in the contra pipeline (and, as usual, disregarding the fact that the administration will use the "humanitarian" aid for any purpose it wishes, and will persist in funding its mercenary forces in other ways, if it so chooses). House Speaker Jim Wright explained that Democrats "don't want to cut off food and medicine. They're not that cruel or heartless or foolish."[58]

The important word is "foolish"; Democrats understand very well what the political consequences would be of refusing to provide "humanitarian" aid for the contra forces maintained in Nicaragua by regular air drops, which will evidently have to continue, in violation of any reasonable interpretation of the Central American agreements or of Nicaraguan sovereignty, just as the Honduran contra bases will have to remain intact. Apart from what this implies about observance of the agreements, the threat of renewed attack at the discretion of the United States thus remains operative, with the consequence that Nicaragua must remain mobilized for war. We can test whether Democrats are not "cruel or heartless," as alleged, by asking whether they also pass legislation providing food and medicine for the victims of U.S. atrocities, or whether they persist in following meekly behind the White House, which not only manages the atrocities but maintains an embargo that has had very serious effects on living standards and health care in Nicaragua. The conclusion is that the Democrats remain "cruel and heartless," though not "foolish." The frank acknowledgement on all sides that the contra forces cannot survive without U.S.-provided aid again expresses their understanding that these are not authentic guerrilla forces, but a foreign-directed mercenary army with no viable social base; no one is proposing that for humanitarian reasons, food and medicine be provided to the Salvadoran guerrillas—who are, at the very least, as deserving as the contras—to enable them to survive during a cease-fire. Another topic off the agenda in the terrorist superpower is any inquiry into how the Salvadoran guerrillas manage to survive, and what is the basis for their popular support.[59]

Henry Kissinger chimed in with an endorsement of the Reagan-Shultz plan to undermine the peace agreements, perhaps chuckling quietly over his success in doing the same in 1973, with the loyal media in tow. "Both sides of our domestic debate should have an interest in" military aid to the contras, he explained: "Congress should vote *contra* aid for an 18-month period on the present scale [that is, at the rate of $100 million annually] to permit a new Administration to set its own policies and to avoid having an issue of fundamental national consequence overwhelmed by the politics of an election year." Note the typical fear that with the heightened attention of the public during an election year, the domestic enemy might have an unwanted influence on the decisions of the state managers. With the grasp of history for which he is famous, Kissinger denounced opponents of contra aid, who "have refused to accept the reality that without the *contras* there would not have been any movement on the negotiating front"; the facts of the matter, we have already reviewed. Contra lobbyist Penn Kemble, identified as president of the National Council of PRODEMCA, "a nonpartisan citizens' education group that supports democratic development in Central America" (in translation: a state-subsidized group that backs the use of terror to prevent any threat of meaningful democracy in Central America), added his recommendations. To ensure the success of the peace plan, "thousands of democrats from other countries" should converge on Managua on November 7 to support returning "resistance leaders" in a public demonstration; no "democrats" need converge on other capitals, because Nicaragua "is surrounded by democratic states": Honduras, El Salvador, and Guatemala come to mind. Furthermore, "The United States must find the means to keep the resistance forces intact, and inside Nicaragua," meaning that the U.S. must continue its daily flights of military and "humanitarian" aid to the "resistance" in explicit violation of the peace agreement that we will support with a demonstration in Managua. The co-author of the memorandum cited earlier calling on the U.S. government to find some way to create a popular base in Nicaragua for its "proxy army," a realist, understands that the "resistance" cannot survive without such regular and massive external assistance, in contrast to indigenous guerrilla forces with a popular base, as in the "democracies" of the region.[60]

In a further effort to elicit a hostile reaction from Nicaragua that could be exploited by the propaganda machine, the U.S. government sent Secretary of Education William Bennett to Managua, where he gave a news conference and delivered a public lecture before an audience of 700 people, most of them from the political opposition, in which he denounced Nicaragua as a despotic tyranny, stating that there would never be freedom in Nicaragua as long as the Sandinistas were in power; announced that "We will support the Contras, we will not abandon the Contras"; and described the contras as "brave men and women" who "fight to secure the blessings of liberty," comparing them with the American patriots who produced the U.S. Constitution, which he lauded in this bicentennial celebration. U.S. Embassy officials kept Bennett from a meeting at the opposition Social Christian Party headquarters because a group of some 40 people were outside, including wounded war veterans, in a peaceful demonstration in which "they were chanting, 'We only want peace, Mr. Bennett, not war'," according to Bennett's aide. "We didn't want a situation in which Sandinista television stations would show the secretary walking past all those war wounded with their stumps and bandaged limbs," a U.S Embassy official told reporters. The U.S. lodged an official complaint with Nicaragua over this incident. Unfortunately, however, despite the deliberate provocation, there was no harsh response from Nicaragua. The U.S. conceded that no barriers were raised to Bennett's trip or public lecture, which was front page news in the Nicaraguan press, and the only response was a statement by Foreign Minister Miguel D'Escoto that "It's a sadly typical North American attitude that Nicaragua has known throughout its history. It's a superior, disrespectful characteristic of this superpower government."[61]

Secretary Bennett was overflowing with self-adulation about the glories of America and its Constitution as he courageously denounced the Sandinista tyrants in their lair. He also gave a judicious appraisal after his one day visit, informing reporters that he had discovered that the Sandinista government has little popular support, but has not yet become "a Marxist-Leninist totalitarian state," though it is well on the way. He did not speculate on what the reaction would have been in the United States, Israel, or other countries that rank high in his esteem to a comparable visit by a spokesman for a hostile power conducting terrorist attacks against the country, making comparable public statements; naturally, for such a visit never would have been permitted in the first place. Nor, according to reports, did this distinguished educator, philosopher, and student of the Constitution include in his patriotic rhetoric any conclusions about how we would react today to a Third World revolution that adopted the practices followed by the Founding Fathers and their descendants, endorsing literal human slavery, organizing genocidal destruction of the native population, disenfranchising males without property, women (for a mere 130 years), and people of the wrong color (for a mere 180 years), and so on—bearing in mind that the American colonies were probably the richest area of the world, and even in absolute terms surpass most of the Third World today in crucial respects. Such thoughts would plainly be inappropriate while denouncing one's victims from on high, just as they are at home.

Secretary Bennett observed that there was "nothing overly coy or subtle" about the decision to send him to Nicaragua, where the freedoms protected by the U.S. Constitution "do not obtain," he proclaimed loftily. Bennett was the only Cabinet member to travel overseas on a presidential mission to mark the anniversary of the Constitution, from which we are to conclude, presumably, that elsewhere the freedoms protected by the U.S. Constitution do obtain, just as we are to assume that they did obtain for dissidents during World War I, Japanese-Americans during World War II, Blacks in Mississippi—to mention a few of innumerable examples during years when the national territory was under no threat.

On the same day that Shultz announced Washington's intentions to disrupt the Central American agreements, the Reagan administration again signalled its displeasure with the errant Costa Rican President who had violated his trust by attempting to pursue a diplomatic settlement. The White House "rejected plans for President Arias of Costa Rica to make a formal speech to a joint meeting of Congress" in late September 1987, as proposed by House Speaker Jim Wright, so that he "will instead deliver more informal remarks to a gathering of legislators, Capitol Hill sources said yesterday."[62]

The President followed with a warning that the Central American peace plan is "fatally flawed"; he "said he believed the requirement that the United States end aid to contras while letting the Nicaraguans still receive aid from the Soviet Union was a fatal flaw, and 'a loophole that the Sandinistas could take advantage of'."[63] This "loophole" could be closed by permitting Nicaragua some other means for self-defense against a terrorist superpower, but that insight appears to be beyond the resources of the Free Press.

Elliott Abrams elaborated further "that the peace plan can be salvaged but only if it is changed to ban Soviet and Cuban aid to Nicaragua," so that the economy, now thankfully ruined by the U.S. assault, will completely collapse, and the country will be defenseless against further U.S. attack; U.S. aid to its clients may persist, however, and U.S. power can continue to be effectively used to ensure that Nicaragua has no other source of support. The leading democrat, Arturo Cruz, went a step further, expressing his hope "that internationalists and solidarity groups stop meddling in Nicaragua." It is important to prevent a Ben Linder from setting up a tiny generator in a remote and impoverished village lacking electricity, and to keep Americans from learning first-hand about a country that their government seeks to destroy. Cruz is not on record as opposing hiring of Israeli mercenaries by "the sons of Reagan" at $10,000 per month, even more than he received from the CIA and Ollie North for his services as front man, or as condemning other U.S. and foreign volunteers for the "freedom fighters"; and "internationalists" who visit Israel to do volunteer work on state-subsidized militarized collectives (from which the non-Jewish citizens of the state are effectively barred) have aroused no visible protest. Nor does the president of Democratic Action for Nicaragua raise objections to U.S. government projects, bringing their form of development to countries of the region. It is only when citizens seek to act on their own that the official "democrats" become concerned; when they are following the orders of higher authorities, all is well.[64]

In a radio speech, Reagan emphasized that "there should be no uncertainty of our unswerving commitment to the contras" in their battle against what the reporter terms "the Moscow-backed Government in Nicaragua," failing to remind us why it is "Moscow-backed."[65] Thus the U.S. government again announced its intention to reject the "indispensable element for achieving a stable and lasting peace in the region," and to persist in the unlawful use of force. And if "the negotiations fall apart" for some unidentified reason, as the reporter puts it, those who did not actively support U.S. international terrorism will bear the burden for the failure. This is a crucial requirement, laying the groundwork for future U.S. violence "in defense of freedom."

And so the travail of Central America moves on to its next phase.[66]

Notes Chapter Seven

1. "Adherence to Agreements: Yalta and the Experiences of the Early Cold War," *International Security*, Summer 1986. A more complete accounting on broader grounds would have to include not only Stalin's duplicity and terror but also, on the Western side, the mass slaughter operations organized by the U.S. in Greece and South Korea and many other operations in the Third World, as well as an analysis of operations in Europe and Japan to ensure a political outcome in the interest of traditional privilege. This has not been seriously attempted since Gabriel and Joyce Kolko's outstanding studies *Politics of War* (Random House, 1968) and *Limits of Power* (Harper & Row, 1972). A great deal of relevant material has since emerged, essentially extending their major conclusions, in my view. See the reference of note 23 p. 37, for review of some recent work on the topic.

2. For the internal U.S. documentary record through the late 1960s, wrestling with these acknowledged problems throughout, see *For Reasons of State*, 1.VI.5. See George Kahin, *Intervention* (Knopf, 1986), for a revealing study of this period. On the immediate U.S. moves to undermine the Paris agreements, announced at once by Washington though suppressed by the media, see my *Towards a New Cold War* (Pantheon, 1982), chapter 3, reprint of a 1973 article. For more on the matter, see Seymour Hersh, *The Price of Power* (Summit, 1983), and on the general background, Gareth Porter, *A Peace Denied* (Indiana U. press, 1975).

3. "Wright plan paves the way to stability in Nicaragua," *BG*, Aug. 10, 1987, reprinted from the *Los Angeles Times*. The concept of "left wing of the Democratic Party" is an intriguing one.

4. See my article in Walker, *Reagan vs. the Sandinistas*, for discussion; the repressive measures instituted during World War I, when there was not even a remote threat of attack against the United States, were still more severe, reaching even as far as a ten-year jail sentence for a presidential candidate who believed absurdly that the right of free expression would be maintained. But we may plead, in extenuation, that this was, after all, only a century and a half after the American revolution, so that the country was still learning democratic ways.

5. *NYT*, Aug. 10, 1987.

6. For discussion and sources below, see *TTT*, 143f.; Burns, *At War in Nicaragua*, 165f.; Smith, "Lies about Nicaragua." For general discussion of the record see Morley and Petras, *The Reagan Administration and Nicaragua* and William Goodfellow's chapter in Walker, *Reagan vs. the*

Sandinistas. The *Times* is not unaware of the facts, and sometimes reports them at least partially; see, e.g., Joel Brinkley, Aug. 6, 1987.

7. *Mesoamerica* (Costa Rica), Sept. 1987.

8. *NYT,* Jan. 8, 1987.

9. José Melendez, *Excelsior* (Mexico City), April 8, 1987; translated in *Central America NewsPak,* March 30-April 12, 1987.

10. On the vicissitudes of the Arias plan, first supported by the Reagan administration when it was able to have a hand in drafting it, then opposed as it was modified to accommodate Central American priorities, see *Central America Bulletin,* Aug. 1987.

11. Pamela Constable, *BG,* March 15, 1987.

12. Rosenfeld, *WP,* June 26, 1987; editorial, *NYT,* June 18, 1987.

13. COHA's *Washington Report on the Hemisphere,* April 15, 1987. On the terms of the plan and a comparison to the Contadora proposal, see "Arias Primer," *International Policy Report,* June 1987.

14. Dennis Volman, *CSM,* June 26, 1987, paraphrasing Habib's briefing as reported by participants.

15. *Central America Report* (Inforpress Centroamericana, Guatemala City), June 26, 1987.

16. James LeMoyne, *NYT,* March 17, 1987.

17. See *TTT,* 157f., for evidence on this matter.

18. See *TTT,* 3.6.3, and for more extensive discussion, Herman and Chomsky, *Political Economy of the Mass Media,* chapter 3.

19. Dennis Volman, *CSM,* June 26, 1987.

20. William Goodfellow and Jim Morrell, Guatemala City, Aug. 4, 1987. Also *Central America Report* (Guatemala City), Aug. 7, 1987. The intervention of Contadora nations seems to have been ignored in the U.S. media. The U.S. government opposition to the peace initiatives of the Latin American states tends to place Contadora under a cloud.

21. Peter Osterlund, *CSM,* Aug. 10; Michael Allen, *WSJ,* Aug. 10, 1987.

22. *Ibid.* See *NYT,* Aug. 12, 1987, for the text of the Central American agreement.

23. *Central America Report,* Aug. 14, 1987.

24. *Le Monde,* Aug. 7; Brummer, *MGW,* Aug. 16, 1987.

25. Ellen Hume and Robert Greenberger, *WSJ,* Aug. 14; Joel Brinkley, *NYT,* Aug. 15, 1987. Shultz quoted by Brinkley, *NYT,* Aug. 6, 1987.

26. *CSM,* Aug. 7, 1987; *NYT,* Aug. 6, 1987.

27. *NYT,* Aug. 7, 6, 1987.

28. *NYT,* Aug. 6, 1987. For a recent review of Reagan administration efforts to evade all forms of negotiation in the face of Nicaraguan pressures to initiate them, see Smith, "Lies about Nicaragua." His record is only partial, excluding, for example, Nicaraguan efforts since 1981, to

settle border issues with international monitoring, obviously intolerable to the U.S., which must attack Nicaragua to deter it from aggression.

29. *NYT*, Aug. 7, 1987; Rosenthal's contributions since retiring as chief editor give much insight into the mentality that animated the *Times* over many years under his stewardship. Some further examples follow.

30. *BG*, Aug. 10, 1987.

31. See p. 136. *NYT*, Aug. 8, 1987.

32. *Central America Report*, Aug. 14, 1987. *Excelsior* (Mexico), Aug 25; in *Central America News Update*, Oct. 1, 1987.

33. Rosenthal, *NYT*, Aug. 21, 1987; Ignatius, *WP Weekly*, Aug. 24, 1987.

34. Editorial, *WP*, Aug. 31, 1987.

35. Ellen Hume and Robert Greenberger, *WSJ*, Aug. 14, 1987.

36. Robert Greenberger, *WSJ*, Aug. 17; Neil Lewis, *NYT*, Aug. 18, 1987.

37. See references cited in note 2.

38. Not entirely, however. See editorial, *BG*, Aug. 21, 1987, which states the facts briefly but accurately, something of a historical event in American journalism. This is, to my knowledge, the first time these critically important facts have ever been stated correctly, or even near correctly, in the mainstream U.S. media, though the facts are transparent, and both the facts, and the astonishing willingness of the media to suppress them in favor of the government version, have been discussed in print since early 1973.

39. "Koch Names 8 to Join Him on Nicaragua Trip, *NYT*, Sept. 14, 1987. For discussion of Freedom House, see Herman and Brodhead, *Demonstration Elections*, Appendix 1: "Freedom House Observers in Zimbabwe Rhodesia and El Salvador." For examination of the Freedom House conception of the nature of a Free Press, see Herman and Chomsky, *Political Economy of the Mass Media*, chapter 5, sec. 5.3 and Appendix.

40. LeMoyne, "Latin Hope and Evasion," *NYT*, Aug. 10, 1987, p. 1. There is an oblique reference to "Nicaraguan officials" who expressed optimism about the accords.

41. Reuters, *Toronto Globe & Mail*, Aug. 10, 1987.

42. James LeMoyne, *NYT*, Aug. 22, 1987.

43. Joel Brinkley, *NYT*, Aug. 28, 1987.

44. COHA's *Washington Report on the Hemisphere*, Sept. 30, 1987.

45. AP, *BG*, Aug. 24, 75 words; Stephen Kinzer, "Nicaraguan Hope Rises For Independent Press," *NYT*, Aug. 24, 1987. On D'Escoto's protest, *BG*, Aug. 25, a few lines in a Reuters story on another topic; AP, *BG*, Aug. 27, 90 words.

46. Philip Bennett, *BG*, Aug. 16, 1987. See also Stephen Kinzer, *NYT*, Aug. 14, citing promises by Vice President Sergio Ramírez to end censorship, free prisoners, abolish special tribunals, etc., if the U.S. stops aid to the contras.

47. Peter Ford, "Sandinista commission raises questions," *CSM*, Sept. 3, 1987. He comments accurately that the "actual political beliefs" of the Commission members are "probably less important than local and international perceptions"; for the U.S., the perceptions will be determined within a framework established in Washington.

48. "Complaint by U.S. Over Latin Panel," Reuters, *NYT*, Aug. 27; Stephen Kinzer, *NYT*, Aug. 30, 1987.

49. Norton, *In These Times*, Sept. 2-8; Norton, *CSM*, Sept. 15, 1987. Norton observes that one of the alternates selected was a member of the small Social Democratic Party, the only gesture to openness in the Commission.

50. *Mesoamerica* (Costa Rica), Sept. 1987. According to this report, "eyebrows were further raised" by this announcement, coming after complaints by Central American diplomats that Honduras was "stalling" during the August meetings. The conference of Honduran Bishops called for the creation of a Commission to "aid the democratic process" and put an end to arbitrary arrests, torture and other atrocities." (*Excelsior*, Aug. 30, 1987, also reporting the refusal of the government to form a Commission as required.) This August announcement was reported on October 1 in the *New York Times* by Lindsey Gruson, noting the pressures from church and other groups after Costa Rica had finally appointed a Commission. President Azcona and the military oppose the formation of a Commission because this "would only provide the small left-of-center and left-wing groups a platform from which to denounce the military and embarrass the country," an argument that easily passes muster in the United States and called forth no impassioned denunciations. See also William Branigin, *WP*, Sept 23, 1987, reporting that General Regalado, chief of the armed forces that effectively rule this "democracy" had "ruled out the establishment of a commission."

51. COHA's *Washington Report on the Hemisphere*, Sept. 30, 1987. The Archbishop, the obvious candidate, was not nominated by the Church, presumably by prearrangement with the government.

52. Sara Scribner, *CSM*, Sept. 29, 1987, selecting an example virtually at random; my emphasis. Scribner is reporting a *Monitor* interview with President Arias, no doubt accurately.

53. *Ibid.*

54. Randolph Ryan, "The sinning Sandinista," *BG*, Sept. 19, 1987, an eloquent critique of the general hypocrisy on these matters; *Mesoamerica* (Costa Rica), Sept. 1987.

55. Philip Bennett, *BG*, Aug. 16; Neil Lewis, *NYT*, Aug. 19, 1987.

56. Steven Roberts, *NYT*, Aug. 14; Neil Lewis, *NYT*, Aug. 17, 1987; Sara Fritz, *BG-LAT*, Aug. 17, 1987, citing House assistant majority leader Tony Coelho. Abrams's statement was bitterly condemned by Costa Rican chancellor Madrigal Nieto (*Excelsior*, Aug. 19, 1987).

57. My emphasis. AP, Sept. 10; Neil Lewis, *NYT*, Sept. 11; text of the agreement, as published by the *New York Times*, Aug. 12. The *Times* used the translation provided by the Nicaraguan Foreign Ministry. For the Guatemalan version, approximately the same, see *Esquipulas II Accord: Plan to Establish a Firm and Lasting Peace in Central America*, Special Document of the *Central America Report*, Aug. 14, 1987.

58. Neil Lewis, *NYT*, Sept. 17; AP, Sept. 17, 1987.

59. See, for example, Jenny Pearce, *Promised Land: Peasant Rebellion in Chalatenango El Salvador* (Latin America Bureau, London, 1986), not exactly a best-seller in the United States. Journalists would also not violate their commitment to objectivity by travelling to these areas to see for themselves, just as they have been careful to avoid refugee camps where they might learn about what is happening within El Salvador from the victims; even congressional reports from refugee camps were effectively banned from the press. See *Towards a New Cold War*, 36f., reprinted in James Peck, ed., *The Chomsky Reader* (Pantheon, 1987).

60. Kissinger, "When Compromise serves no Purpose," *LAT*, Sept. 6, 1987. On Kissinger's historical fantasies, see *Towards a New Cold War*, chapter 6. Penn Kemble, "Put Eyes of the World on Sandinistas; A Nov. 7 Rally in Managua Could Give Freedom a Chance," *LAT*, Aug. 27, 1987.

61. Julia Preston, "Bennett Criticizes Peace Plan," *WP*, Sept. 18; AP, "Secretary Bennett attacks Sandinistas," *BG*, Sept. 18; AP, Sept. 17, 18, 1987.

62. AP, *BG*, Sept. 11, 1987; 80 words. Not reported in the national press.

63. Neil Lewis, *NYT*, "Reagan Attacks the Central American Peace Plan," Sept. 13, 1987.

64. Abrams cited in a telephone interview by Norman Kempster, *LAT*, Sept. 13, 1987. Cruz, "Arias Plan is the Best Hope for Peace, But Central American Pact Needs to Avoid a New Bay of Pigs," *LAT*, Aug. 20, 1987. On Israeli mercenaries for the contras, see *TTT*, 133. Benjamin Linder was assassinated by contras while taking measurements for a dam that was to provide electric power for a "poor and backward village" in northern Nicaragua. According to his father, a pathologist, the autopsy reports show "that they blew his brains out at point-blank range as he lay wounded" (Stephen Kinzer, "Nicaragua Village Mourns American," *NYT*, May 6; Philip Bennett, "Contras killed wounded American at close range, autopsy shows," *BG*, May 6, 1987). His murder evoked a debate over whether he might have carried a rifle, or someone nearby might have been armed, in which case he presumably got what he deserved.

65. Neil Lewis, *NYT*, "Reagan Attacks the Central American Peace Plan," Sept. 13, 1987.

66. For a discussion of the dedicated U.S. efforts to undermine the accords during the inital three-month phase, and the achievements of the Free Press in suppressing the facts, see my article "Is Peace at Hand?," *Z Magazine*, January 1988.

8

The Reality That Must Be Effaced: Iran and Nicaragua

While the damage control project requires that we shake our heads in dismay over the foolishness and incompetence of those who have strayed from the American Way in their passion for democracy, the real world suggests a rather different picture. Here we find that the policies of the planners for whom Reagan serves as a figurehead are simply adaptations of traditional practice and principles to current conditions, and they have been anything but stupid. It should be recalled that as the Reaganites took command, there appeared to be real possibilities for democracy and social reform in Central America, with meaningful participation on the part of normally suppressed segments of the population. But these dangers were successfully overcome. Honduras was converted into a U.S. military base and the power of the domestic military and the oligarchy was further entrenched, while in El Salvador and Guatemala, state terror succeeded in protecting the rule of similar elements from any popular challenge. There were also substantial achievements in deterring significant reform and economic progress in Nicaragua and punishing it for its departure from "the Central American mode" of subordination to U.S. power, though the further goal of "restoring democracy" in the approved sense remains elusive. Furthermore, the bloodshed and torture were largely removed from American eyes—a remarkable accomplishment, given its scale and character—and the costs at home were limited. All in all, not an unimpressive chapter in the annals of international terrorism.

More generally, the application of the Reagan Doctrine reveals considerable sophistication, and a global vision that is impressive, in formulating and executing projects that are broadly supported by the elite consensus. The conclusion holds of both of the components of the operations partially exposed in late 1986: (1) the attack against Nicaragua, and more generally, the international terror network constructed to carry out this and other covert actions; and (2) the dealings with Iran, linked to these terrorist operations, but conducted for quite different purposes. Let us turn to these topics, now departing from the historical amnesia that is a condition of respectable discourse. With even a cursory look at recent history, essential details of what has been revealed—most of which, in fact, was long known, apart from details—fall into place within the normal spectrum of planning and execution.

Both Nicaragua and Iran were ruled until 1979 by U.S. clients—brutal, barbarous, corrupt murderers and torturers—who had been placed in power by U.S. violence (the Shah, by a CIA coup in 1953; the Somoza dynasty, by the Marine intervention of the late 1920s) and kept in power by the U.S., in the last years, with the aid of Israel in both cases. Furthermore, Nicaragua and Iran each played a leading role in U.S. strategic planning, so that the loss of these client states in 1979 was a serious matter.

Nicaragua under the Somozas had been the major base for U.S. subversion and terror in the region. Iran was part of a tripartite alliance (Iran, Israel, Saudi Arabia) constructed by the United States in the 1970s (with earlier roots) as a component of the Nixon Doctrine, which recognized that the U.S. no longer had the capacity to carry out military intervention everywhere and must therefore rely on surrogate states. As explained by Defense Secretary Melvin Laird, "America will no longer play policeman to the world. Instead we will expect other nations to provide more cops on the beat in their own neighborhood"—though police headquarters, it is understood, remains in Washington. In Henry Kissinger's rhetoric, other states must pursue their "regional interests" within the "overall framework of order" managed by the United States. In the Middle East, Israel and Iran were the "cops," protecting Saudi Arabia and its oil-rich neighbors from the usual enemy, the indigenous population, who may be affected by strange and unacceptable ideas about control over our resources in their lands; the conventional code phrase for these concerns is "defense against the Soviet Union." As explained by the Senate's leading specialist on the region, Senator Henry Jackson, an alliance developed between Israel, Iran and Saudi Arabia (meaning: the tiny elite that dominates Saudi Arabia and that is closely linked to the U.S.), in furtherance of these objectives.[1] It comes as no surprise, then, that there should be efforts to reconstruct this system of power with the cooperation of Israel and Saudi Arabia, as revealed in the late 1986 scandals—Israel having "become just another federal agency, one that's convenient to use when you want something done quietly," in the words of one Israeli analyst,[2] a status to which the Saudi elite no doubt aspire as well.

In both cases, these subsystems of U.S. global power fit squarely into the more general framework of U.S. geopolitics. Loss of control over Iran is a particularly serious matter. Since World War II, the U.S. has been committed to dominating the Gulf and the world's major energy reserves nearby. The fundamentalist regime in Teheran might, if successful in its aims, enflame Islamic nationalist efforts to take control of the critical resources of the region, a prospect that is particularly dangerous because of the large Shiite population in the oil-producing areas that might be particularly responsive to Khomeinist appeals. The problem is further exacerbated by the rise of fundamentalism throughout the Islamic world, in part a reaction to the failures of secular nationalism. From the U.S. perspective, the Khomeini regime poses threats to U.S. hegemony that are reminiscent of the "radical nationalism" of Egypt's Nasser, also intolerable to the United States. For these reasons alone, the U.S. and Iran are on a collision course, as matters now stand, and it is readily understandable that the U.S. should seek to reincorporate Iran as an obedient participant within its global system; or failing this, to maintain physical control of the Gulf with naval forces and bases nearby, if they can be obtained from the reluctant neighboring states.

With regard to Central America, a prime concern is to "protect our resources" in the words of State Department doves, who explain that this commitment often requires reliance on police states since more liberal elements cannot be trusted to crush dissidence.[3] Secret documents explain further that Latin American legal systems pose problems, because they require evidence of crimes, thus impeding steps to suppress "anti-U.S. subversion"; and worse still, they do not impose the kinds of barriers to travel that protect the Land of the Free from unwanted ideas, as when a member of CoMadres—the Committee of Mothers and Relatives of Political Prisoners, Disappeared and Assassinated of El Salvador—who had recently been released from imprisonment and torture by the Duarte government is refused entry to the United States to attend meetings at small towns organized by NOW chapters to celebrate International Women's Day, facts too insignificant to be reported in the quality press.[4] This willingness of the excessively liberal Latin American culture to tolerate "anti-U.S. subversion"—what George Shultz, following the usual practice, calls "alien ideologies"[5]—has always been a severe annoyance to enlightened American opinion.

The *Toronto Globe & Mail*, commenting on Shultz's phrase, observes that "it would be hard to call the ideology of the elected Nicaraguan government 'alien' to Nicaragua. The idea seems to be that Nicaraguans should be free to choose any government they wish, as long as it is one the US government can live with." Note that the Canadian journal falls into the same error as the mainstream British press cited earlier (p. 51), referring to the elected Nicaraguan government as "elected"; one would be hard put to find a similar deviation in their U.S. counterparts.

It has, in fact, long been U.S. policy, expressed in the secret as well as the public record, that the U.S. government has the right to demand conformity to its dictates in the hemisphere, a minor footnote to the posturing about how "We believe in freedom" (Krauthammer). In contrast, the Brezhnev Doctrine of 1968 insisting on ideological conformity in the East European satellites—through which the Soviet Union was attacked and almost destroyed a generation ago—is regarded as the ultimate demonstration of Communist depravity.

This demand for obedience to U.S. wishes is regularly accompanied by hysteria about the colossal consequences of any deviation from conformity. Thus UN Ambassador Vernon Walters, speaking to "democrats" of the Nicaraguan American Bankers Association, described Soviet influence in Nicaragua, a "cancer from outside the Americas," as "the greatest threat to the integrity of the Americas since we became free" (exactly who in the Americas became free, he does not say). Nicaragua could be the "landing beach" for "destabilizing Mexico," and Texas is just beyond, as Reagan warned.[6] Similarly, the U.S. has the right to ensure that there is no hostile military presence anywhere near its borders,[7] while the USSR must be ringed with powerful military forces at its borders with U.S. bases and missiles on alert aimed at its heartland—what is called "containment."

The premises of discourse in the United States merit close examination; they reflect imperial pretensions with few counterparts in history.

The secret documents on Latin America explain further that we must oppose "nationalistic regimes" that are responsive to "increasing popular demand for immediate improvement in the low living standards of the masses" and that are thus concerned "to increase production and to diversify their economies." These regimes respond to the wrong national interest—that of the domestic society, not the "national interest" represented by U.S. corporations. We must foster export-oriented production, protect U.S. investment, and prevent "anti-U.S. subversion" in the hemisphere. This requires that the U.S. gain "predominant influence" over the Latin American military and ensure their "understanding of, and orientation toward, U.S. objectives." The primary role of the Latin American military is "internal security"; specifically, as the Kennedy liberals explained, "in the Latin American cultural environment," the role of the military is to "remove governmental leaders from office whenever, in the judgment of the military, the conduct of these leaders is injurious to the welfare of the nation"—that is, the welfare of Big Brother, once the military have come to understand and accept "U.S. objectives." U.S. planners perceive that "the contemporary ferment in Latin America is giving rise to a revolutionary struggle for power among major groups which constitute the present class structure." Naturally, the U.S. and its local clients must position themselves properly to determine the outcome of this class struggle, the internal security forces being the essential element, since they are "probably the least anti-American of any political group [sic] in Latin America." All of this follows from the fact that the primary root of U.S. interest in Latin America is "the economic root," including investment and trade.[8]

It is noteworthy that such perceptions of the world within the framework of a rather vulgar form of Marxism are not uncommon in the documentary record of state planning and in the business literature (see, e.g., p. 33, above).

The objectives of U.S. planners are clearly articulated in internal documents, as is their awareness that these objectives require reliance on force and organization of indigenous elements that can apply it properly. Such thinking explains the systematic features of U.S. foreign policy exhibited in practice, not only with regard to Latin America. The gap between the documentary record and standard incantations being vast, the former must be rigorously ignored.

In this context, it is not surprising that Carter's Human Rights Administration should have strongly supported both Somoza and the Shah. Congressional legislation, reflecting popular dissidence from the late 1960s, placed constraints on direct aid to Somoza, so the Carter administration was compelled to rely on Israel to provide arms and advisers while Somoza's National Guard killed some 40-50,000 people in its final paroxysm of violence.[9]

When it became impossible to save Somoza, Carter attempted to ensure the rule of the National Guard and to exclude the Sandinistas from power, since they were clearly "nationalists" who responded to the wrong "national interest" and "class interest." When this proved impossible, elements of the National Guard were rescued and reconstructed as a terrorist force to attack Nicaragua from Honduran bases, at first through the medium of what are openly called "proxy" states[10]: El Salvador, Taiwan, Argentina (then under the rule of the neo-Nazi generals, hence an acceptable "proxy"), and Israel. The Reagan administration even flew its friend General Leopoldo Galtieri, an Argentine criminal "who seems to have had no compunction about ordering the arrest and torture of suspects during the Dirty War,"[11] to Washington in November 1981 "to devise a secret agreement under which Argentine military officers trained Nicaraguan rebels, according to an administration official familiar with the agreement." These operations still being too limited, the U.S. soon took them over directly.[12]

In the case of the Shah, who was regularly cited by Amnesty International and other human rights organizations as one of the worst human rights violators of his day, President Carter praised his "progressive administration" and "move toward democracy" on October 31, 1978, shortly after his U.S-trained troops had murdered thousands of demonstrators in the streets. Earlier, Carter had explained that "there is no leader with whom I have a deeper sense of personal gratitude and personal friendship" than the Shah. Carter was particularly impressed by the "stability" in Iran "under the great leadership of the Shah": "This is a great tribute to you, Your Majesty," he declared, "and to your leadership, and to the respect, admiration and love which your people give to you." Meanwhile U.S. arms flowed in abundance while the CIA instructed the Shah's secret police in torture techniques devised by the Nazis, with the help of Israeli specialists.[13]

Unaware of the love they felt for the Shah, the Iranian people overthrew his regime. General Robert Huyser was dispatched to Iran in an effort to organize the Iranian military to carry out a military coup if the U.S.-backed government could not maintain itself. As he demonstrates in his personal record of these events, General Huyser approached the Iranian generals with exactly the assumptions on the role of local military forces and their U.S. supervisors that are outlined in the high level secret documents just discussed—not only "in the Latin American cultural environment." When Prime Minister Bakhtiar seemed unwilling to "face the prospect of a military takeover," General Huyser "came back hard and insisted that as military people, that was just the type of action we should expect to be called on to take." When the Iranian chief of staff seemed to him "not the man to head [a military takeover]," Huyser realized that "if the bottom line was reached, we were anyway going to have to put somebody else in charge." With "prudent planning," he felt, the military could "seize control" and "the masses could not hope to dislodge them." The opposition held that they were "controlling [the economy] for the people, and could cut it off at any moment, and they were absolutely right. The only way to change that fact was to introduce military control, and make it work." The military would have to take over "should the people get out of control." But against "the elemental power of this popular movement, we had made little headway." The military leadership proved unsuited for the task, though Carter's national security adviser Zbigniew Brzezinski remains convinced that "procrastination and bureaucratic sabotage prevented the U.S.-sponsored military coup" that he advocated and "that might have saved Iran from Khomeini"—and "the masses."[14]

Since shortly after the failure of these efforts to instigate a military takeover, the U.S. has—at least tacitly—authorized arms sales to Iran through its Israeli client, a natural choice in the light of the very close alliance between Israel and Iran under the Shah.[15] This is not a discovery of late 1986. In July 1981, a plane carrying military supplies from Israel to Iran crashed in the Soviet Union near the Turkish border; the incident revealed Israeli arrangements to supply Iran with arms, including U.S.-made spare parts and ammunition, involving many flights and supply operations from 1979. Zbigniew Brzezinski reported in his 1983 memoirs that the Carter administration had learned in 1980 of secret Israeli shipments of U.S. armaments to Iran.[16] In 1982, a front-page story by current *New York Times* editor Leslie Gelb reported that half of the arms to Iran were "being supplied or arranged by Israel"—surely with U.S. knowledge and authorization, given the relations between the U.S. and its mercenary state—"and the rest by free-lance arms merchants, some of whom may also have connections with Israeli intelligence," while the CIA was carrying out covert actions against the Khomeini regime from its bases in eastern Turkey. A lengthy chronology from the public record in Israel's leading journal is appropriately headlined: "the most open secret."[17] It is hard to take very seriously the show of surprise on these matters after the Fall 1986 scandals erupted, or such "scoops" as *Times* columnist Flora Lewis's revelation in August 1987 that "the C.I.A. knew about the shipments" of arms from Israel to Iran, as she was informed by CIA deputy director Bobby Ray Inman in mid-1982, according to her recollection, but in any event well after they had been publicly discussed in the *New York Times* and elsewhere.[18]

The *London Observer* reports that documents it has obtained show that Israeli arms dealer Yaakov Nimrodi, with close Israeli government and Mossad connections and intimate ties to the Iranian military from earlier years, "has been supplying Iran with the latest US military hardware" since 1981, including Lance missiles and "the latest laser-guided Copperhead anti-tank shells, which only went into production the previous year." The documents include a July 1981 contract between Nimrodi's company and the Iranian Ministry of National Defense. The order was so substantial in scale that "military and diplomatic sources in London, Washington and Jerusalem confirmed" that the deal "could only have been made with official sanction. The order for Copperhead alone was larger than the US Army order for 1981." The operations proceeded with the knowledge of the British government, and, surely, the U.S. government as well.[19]

By November 1984—long before the first consideration of arms shipments to Iran according to the Tower Commission and the congressional hearings—Col. North approached British arms dealers to arrange shipments of missiles to Iran, the *London Observer* reports on the basis of documents it obtained. The deal involved CIA director William Casey, ex-CIA operative Theodore Shackley, the Iranian businessman Manucher Ghorbanifar who figured prominently in the later arrangements, U.S. Embassy officials in London, and "a former mercenary with close links to US intelligence," flown by the U.S. Air Force to Frankfurt to meet

Casey and given a letter to the Iranian Ambassador in Bonn, dated December 6, 1984, "which confirmed the deal." All of this is confirmed by "US intelligence sources" and is flatly inconsistent with North's sworn testimony that his involvement began after Israeli initiatives in June 1985. The West German press has reported that North himself met with the Iranian ambassador to West Germany in Hamburg in 1984 to arrange the purchase of 20,000 U.S.-made TOW anti-tank missiles, a deal that fell through when an Iranian contact disappeared with a letter of credit. In October 1985, the State Department blocked a U.S. Customs Service investigation of the delivery of U.S. TOW missiles by Israel to Iran, advising Customs personnel to "forget the whole incident," according to a Customs memorandum; Secretary of State George Shultz claims to have known nothing about all of these arms shipments until December 1985.[20]

The available record suggests that arms shipments flowed to Iran from U.S. allies, with U.S. government authorization or initiative, from shortly after the fall of the Shah.

Public reports of Israeli shipments of arms to Iran, including U.S.-supplied arms, continued prior to the November 1986 "disclosure" of the scandals, though they were suppressible, much as in the case of the extensive supply operations for the contras in violation of congressional directives. Israeli senior Foreign Ministry spokesman Avi Pazner confirmed in an April 1986 interview that in 1982 Israel had sent Iran military supplies with the approval of the U.S., including spare parts for U.S.-made jet fighters.[21] In May, Patrick Seale reported that "Israeli and European arms dealers are rushing war supplies to Iran," as Israel now dispenses with "the usual roundabout arms routes"; "for example, a ship now at sea, carrying more than 25,000 tonnes of Israeli artillery, ammunition, gun barrels, aircraft parts and other war supplies" was ordered to proceed directly to Iran instead of transshipping through Zaire.[22]

One major purpose of these arms supply operations was to locate what are called "moderates." Thus the *Los Angeles Times* reports that Israeli arms shipments to Iran apparently began in 1979, hence shortly after General Huyser's failure to instigate a military coup, to "help keep channels open to moderate or pragmatic elements in Iran, particularly in the military, who would one day overthrow or at least inherit the power."[23] The terminology ("moderate," "pragmatic") is standard Newspeak, but this report is unusually honest in recognizing the reasons. The

concept of "moderate" is explained by Uri Lubrani of the Labor
Party, former de facto Israeli Ambassador to Iran under the Shah,
now in charge of Israeli operations (terrorism, to be honest) in
southern Lebanon. Outlining the motivation for the Israeli arms
sales over BBC in February 1982, Lubrani said:

> I very strongly believe that Tehran can be taken over by a very
> relatively small force, determined, ruthless, cruel. I mean the
> men who would lead that force will have to be emotionally
> geared to the possibility that they'd have to kill ten thousand
> people.

In short, these men would be "moderates," in the technical Orwellian sense, who could carry out a coup that would, it was hoped,
restore the Israel-Iran-Saudi Arabia alliance. In October 1982, the Israeli Ambassador to the U.S., Moshe Arens, informed the press that
Israel was providing arms to Iran "in coordination with the U.S.
government...at almost the highest of levels" in the hope of establishing relations with Iranian officers who could carry out a military
coup, or who "might be in a position of power in Iran" during the
post-Khomeini succession. The same analysis was presented
publicly in 1982—though kept from a U.S. audience—by other
high-ranking Israeli officials, including David Kimche and Yaakov
Nimrodi, who are now identified as the earliest intermediaries in
the 1985 operation of secret arms supply to Iran, perhaps its in-
itiators.[24]

The occasional oblique references to these facts in the media
generally suppress the reasons explicitly presented by the high
Israeli officials involved. Thus the *Times* reports that Israeli arms
shipments to Iran "since 1979" were part of a "broad strategy,"
namely, to protect Jews in Iran and to prolong the Iran-Iraq war.
The still "broader strategy" undertaken in coordination with the
U.S. government is unmentioned.[25]

Israel's leading journal, *Ha'aretz*, reports that "the truth,
according to reliable [Israeli] sources," is that the 1985
U.S.-Israel-Iran connections were advocated by David Kimche in
order to overcome the negative effects of the Jonathan Pollard spy
affair on Israeli-U.S. relations. Robert McFarlane testified in the
Senate that David Kimche had initiated the idea of supplying
arms.[26] Both Kimche and Nimrodi have recently expressed
publicly the deep humanitarian commitments that impelled them
to become involved in the efforts from 1985 to "rescue American
hostages." They have not been asked to explain when their
conversion to humanitarian concerns took place, and why they

abandoned the motives that they had expressed a few years earlier while pursuing the same policies.

The efforts to inspire a military coup in Iran were publicly endorsed in February 1982—with some skepticism as to the prospects—by U.S. commentators, including Richard Helms (former CIA chief and Ambassador to Iran), Robert Komer (high Pentagon official under the Carter administration and "pacification" chief in Vietnam, and one of the architects of Carter's Rapid Deployment Force, which, he observed, could be used to support a military coup in Iran), and others. Again, all of this was out of earshot of the American public, except for publications that are easily ignored in the United States.

There is no reason to believe that the plans have ever been shelved, despite problems that have arisen in carrying them out. Israeli officials report that their Iranian contacts were caught and executed in "the mid-1980's" and that contacts were renewed "in early 1985."[27] The U.S. supply of arms to Iran through Israel with Saudi Arabian funding since 1985 is, very likely, a renewal of these earlier efforts, combining with earlier U.S. initiatives, already under way.

These programs may well be continuing, despite the disruption caused by the partial exposures of Fall 1986. The Labor Party press in Israel reports from Copenhagen that "Israeli arms continue to flow to Iran," citing reports from the Danish Seaman's Union, which publishes a record of shipments under the Danish flag. In its records from September 1986 to March 1987, "Israel captures first place"; ten out of 24 shipments left from Israel, followed by West Germany, Spain, Chile, South Africa and Portugal. Earlier reports from this source were generally ignored by the press, then cited briefly after the 1986 scandals broke. The same Israeli journal reports that Israel provides training in logistics and weapons handling to Iranian Revolutionary Guards (Pasdaran)—while Ha'aretz reports in January 1987 that Israeli instructors are training contras in Honduras, possibly paid by the U.S. government, according to Israeli military sources.[28]

Again, it is plain that such Israeli programs proceed with U.S. authorization, at least tacit. The Israeli press describes Israel as "the Godfather's messenger," undertaking the "dirty work" for the Godfather, who "always tries to appear to be the owner of some large respectable business,"[29] an apt analogy.

The Tower Commission cites a memorandum that they attribute to Oliver North, which was apparently the basis for

information provided to Secretary of State Shultz by national
security adviser John Poindexter outlining U.S. interests in the
"transaction" with Iran. The first of these interests is "a more
moderate Iranian government," which "is essential to stability in
the Persian Gulf and MidEast. Such a change of government in
Iran is most likely to come about as a consequence of a credible
military establishment," based on the professional Iranian army
(that is, a military coup). With a proper interpretation of the terms
"moderate" and "stability," this is a plausible formulation of the
primary and persistent U.S. objective. Further interests are:
blocking the spread of "Shia fundamentalist terrorism" and "the
return of the American hostages [which] will relieve a major
domestic and international liability—in addition to its obvious
humanitarian aspect."[30]

There is little doubt that the Reagan administration very much
wanted to secure the release of CIA operative William Buckley,
who they assumed would be tortured to obtain information, and
release of other hostages would undoubtedly have been a political
plus. Retired House Speaker Thomas (Tip) O'Neil may have been
the first to state openly what has surely crossed the mind of every
observer: that the Iran arms deal was "inspired by the White
House's desire to get the hostages back before the 1986 elections to
hold onto Republican control of the Senate," with wonderful
photo opportunities on the White House lawn properly timed
before the vote.[31] Nevertheless, the fact that essentially the same
policies were pursued before there were any hostages suggests that
the ranking of aims given in the North-to-Poindexter-to-Shultz
memo is realistic, putting aside the humanitarian passion that is
emphasized in public discussion of Reagan's zeal to rescue the
hostages, a quality that has been so dramatically revealed under
the Reagan Doctrine.[32]

Furthermore, the pattern of the "transaction" is a classical one;
hostility to some government is regularly accompanied by efforts
to strengthen connections with the military, for quite obvious
reasons—essentially those explained in the 1965 Pentagon
memorandum cited earlier and by Carter's emissary General
Huyser: it is the role of the military to take power when necessary,
overthrowing unacceptable civilian governments in accordance
with their "understanding of, and orientation toward, U.S.
objectives," firmly implanted through their association with the
Godfather.

Examples are numerous, several of them similar to the Iranian episode. Thus, relations between the U.S. and Indonesia became bitterly hostile in the 1950s, so much so that the CIA sponsored an invasion and coup attempt in Indonesia in 1958. After the failure of this attempt to overthrow the Sukarno regime, the U.S. continued to provide it with arms. In late 1965, the pro-American General Suharto carried out a military coup, leading to the slaughter of several hundred thousand people, mostly landless peasants, and the destruction of the only mass-based political organization in Indonesia, the Indonesian Communist Party. Indonesia was thus restored to the Free World, opened to robbery and exploitation by U.S., Canadian, European and Japanese corporations, impeded only by the rapacity of the ruling generals, who imposed a corrupt and violent dictatorship. These developments were warmly welcomed by enlightened opinion in the West, and regarded by American liberals as a vindication of U.S. aggression against South Vietnam, which provided a "shield" that encouraged the generals to carry out the necessary purge of their society. In Senate testimony after the slaughter, Defense Secretary Robert McNamara was asked to explain the supply of arms to Indonesia during the period of intense hostility between the two countries. He was asked whether this arms supply had "paid dividends" and agreed that it had—some 700,000 dividends at that point, according to his Indonesian friends. A congressional report held that training and continued communication with military officers paid "enormous dividends" in overthrowing Sukarno.[33]

And sure enough, Suharto's accomplishments qualify him as a "moderate": "Many in the West were keen to cultivate Jakarta's new moderate leader, Suharto," the press comments accurately, using the term "moderate" in its approved Orwellian sense. The London *Economist* goes so far as to describe this extraordinary mass murderer and torturer as "at heart benign" in a lengthy ode to Indonesia under his rule—presumably on the basis of his kindness to international corporations, which is not in doubt. The same issue of the *Economist* continues the regular berating of "the Sandinists," who have quite the wrong priorities.[34] An accompanying chart lists "political killings" in Central America since 1979, including 15,000 in Guatemala and 70,000, the record, in Nicaragua, which the reader is presumably to attribute to "the Sandinists." The hysteria they arouse in business circles is wondrous to behold.

To take another example from Southeast Asia, after many years of corrupt and brutal military rule backed enthusiastically by the United States, Thailand began to move towards a democratic government in 1973, arousing concerns in Washington over the threat to its major base for aggression and subversion in the region; Thailand was to be the "focal point" for covert operations to undermine the Geneva accords on Indochina in 1954, as the National Security Council determined in its secret reaction to the perceived "disaster" of the political settlement, and later a source of mercenaries and base for bombers for the U.S. wars in Laos and Vietnam. The U.S. offered no support, even verbal, for incipient Thai democracy but instead reduced badly needed economic aid while sharply increasing military aid to strengthen the security forces it had established, which duly carried out a bloody coup in 1976, allaying concerns.[35]

Turning to Latin America, according to Pentagon sources, "United States military influence on local commanders was widely considered as an element in the coup d'état that deposed Brazil's leftist President João Goulart in 1964,"[36] to the enthusiastic acclaim of Kennedy liberals, installing a National Security State complete with torture, repression, and profits for the foreign investor. The story was re-enacted in Chile a few years later. During the Allende regime, the U.S. continued to supply arms while doing its best to bring down the regime, and was rewarded with the Pinochet coup, which again it welcomed.

The Iranian operations conform to a familiar pattern of policy planning, which is quite understandable and sometimes realistic. "The US may have wanted its hostages back," ABC Middle East correspondent Charles Glass writes—in Europe—"but it also wanted to find an Iranian Pinochet."[37]

These achievements in Southeast Asia and Latin America were no small matter, and it would be most surprising if U.S. planners were unaware of the lessons. The 1965 Pentagon memo cited earlier, explaining the role of the military in overthrowing civilian governments (under U.S. influence and control), was transmitted shortly after the bloody military coup in Brazil and was followed a few months later by the far more murderous coup in Indonesia, which dramatically reaffirmed the doctrine. The coup in Brazil, furthermore, had a significant domino effect in Latin America. In the major study of human rights and U.S. policy in Latin America, Lars Shoultz points out that the new forms of "military authoritarianism" that swept over the continent beginning with the U.S.-backed military coup in Brazil were novel in that they aimed "to destroy permanently a perceived threat to the existing structure of socioeconomic privilege by eliminating the political participation of the numerical majority, principally the working or (to use a broader, more accurate term) popular classes." These National Security States developed in response to "increased popular political participation," he observes.[38] This phenomenon is unacceptable to the United States, inconsistent with the traditional and well-motivated antidemocratic thrust of U.S. policy, as events in Central America during the 1980s demonstrate once again.

The standard procedures are in process elsewhere as well. In Haiti, for example, the Reagan administration turned against the Duvalier dictatorship only when it was clear that it was unraveling and that the U.S.-linked elites were turning against the regime, as in the Philippines at the same time.[39] What lies behind the enthusiasm for "democracy" that was aroused when the dictatorship could no longer be sustained is revealed in a *Times* report headlined "Haitian Democracy Imperiled By a Rising Tide of Violence." It warns that "Haiti is caught up in such a tide of violence that it is doubtful whether elections can be held"—namely, as we find when we look behind the useful passive voice, violence by the security forces and by mobs organized by landowners and other right-wing elements. The conclusion? "The United States, which argues that elections are the best hope for restoring order to the country, has given Haiti more than $400,000 worth of riot control gear" and has trained the security forces "in riot-control techniques,"[40] measures likely to strengthen the most anti-democratic elements and to facilitate continuing effective military control, whether elections are formally held or not.

To restore the convenient arrangements of earlier years with Iran is plainly in the interest of the U.S., Israel, and their Saudi allies. It should come as no surprise that Saudi Arabia, through the medium of the billionaire Adnan Khashoggi, was cooperating with its tacit Israeli ally under the coordination of the U.S. in supplying armaments to Iran—not enough to terminate the useful Iran-Iraq mutual slaughter on Iranian terms, but enough, it was hoped, to locate those Iranian "moderates" in the military who would be able to serve the function of Suharto, the Thai and Brazilian generals, and Pinochet.

The idea of linking these efforts to the attack against
Nicaragua—and possibly Angola as well, among other cases yet to
be investigated[41]—was by no means foolish, apart from the
possibility of exposure. On the contrary, all of these plans reflect a
considerable degree of sophistication and geopolitical insight,
applied within the limits imposed by a largely dissident
population, which must not be aroused from its passivity.

The Reagan policies were well within the normal framework
of U.S. planning and geopolitics. True, the Reagan planners
worked through "secret teams," as did their predecessors, and
established an international terrorist network on a hitherto
unprecedented scale. But the policies remain those laid out in the
secret record in liberal as well as conservative administrations,
and implemented in practice for many years. The resort to
clandestine means, covert operations, and ad hoc executive
structures is natural and to be expected when the normal means of
excluding the public from any influence on policy lose their
efficacy. Functioning democracy can be tolerated at home no more
than it can in Central America or elsewhere, for reasons that are
solidly grounded in the socioeconomic institutions of capitalist
democracy, particularly in the variety that has evolved in the
United States with its special features. The historical record can be
readily understood, if we approach it without illusion and dogma.

The Reagan planners have, however, faced certain unavoidable
contradictions in their efforts. One problem has to do with the
program of driving Nicaragua to dependence on the USSR while at
the same time depriving it of the means of survival. It has surely
occurred to Reagan planners that a program of Kissinger-style
"linkage" might engage the USSR in the enterprise of strangling
Nicaragua in tacit association with the extensive network already
constructed to that end, possibly in exchange for an arms
agreement of the sort that the U.S. had been seeking to avoid
during the Reagan years. Reagan made the point explicit in a radio
address announcing that such an agreement was "close," but
warning that that this would be a "particularly good time" for the
Kremlin to renounce military adventurism throughout the world.
Specifically, President Reagan said: "They can stop helping the
Sandinista regime in Nicaragua subvert their neighbors"—to
decode from presidential Newspeak, they can stop providing
Nicaragua with means to defend itself from U.S. attack. "If the
world is to know true peace," Reagan continued, "the Soviets must
give up these military adventures."[42] There are signs that such

initiatives may have been undertaken, e.g., the Soviet decision to cut back desperately needed petroleum supplies. But such moves fly in the face of the necessity to ensure Nicaraguan dependence on the Soviet Union so as to market the attack against Nicaragua at home in terms of self-defense in an East-West confrontation. This would be a difficult problem to resolve even for the most sophisticated planners.

Other problems have arisen in dealing with another major enemy: the population of the United States. As discussed earlier, the major programs of the Reaganites have always been opposed by the general public, in particular, the right-wing Keynesian program of forcing the public to subsidize high technology industry through the military system. There is a classic method for obtaining the acquiescence of the public to policies it strongly opposes: induce fear. If the populace can be led to believe that their lives and welfare are threatened by a terrible enemy, then they may accept programs to which they are opposed, as an unfortunate necessity. To induce fear, the propaganda system must be put to work to conjure up whoever happens to be the current Great Satan. Other powers have their own favorites; at various moments of U.S. history the enemy invoked to justify aggression, subversion and the resort to terror has been Britain, Spain or the Huns, but since 1917 the Bolshevik threat has been the device most readily at hand. Hence the renewed appeal under Reagan to the threat of the Evil Empire, advancing to destroy us.

At this point, however, a new problem arises: confrontations with the Evil Empire might prove costly to us, and therefore must be avoided. The problem is to confront an enemy frightening enough to mobilize the domestic population, but weak enough so that the exercise carries no cost—for us, that is. The solution is obvious enough: we must confront not the Evil Empire itself, but rather its *proxies*, little Satans, states or groups sufficiently weak and defenseless so that we can attack them and torture and kill without fear that we might also suffer. Predictably, then, the Reagan administration came to office declaring that it would dedicate itself to eliminating the plague of international terrorism, as it prepared to launch programs of international terrorism on an unprecedented scale. Predictably, this was all accepted uncritically by the educated classes, abroad as well, and still is.[43]

The Reagan Public Relations system proceeded at once to construct a series of appropriate demons: Qaddafi, the PLO, the Sandinistas, and so on. They can be attacked by us or our allies without fear that we will suffer in the process, and can be designated as Soviet clients, or forced into that position. Libya was particularly well-suited to the role against the background of anti-Arab racism in the United States, and Reaganite Agitprop specialists have skillfully concocted a series of incidents and threats, timed in each case to domestic political needs, to which Reagan and Shultz have been able to respond with appropriate heroic posturing.[44] The Sandinistas too are depicted as terrorists attempting to conquer the hemisphere as agents of Soviet aggression, so that liberal voices in the media and Congress call for "containing Nicaragua" and compelling Nicaragua to "rein in its revolutionary army." The "terrorists" in El Salvador are also "aiming at the whole of Central and South America [and] I'm sure, eventually, North America" as well, Reagan explained in March 1981.[45] It would be difficult to convince the American people that these monsters really threaten our existence, but if they are all tentacles of the Evil Empire, poised to encircle and destroy us—intending "to sweep over the United States and take what we have" as Lyndon Johnson wailed, referring to those beyond our borders who "outnumber [us] 15 to 1"—then the threat becomes more credible. And there is no doubt that the propaganda campaign has been effective.

One aspect of the brilliantly conceived propaganda campaign regarding (properly selected) acts of terrorism has been exalted rhetoric about the need to isolate these criminals and to refuse any contacts with them; the fact that such words can be pronounced by Reagan, Shultz and their associates without eliciting international ridicule is a measure of the cultural colonization of much of the world by U.S. power. In general, the device has worked magnificently. But it came to grief when the Iran operation was exposed, revealing that the U.S. itself was violating its lofty prescriptions about "dealing with international terrorists."

If the media proceed to expose the probable U.S. government complicity in the international drug racket, that will engender similar problems, given the effort to exploit the drug problem as an additional device to mobilize the public and bring it to accept the strengthening of state power and the attack on civil liberties that is yet another plank of the "conservative" agenda.[46]

Through 1986, the media largely skirted the issue. To mention one interesting case, on March 16, 1986, the President gave an impassioned address denouncing the Sandinistas for every conceivable crime including involvement in the drug trade; this, he said with great emotion, would cause "every American parent...[to] be outraged." His statements were reported without comment, but partial exposures of this and other fabrications did appear later.[47] The reports on the President's evening address, however, refrained from mentioning that the morning edition of the *San Francisco Examiner* on the same day had a lengthy story describing how "a major Bay Area cocaine ring helped to finance the contra rebels in Nicaragua according to federal court testimony and interviews with the convicted smugglers."[48] Furthermore, sealed court records obtained by the *Examiner* revealed that the Federal authorities returned to one convicted smuggler "$36,020 seized as drug money after he submitted letters from contra leaders saying it was really political money for 'the reinstatement of democracy in Nicaragua'." The money was returned at the initiative of a U.S. District Attorney. The report proceeds to discuss evidence distributed months earlier by AP, but not generally reported, of contra involvement in drug smuggling. Thus the media might have accompanied the report of the President's charge with two facts that they knew: the charges against the Sandinistas had long been dismissed by his own Drug Enforcement Agency, but U.S. Federal authorities might well be guilty of the charge. Nothing of the sort happened, however.[49]

A more thorough news analysis might have noted that U.S. government involvement in drug trafficking can be traced to the earliest days of the CIA, when the CIA and the U.S. labor bureaucracy recruited goon squads and scabs from the underworld to break French labor unity and prevent interference with arms shipments for the French reconquest of Indochina, and continued through the Indochina wars. If U.S. officials have been involved in drug smuggling to obtain weapons for the contras, or have been looking the other way to permit it to proceed as recent testimony by drug smugglers indicates, this would simply be another chapter in a long history.[50]

Such are the problems that arise with complex and sophisticated global planning in the service of international terrorism, forced underground by popular dissidence.

Notes Chapter Eight

1. See my *Towards a New Cold War* and *Fateful Triangle*. Laird, cited in Ferguson and Rogers, *Right Turn*, 97. On the role of Nicaragua under Somoza as a base for U.S. operations, see *TTT*, 98.

2. Glenn Frankel, *WP*, Nov. 19, 1986.

3. See *TTT*, chapter 2. On the documents discussed below, see *PI*, chapter 1.

4. *Cape Codder* (Orleans, Mass.), Feb. 20, March 10, 1987. On the ordeal of the CoMadres leader who was refused entry, Maria Teresa Tula Pinto, see Marjorie Miller, *LAT*, Sept. 24, 1986; see also *TTT*, pp. 22f., on the earlier record, largely suppressed here. See p. 196 for another example. There are numerous others, mostly unknown; for example, the Canadian publisher of *TTT* and *PI*, prevented from crossing the border because of his outspoken opposition to the U.S. wars in Indochina.

5. *Toronto Globe & Mail*, Nov. 13, 1986.

6. AP, March 21, 1987.

7. Recall that there is one major foreign military base in Cuba, namely, the U.S. base at Guantanamo, and the Kennedy administration was prepared to blow up the world to ensure that Cuba did not mirror the status of Turkey.

8. NSC 5432, "U.S. Policy Toward Latin America," Aug. 18, 1954; "Study of U.S. Policy Toward Latin American Military Forces," Secretary of Defense, 11 June 1965. The former replaces NSC 5419, 5419/1, "U.S. Policy in the Event of Guatemalan Aggression in Latin America," a threat overcome by the successful destruction of Guatemalan democracy. See *PI* for further details and more extensive quotes; also Bowen, "U.S. Policy Toward Guatemala." The secret discussion relating to NSC 5419 expands on the right of the U.S. to block arms shipments to Guatemala from any source on grounds of "self-defense and self-preservation," as an "application of the general rule of preventing the extension of the Communist conspiracy to the Western Hemisphere." It is also noteworthy for the hysterical fantasies apparently advanced by intelligence; the concern over Guatemalan-inspired "internal subversion" elsewhere, such as a strike in Honduras; and the outrage expressed over "the Communist line being followed" by the *New York Times*, "the most untrustworthy newspaper in the United States" according to President Eisenhower. Communists seeking to destroy us are everywhere.

9. Israel's role in supporting Latin American state terror dates from 1977, reflecting the constraints imposed on the U.S. executive. The common argument that the Carter administration was unaware of this, or could do

nothing to affect it, is hardly credible. In 1977-8, U.S. aid to Israel vastly increased, reaching close to 50% of total U.S. foreign aid worldwide for several years. On these matters, see *Fateful Triangle*, and for illuminating discussion from a partially shared but somewhat different perspective, see Cheryl Rubenberg, *Israel and the American National Interest* (U. of Illinois, 1986). See also the references of chapter 3, note 41.

10. See *TTT*, p. 201.

11. John Simpson and Jana Bennett, *The Disappeared* (St. Martin's Press, 1985), 311.

12. Alfonso Chardy, *MH*, July 5, 1987. See *TTT*; also Walker, *Reagan vs. the Sandinistas*.

13. Seymour Hersh, *NYT*, Jan. 7, 1979, citing the former chief CIA analyst on Iran; Richard Sale, *WP*, May 9, 1977. On Carter's record, and his horrendous human rights record generally (soon to be far surpassed by Reagan), see my "The Carter Administration: Myth and Reality," reprinted in C. P. Otero, ed., *Radical Priorities* (Black Rose, 1981); Chomsky and Herman, *The Political Economy of Human Rights* (on Iran, vol I, 13f., 369); and *Towards a New Cold War*.

14. Huyser, *Mission to Tehran* (Harper & Row, 1986), 158-60, 194, 199, 231, jacket cover comment by Brzezinski. Huyser nevertheless convinced himself that the population would have welcomed a military coup; 289.

15. On the remarkable extent of this alliance, revealed in the Israeli press after the Shah's fall, see *Towards a New Cold War*, 455. Had the U.S. wished to see these operations terminated by its Israeli client, it could doubtless have achieved this objective.

16. Scott Armstrong et al., *The Chronology: The Documented Day-by-Day Account of the Secret Military Assistance to Iran and the Contras* (National Security Archive, Warner, 1987), 7-8, citing the *Washington Post*, July 27, 1981, and Brzezinski's *Power and Principle*.

17. Gelb, *NYT*, March 8, 1982; *Ha'aretz*, Nov. 24, 1986. There is occasional reference to the facts in the extensive coverage of the late-1986 scandals; e.g., Stephen Engelberg, *NYT*, Nov. 15, 1986, last paragraph, noting evidence that "the United States was tacitly approving violations of its arms embargo on shipments to Iran" through Israel from 1982; John Walcott and Jane Mayer, *WSJ*, Nov. 28, 1986, noting that U.S. authorization of Israeli arms sales to be compensated by the U.S. goes back to 1981, with the knowledge of Haig, Weinberger, Shultz, etc.; Glenn Frankel, *WP*, Nov. 19, 1986. For accurate discussion, see Alexander Cockburn, *WSJ*, Nov. 13, 1986, which may well have elicited the oblique references just cited; *In These Times*, Nov. 26, 1986.

18. *NYT*, Aug. 3, 1987.

19. Simon du Bruxelles and Farzad Bazoft, *Observer*, Nov. 30, 1986.

20. Simon de Bruxelles and Hugh O'Shaughnessy, *London Observer*, July 26, 1987; *Die Welt* (Bonn), Sept. 29, 1987; *Newsday-BG*, Aug. 3, 1987.

21. Michael Widlanski, "The Israel/U.S.-Iran connection," Tel Aviv, *Austin American-Statesman*, May 2, 1986.

22. Patrick Seale, "Arms dealers cash in on Iran's despair," *London Observer*, May 4, 1986.

23. *LAT*, Nov. 22, 1986.

24. For sources and discussion, here and below, see *Fateful Triangle*, 457ff.

25. Stephen Engelberg with Jonathan Fuerbringer, *NYT*, Dec. 23, 1986.

26. *Ha'aretz*, Nov. 28, 1986; *NYT*, Dec. 5, 1986.

27. Thomas Friedman, *NYT*, Nov. 26, 1986.

28. *Davar*, April 21, Feb. 2, 1987, citing the Paris *Nouvel Observateur*. *Ha'aretz*, Jan. 12, 1987.

29. Nathan Shaham, *Yediot Ahronot*, Nov. 28, 1986.

30. *The Tower Commission Report* (Bantam-Times, 1987), 179-80. The major fear of the spread of "Shia fundamentalist terrorism" probably has to do with Saudi Arabia, where the Shi'ite population might be aroused by Iran, posing a threat to the oil fields, situated in Shi'ite areas.

31. David Nyhan, *BG*, Aug. 30, 1987, paraphrasing O'Neil's earlier surmise, endorsed by a letter in the *New York Times*, Aug. 23, by Frederick Rarig, former special assistant to the Attorney General in the Criminal Division of the Justice Department.

32. Christopher Hitchens has compiled evidence suggesting that the arms flow to Iran may have been in part a "payoff" by the Reagan administration to Khomeini for delaying the release of the Embassy hostages until after the November 1980 elections, to avoid an "October surprise" that might have swung the election to Carter. See *Nation*, June 20, July 4, 1987; and for confirming evidence from Reagan staff worker Barbara Honegger, see Honneger and Jim Naureckas, *In These Times*, June 24, 1987. Flora Lewis reports confirming evidence from former Iranian president Bani-Sadr for a Reagan-Khomeini deal to delay the hostage release until after the election in exchange for arms shipments, noting also similar charges with regard to Prime Minister Jacques Chirac of France; *NYT*, Aug. 3, 1987.

33. Miles Wolpin, *Military Aid and Counterrevolution in the Third World* (Lexington Books, 1972), 8, 128.

34. John Murray Brown, *CSM*, Feb. 6, 1987; *Economist*, Aug. 15, 1987.

35. See Chomsky and Herman, *Political Economy of Human Rights*, I, 4.2.

36. *NYT*, Nov. 1, 1970; cited by Wolpin, *Military Aid*.

37. *Spectator* (London), Feb. 7, 1987. Glass was himself held hostage in Beirut from June 1987 until his remarkable escape two months later. The *New Republic* editors chose the occasion to berate him for not meeting their standards of support for Israel; July 21, Aug. 31, 1987, both published during the period when Glass was held hostage.

38. Lars Shoultz, *Human Rights and United States Policy toward Latin America* (Princeton, U. press, 1981), 7.

39. On the background in Haiti, see *PI*, 67f.

40. Joseph Treaster, *NYT*, Aug. 10, 1987.

41. Among them, possibly Mozambique (see p. 58) .and Cambodia, where the U.S. provides support for the Pol Pot-based Democratic Kampuchea coalition; see Herman and Chomsky, *Political Economy of the Media.* As for Angola, the London *Observer* reports that there is considerable evidence that the Reagan administration circumvented Clark Amendment restrictions barring aid to the South African-backed UNITA forces in much the ways illustrated in the case of the Boland Amendments and Nicaragua: networks of private wealth in part through the World Anti-Communist League; client states, primarily Saudi Arabia and Morocco; self-financing trading and service companies to generate funds, supply arms, etc., including Southern Air Transport, with close CIA and South African links. Steve Mufson, *Toronto Globe & Mail* (*Observer* service), July 28, 1987. Recall the comments of Jonas Savimbi, p. 56.

42. AP, *BG*, Aug. 30, 1987. The brief *New York Times* report of Reagan's speech the same day omitted these crucial remarks (special, Aug. 30, p. 14).

43. For discussion of these matters in the early days of the Reagan administration, when the course of planning was already obvious, see Edward Herman, *The Real Terror Network* (Black Rose 1982); *Towards a New Cold War*, 47ff.

44. See *Fateful Triangle*, 209-10; *Pirates and Emperors*, chapter 3.

45. Ronald Reagan, March 6, 1981; *NYT*, March 7, 1981.

46. For one recent example, see the decision written by Reagan Supreme Court appointee Antonin Scalia, in an Appeals Court, ruling that the government may install warrantless wiretaps if a "reasonable jury" would have found "that a national security justification was reasonable," even if it would (if called) have disagreed with the decision to wiretap. AP, Dec. 5, 1986.

47. See Joel Brinkley, "Drug Agency Rebuts Reagan Charge," *NYT*, March 19, 1986. The President's lies in that talk were so outlandish that even the editors of the *New York Times* felt called upon to issue a gentle admonition; editorial, March 20. For a partial record of the lies in this speech and elsewhere, see COHA, "Misleading the Public"; "Talk of the Town," *New Yorker*, March 31, 1986. See *TTT* and sources cited for an earlier record, particularly, Americas Watch, *Human Rights in Nicaragua: Reagan, Rhetoric and Reality*, July 1985. See also Thomas Walker in Kenneth Coleman and George Herring, eds., *The Central American Crisis* (Scholarly Resources Inc., 1985), and Wayne Smith, "Lies About Nicaragua," among others.

48. Seth Rosenfeld, *San Francisco Examiner*, March 16; carried on the wire services and hence readily available.

49. The *New York Times* mentioned the report, and the failure of Congress to investigate it, on July 10 (David Shipler, page B6, second section; there is also an oblique reference in "Washington Talk," Jan. 13, 1987). On some aspects of the media duplicity on this issue, see Joel Millman, *Columbia Journalism Review*, Sept./Oct. 1986. After the 1986 scandals erupted, reports on probable U.S. government involvement in the contra drug operations began to appear; see p. 72.

50. See Alfed McCoy et al., *The Politics of Heroin in Southeast Asia* (Harper & Row, 1972), primarily concerned with the CIA role in drug flow from the Golden Triangle in the Thailand-Burma-Laos region in connection with its secret wars in Indochina; Roy Godson, *American Labor and European Politics* (Crane, Russak, 1976, 80f., 135), a semi-official labor history that takes pride in the achievements in France, skirting the mafia connection; also Henrik Krueger, *The Great Heroin Coup* (Black Rose 1980). The *Times* managed a story on U.S. efforts to stop the drug flow from the Golden Triangle, including historical background, with not a word on the U.S. role; Peter Kerr, *NYT*, Aug. 10, 1987.

PART TWO

Further Successes of the Reagan Administration

9

Accelerating the Race Towards Destruction

It is not only with regard to Central America that the Reagan administration has been been compelled to deal with a recalcitrant public. National security policy provides another example of this pervasive problem.

Elite circles in the United States are united in their commitment to the Pentagon system, which serves as an essential device to ensure a public subsidy to high technology industry and provides a nuclear umbrella for U.S. intervention worldwide, deterring any response.[1] Accordingly, there was little reaction here to Gorbachev's proposals in early 1986 for the U.S. to join the unilateral Soviet test ban, for removal of the U.S. and Soviet fleets from the Mediterranean, for steps towards dismantling NATO and the Warsaw Pact, for outlawing of sea-launched cruise missiles, and similar measures.[2] But matters could get out of hand. Small wonder, then, that Secretary of State George Shultz called on Gorbachev to "end public diplomacy," which was beginning to cause acute embarrassment in Washington[3]; Shultz was much praised for this statesmanlike reaction. Similarly, the U.S. alone boycotted a UN disarmament conference in New York called "to examine how money saved under future disarmament agreements could be used to stimulate economic development, particularly in the third world." The reason, according to U.S. officials, is that the conference "would enable Moscow to discredit President Reagan's space-defense program and his opposition to a nuclear test ban in third-world eyes by presenting them as obstacles to disarmament and thus to the developing world's advancement," quite accurately. The conference was originally proposed by France, which backed down after U.S. objections, though France along with all U.S. NATO allies and all members of the Warsaw Pact attended. The State Department denied a visa to a leader of the Salvadoran Human Rights Commission, preventing him from attending the UN conference to which he was a delegate. Neither this, nor a protest by the Commission in San Salvador, were reported, and the UN conference also disappeared from view.[4]

The Gorbachev proposals that were successfully evaded in 1986 would have been beneficial to U.S. security and the proclaimed ends of policy. A comprehensive test ban would over time reduce confidence in offensive weapons, hence the likelihood of a first strike, while preserving the deterrent, which does not require a high level of confidence. Removal of fleets from the Mediterranean would reduce the possibility of superpower confrontation there, a threat that has repeatedly come all too close to realization in the context of the Arab-Israeli conflict, and that continues to pose a serious—perhaps the most serious—threat of nuclear war. The same would have been true with regard to the Soviet proposal to reduce the superpower military presence in the Gulf in mid-1987, when the Reagan administration, seeking to counter the effect of the Iran-contra hearings,[5] decided to gamble on a confrontation with Iran, risking consequences that might prove disastrous. For obvious historical and strategic reasons, moves towards dismantling the pact system would be a necessary (though not sufficient) condition for relaxing the Soviet grip over Eastern Europe, and should reduce tensions in the area generally. Sea-launched cruise missiles, as strategic analysts have observed, would render any ballistic missile defense largely irrelevant and would pose a severe threat to the U.S. with its long coastlines.

Whether these options are realistic, we do not know, since the U.S. either ignored or rejected the Gorbachev initiatives, with no noticeable comment here in elite circles. New problems arose in subsequent months, as Gorbachev unexpectedly accepted U.S. proposals on reduction of missiles in Europe; these had been offered on the assumption that they would be rejected, as part of the procedure for evading serious impediments to the arms race while pacifying public opinion. Efforts to evade Gorbachev's annoying moves by continually raising the ante[6] were accompanied by steps to increase tension and hostility, for example, naval maneuvers led by the battleship New Jersey in the

Sea of Okhotsk north of Japan, bordered on three sides by Soviet territory and considered by the USSR as "their play pond" according to a source quoted. These operations were undertaken in "response to a recent large-scale Soviet exercise in the area" in summer 1986, practicing how the USSR would "defend the Sea of Okhotsk and later, how a battle group would break from the sea through the Kuril Islands into the Pacific." Naturally we must "respond" with a display of force, just as we would expect them to respond in a similar manner to U.S. maneuvers off the coast of Texas. This U.S. response merited no mention in the national press.[7]

These developments provide confirming evidence for a conclusion supported by the entire history of the postwar arms race: security is only a marginal concern of security planners.[8] It will be no small matter to move towards arms agreements that threaten the major functions of the Pentagon system just mentioned: its utility for state economic management (organizing public subsidies for the costly phase of research and development before the state subsidized "private corporations" can take over for profit, maintaining a substantial state-protected market for high technology industry, etc.); and its role in "deterrence," that is, providing an umbrella for global intervention. Systems that are only marginally useful for these purposes can be sacrificed, but to reach an agreement that interferes with these essential functions is a different matter.

After the 1986 Reykjavik summit, widely portrayed in the United States as a great triumph for Reagan, the U.S. Information Agency commissioned a classified opinion poll to assess the reaction among NATO allies. The results showed that Reagan was generally blamed for the summit failure, in Britain by 4 to 1, in Germany by 7 to 1; only in France were both sides blamed equally. The results were leaked and published in Europe, but I found no mention here.[9]

Notes Chapter Nine

1. For discussion of the background for recent developments surveyed briefly here, see *TTT*, *PI*.

2. Serge Schmemann, *NYT*, March 30, 27, 1986; AP, Berlin, April 21, 1986; Joseph Nye, *Foreign Affairs*, Fall 1986.

3. Bernard Gwertzman, *NYT*, March 31, 1986.

4. Paul Lewis, *NYT*, Aug. 22, 1987. AFP, Sept. 5, 1987; *Central America News Update*, Oct. 1, 1987.

5. While the timing suggests that this was the proximate cause, there are far more serious issues in the background, as discussed in chapter 8.

6. Some of the Soviet concessions are rather surprising, for example, their willingness to exempt French and British nuclear forces and missiles, which are no less threatening to them than American ones and are by no means trivial in scale. According to secret U.S. reports obtained through the Freedom of Information Act, Britain (with other NATO governments) has been implementing plans to add several thousand new nuclear weapons with ranges of 500 to 900 kilometers, including very long range artillery, a successor to the Lance surface-to-surface missile, and short-range cruise missiles that can be launched from American or European aircraft. The nuclear warheads for these programs, which the British government falsely denied were under way, are to be paid for by the United States. Ian Mather, *Observer* News Service, *Toronto Globe & Mail*, March 23, 1987. Such techniques, along with offshore deployment, might serve to impede further and more meaningful arms reductions.

7. AP, September 29; *BG*, Sept. 30, 1986.

8. See *TTT* and *PI* for further discussion.

9. *MGW*, Nov. 9, 1986.

10

Controlling "Enemy Territory"

Some concern was felt in elite circles over the Reagan administration's decision to exceed the SALT II limits. In the military authorization bill of October 1986, both Houses of Congress called on the Executive to comply with SALT II, in the interest of national security. A few weeks later, the Reagan administration announced that it was proceeding to exceed the SALT limits. An administration spokesman explained: "Congress is out of town and the summit in Iceland is past,...so what's holding us back"?[1] In other words, the cop is looking the other way, so why not rob the store? In actual fact, Congress is "out of town" even when it is in town, as the administration knows very well, and it is not too difficult for a gang of street fighters to ride roughshod over the generally pathetic opposition, which is in fundamental agreement with their objectives despite occasional tactical objections.

It is hardly surprising that the Iran-contra hearings became a forum for contra propaganda. Contra supporters at least have the courage of their convictions, while the opposition, with largely tactical objections, had long surrendered any moral basis for their critique and could therefore only look on in embarrassed silence at the flow of "patriotic" tirades.

The attitude of the statist reactionaries of the Reagan administration towards their domestic enemy, the general public, is demonstrated by the large increase in the traditional resort to clandestine operations to evade public scrutiny, as discussed earlier. Their contempt for Congress—meaning, whatever limited role the public plays in the political system through its elected representatives—was revealed dramatically in the Iran-contra hearings, particularly during Oliver North's testimony. The public reaction was also illuminating. While elite elements were disturbed by this glimpse of the face of fascism, there was a notable, if brief, wave of popular enthusiasm. This was widely interpreted as an expression of popular antagonism towards the role and behavior of Congress, perhaps rightly, though we should recall that the public "trust Congress over Reagan when it comes to solving the nation's major problems by nearly a 2-1 margin." But at a deeper level, the immediate public response illustrates the insight of the 18th century European Enlightenment that the value and meaning of freedom are learned through its exercise, and that the instinctive desire of "all free peoples to guard themselves from oppression" (Rousseau) may be repressed among a subordinated population, effectively removed from the political system, disengaged from the struggle against state and other authority, and in general, objects rather than agents.[2] In the absence of organizational forms that permit meaningful participation in political and other social institutions, as distinct from following orders or ratifying decisions made elsewhere, the "instinct for freedom" may wither, offering opportunities for charismatic leaders to rally mass popular support, with consequences familiar from recent history.

The attitude of the state authorities towards the public is revealed still more clearly by what one Reagan official called "a vast psychological warfare operation" designed to fix the terms of debate over Nicaragua, a vast disinformation campaign called "Operation Truth"—Goebbels and Stalin would have been amused. The campaign was largely successful, along with similar operations with regard to Libya, international terrorism, the arms race, and numerous other matters. The pioneers of modern totalitarianism would also have nodded their heads in approval over the formation of a State Department Office of Public Diplomacy, reported to be controlled by Elliott Abrams under the supervision of the National Security Council, dedicated to such maneuvers as leaking "secret intelligence [that is, constructions of state propaganda disguised as intelligence] to the media to undermine the Nicaraguan government." This "vast, expensive and sophisticated worldwide campaign aimed at influencing international opinion against the Sandinistas," and crucially, designed to control the media and public opinion at home and to "influence congressional debate in favor of the rebels" attacking

Nicaragua, is explained in a March 1985 "15 page mega-memo" from Oliver North to Robert McFarlane, given little notice in the media that were one prime target of the enterprise. The Office of Public Diplomacy was "one of the least known but perhaps must influential programs of the Reagan administration."[3]

These measures to control "the public mind," in the terminology of the Public Relations industry, were quite successful in setting the agenda of discussion and fixing its narrow bounds. A senior U.S. official "familiar with the effort" describes the enterprise as "a huge psychological operation of the kind the military conducts to influence a population in denied or enemy territory." The terms are well chosen to express the perception of the public and Congress within contemporary "conservatism": enemy territory.

Notes Chapter Ten

1. Jeffrey Smith, *WP*, Nov. 9, 1986.

2. On the development of these ideas, important for understanding modern Western society as well as the early stages when oppressed people break their bonds, see my "Language and Freedom," reprinted in *For Reasons of State* and in Peck, *Chomsky Reader*. Also chapter 2 of my *Problems of Knowledge and Freedom* (Pantheon, 1972).

3. Alfonso Chardy, *MH*, Oct. 13, 1986; July 19, 1987.

11

Freedom of Expression in the Free World

In the case of Nicaragua, the compliance of elite opinion is revealed very clearly by what is called "the debate" over the U.S. intervention. This "debate" reached its peak in the first three months of 1986, as Congress prepared to vote on contra aid. During this period, the two major national newspapers—the *New York Times* and the *Washington Post*—devoted to this matter no less than 85 opinion pieces by regular columnists and invited contributors.[1] All 85 were critical of the Sandinistas, the overwhelming majority bitterly hostile; thus total conformity was maintained on the central issue. In 85 columns, there was not a single phrase noting that in sharp contrast to our loyal allies and clients, the Sandinista government, whatever its sins, does not slaughter its own population; the irrelevance of this evidently insignificant fact is just another indication of the ease with which we tolerate horrendous atrocities committed by "our side." In 85 columns, there were two phrases referring to the fact that the Sandinista government attempted social reforms before this dangerous development was aborted by the U.S. terrorist attack.

Naturally, there could be no contribution to the "debate" by the charitable development organization Oxfam, which reports that "Among the four countries in the region where Oxfam America works [Guatemala, El Salvador, Honduras, Nicaragua], only in Nicaragua has a substantial effort been made to address inequities in land ownership and to extend health, educational, and agricultural services to poor peasant families"; "from Oxfam's experience of working in seventy-six developing countries, Nicaragua was to prove exceptional in the strength" of the commitment of the political leadership "to improving the condition of the people and encouraging their active participation in the development process."[2] Oxfam adds that it has been compelled to shift its efforts from development to war relief, a grand success for the American war, which also provides U.S. moralists with a welcome opportunity to denounce Sandinista failures and "mismanagement." None of this can be known apart from narrow circles that escape the constraints of the indoctrination system, and it is inexpressible in the opinion pages of the national press when the time comes to "debate" the propriety of an escalation of the attack against Nicaragua.

The uniformity and obedience of the media, which any dictator would admire, thus succeeds in concealing what was plainly the real reason for the U.S. attack, sometimes conceded openly by administration spokesmen. "Few US officials now believe the contras can drive out the Sandinistas soon," Central America correspondent Julia Preston reports. "Administration officials said they are content to see the contras debilitate the Sandinistas by forcing them to divert scarce resources toward the war and away from social programs."[3] These horrifying statements are blandly reported, evoking no comment, quickly forgotten. The U.S. will not permit constructive programs in its own domains, so it must ensure that they are destroyed elsewhere to terminate "the threat of a good example." And elite ideological management will ensure that no such topics enter the arena of discussion, within respectable circles. Rather, the framework of discussion established by Operation Truth must be adopted, with no deviation tolerated, though it is then permitted to raise timid questions about whether the administration has selected the right means to achieve its "noble objectives."

The narrow conformism of the media is in part a response to the needs of the state propaganda system, in part a contribution to guaranteeing its effectiveness. The task is also surely consciously pursued. It is intriguing, for example, to see how rarely professional Latin Americanists are called upon for comment, in striking contrast to other regions and other topics, where the academic profession can be relied on to provide the desired opinions, thus protecting the fabled "objectivity" of the press. To select one example, it is a staple of Operation Truth that the 1984 elections in Nicaragua were a hopeless fraud while those in El

Salvador at the same time were a dramatic victory for democracy. Therefore, it is necessary to suppress the official report of the Latin American Studies Association (LASA) on the Nicaraguan elections, along with corroborative reports by a balanced Irish Parliamentary Delegation and others, because it simply drew the wrong conclusions after a careful inquiry by American academic specialists on Nicaragua. Similarly, it was necessary to exclude or to falsify commentary by international observers on both elections, including even those highly supportive of the American project, because they compared the Nicaraguan elections quite favorably with those in El Salvador, concluding that in Nicaragua the elections "were more open than in El Salvador" and that by the elections, "the legitimacy of the government is thus confirmed."[4] Plainly such material is inappropriate, given that editors and other commentators have a serious responsibility: they must contrast "the elected governments" of the "fledgling democracies" and their "elected presidents" with the Marxist-Leninist dictatorship of Nicaragua, just as their counterparts in *Pravda* must laud the "peoples democracies" of the peace-loving states of the Eastern zone, and contrast them with the warmongers controlled by fascists.

The practice is far more general, and it is understandable. Pursuing their commitment to objectivity in reporting on "the fledgling democracies" and "the resistance" to tyranny in Nicaragua, the national press can hardly be expected to report the conclusions of international observers who found that the Salvadoran elections of 1984 were conducted in an "atmosphere of terror and despair, of macabre rumour and grisly reality,"[5] or to approach mainstream scholars who describe the contras as "a hopeless band of blood-thirsty mercenaries" and observe that "The willingness of the Nicaraguan population to fight in defense of their revolution is what turned back the Contra attacks and gave pause to policy makers contemplating an invasion."[6]

The media have, in fact, been compelled to develop a new cadre of experts who can be called upon to define the approved spectrum of opinion. Thus in the news columns of the *New York Times*, R. W. Apple presents the spectrum of responsible opinion, ranging from Mark Falcoff of the American Enterprise Institute to contra lobbyist Robert Leiken. Falcoff tells us that the Reaganites whom he supports have been "stupid and maladroit" while "the Democrats on the Hill keep pretending that this Government in Managua is a Social Democratic humanist regime bumbling its way toward democracy" (in the real world, congressional opinion is as uniformly anti-Sandinista as the press[7]). And Leiken comments that "both sides are basically hysterical," refusing to "cope with reality," the reality being that Nicaragua is caught in a "contest between Moscow and Washington" with the superpowers represented locally by the "Soviet-backed expansionist Sandinista regime" for which popular support has "virtually vanished," and the peasant-based "resistance" that he supports, which expresses "the antihegemonist sentiments of the Nicaraguan people" and must undertake a "protracted struggle" of "armed resistance to the Sandinistas," leading the defense of Latin America against "Soviet hegemonism."[8] Beyond the respectable Falcoff-Leiken spectrum, the *Times* news columns inform us, the "issue's subtleties" are "buried in epithets," mere "mudslinging," entirely unserious.

Other views could be discovered, even within the narrow ideological confines of the media. They include not only charitable development agencies with ample experience in the region and elsewhere and professional Latin Americanists, but also respected Latin American figures with long and close associations with the United States: for example, the founding father of Costa Rican democracy, three-time President José (Pepe) Figueres, who describes Nicaragua as "an invaded country" and calls upon the United States to allow the Sandinistas "to finish what they started in peace; they deserve it":

> After all, the Sandinistas were elected as fairly as anyone else in Central America, except for Costa Rica, where we have a real democratic tradition that the other countries lack... All my life I fought against the Somoza dynasty because it was expansionist. They bought large properties in Costa Rica and persistently interfered with our internal affairs. Moreover, they were accomplished torturers and villains. The U.S. embassy in Managua supported them. I helped to organize countless movements to overthrow them and am grateful to the Sandinistas for finally achieving their ouster. Now, for the first time, Nicaragua has a government that cares for its people. I would have preferred a different approach to government in Managua. I am a fervent democrat and favor an electoral system along with freedom of the press. I was very sorry that they recently closed *La Prensa* but I also understand that Nicaragua is a nation at war, besieged by the United States and the regional oligarchies. When Somoza invaded Costa Rica in 1948 and again in 1955, we too established censorship of the press until the threat was over. As much as I disagree with the closing of *La Prensa*, I also understand why it happened.[9]

Clearly these sentiments do not serve the needs of Operation Truth, so the media must be careful to protect the inhabitants of "enemy territory" from the pernicious influence of the leading democratic figure in Central America.

As distinct from Leiken and other media favorites, Figueres reports that he found "a surprising amount of support for the government" on a recent visit. The same is true of other visitors, e.g., British TV correspondent Trevor McDonald who concludes that Daniel Ortega's "greatest achievement is that he has been able to convince most Nicaraguans that the Sandinista revolution is still worth fighting and suffering for."[10]

While the founder of Costa Rican democracy is not worth hearing, Costa Rican opinion is not excluded in principle from the media. Thus there is space for a columnist of the ultra-right-wing journal *La Nación* condemning Nicaragua for such sins as "its defamatory claims about Costa Rica"—meaning, its true charges about use of Costa Rican territory for attacks against Nicaragua, brought by Nicaragua to the World Court in accordance with international law, an infuriating violation of good form by the standards of a terrorist culture.[11]

Or the press might report the conclusions of Argentine Nobel Peace Prize winner Adolfo Perez Esquivel, whose visit to Central America showed him "the intervention, the repression, and the grave violation of human rights which the United States is committing" and who condemns the U.S. violation of international law and its efforts to undermine negotiations.[12] Or the Catholic Institute of International Relations in London, which identifies the "fundamental cause for the conflict between the US and Nicaragua" as "the relations between rich and poor on the Latin American continent":

> The Sandinistas have brought about a shift of power within Nicaragua from the rich to the poor. Their chief opponents in Nicaragua are those who have lost wealth or status through the revolution. It is with these people, and with their like throughout Latin America, that U.S. governments are allied, militarily, through investment and commercial relations and by ties of friendship. The consequences of these links have been demonstrated on many occasions, from Guatemala in 1954, through Chile in 1973 to El Salvador today. To most of the population of the continent, therefore, President Reagan's talk of freedom means the freedom of the rich to humiliate, exploit, and, if they judge it necessary, murder the poor

—the "Fifth Freedom" that is a determining factor in U.S. policy planning.[13] "The practical achievements of the Nicaraguan revolution," they continue, offer the poor "an alternative model and make Nicaragua a symbol of the hope that, despite all the odds, a better life is possible."[14]

Similarly, one is unlikely to find in the U.S. media a November 26, 1985 message to the Nicaraguan people by Fr. Manuel Henrique, president of the Brazilian National Commission of Clergy, expressing

> our solidarity with your struggle for a democratic and free nation based on justice. We condemn the cowardly aggression inflicted on your land by the Reagan administration, and we protest against every form of slavery imposed by the capitalist powers on our poor countries. That enslavement is sinful.

Even statements by Nicaraguan church groups critical of the Sandinistas are inappropriate when they are not useful for the cause, for example, the Pastoral Letter of the Baptist Convention of Nicaragua of May 1985, denouncing the "illegal...blockade carried out by the United States Government" and expressing their "hurt" over the fact that

> in the last few months more than 150 children have been murdered by the aggression financed and sustained by the United States Government... 9000 people have been murdered by the counter-revolution, 900 adult education centers have been obliged to close, with 250 of their participants being murdered; 17 schools were totally destroyed and 360 have been forced to close; 170 teachers were murdered and 180 kidnapped, 150 agrarian cooperatives were destroyed and 11 infant care centers have been closed down. It hurts us deeply that a country like Nicaragua—small, poor, indebted and lashed by every kind of calamity—suffer economic damages that already surpass $1 billion.[15]

Equally abhorrent to the Free Press is the Resolution of the Conference of the Interparliamentary Union, convening in Managua in April-May 1987 with delegates from 90 nations. Approved unanimously except for El Salvador, whose proposal to add their contention that their country was being attacked by a foreign power was rejected, the Resolution "Calls on the United States to pay heed to the findings of the World Court, to cease all military activities within and against Nicaragua," and condemns the U.S. embargo.[16] It was not mentioned in the *New York Times* or *Washington Post* (or elsewhere, to my knowledge), though the press reported the conference, dismissing it as "of little real importance"[17]—as indeed it is, given the realities of power and the doctrines of Operation Truth.

Nor is attention likely to be drawn to the denunciation of U.S. policy by the representatives of the elected legislatures in Latin America, meeting in April 1986 under the auspices of the World Parliamentary Union, whose declaration, adopted unanimously, said: "Deserving special condemnation is the open intervention in the problems of Nicaragua by the U.S. government and sectors of the U.S. Congress," an intervention in "flagrant violation of international law" that is a "threat to the sovereignty of the republics of Latin America."[18]

Such conclusions, or the evidence that supports them, would not be consistent with the required image of Nicaragua as a totalitarian dungeon and of the U.S. as engaged in the "noble cause" of bringing "democracy" to its suffering people, as it has done under the Reagan Doctrine in El Salvador, Guatemala and Honduras. Consequently, the media must be careful to exclude such perceptions rigorously, keeping to the approved guidelines as to how facts may be selected, presented and interpreted, in accordance with the dictates of the Office of Public Diplomacy. And so they do, with impressive consistency and only rare departures, as illustrated in the sample of the national press on page 203.

It is striking that even this level of media subservience to the state propaganda system does not suffice for the respected "democrats" of the Nicaraguan opposition or their advocates here. Thus in a cover story of the *Los Angeles Times Magazine*, Arturo Cruz, Jr. informs us that "the contras, so charismatic in Nicaragua, were always terrible at public relations in America" where the Sandinistas "won the [Madison Avenue] war handily." "They learned how to please America and how to play with American public opinion... The Sandinistas have hired the effective American mercenaries: not the soldiers, but the public relations firms—American mercenaries of ideas." American Senators want "to align with" the Sandinistas "so that they could take their alignment back to the United States and pose with it for their constituency," which explains the constant stream of pro-Sandinista propaganda on the Senate floor and in the mass media. The problem faced by the contras, he explains in the *New Republic*, is they they are "unable to speak the very special language necessary to communicate with American journalists," offering responses that are considered "too pedestrian and tacky to be truly revolutionary" by the ultraleftists who dominate the U.S. press.[19] Cruz Sr., the leading official democrat, chimes in as well. As distinct from José Figueres and others, his thoughts are reported in the Free Press, which naturally takes his perceptions to be accurate, describing him as the spokesman of "the center-left leadership":

> After watching the leftist Sandinista government of Nicaragua consistently score public relations victories in the United States, notes Mr. Cruz, [Oliver] North's riveting testimony has turned the tables. "This could be the first time the contra movement has had its day in court, so to speak, in this country," Cruz says.[20]

Finally, through the intervention of the great democrat Oliver North, the contras were able to break through the incessant barrage of pro-Sandinista propaganda that floods the U.S. media and Congress, and to overcome the barriers erected by the Sandinista-dominated media to the expression of any criticism of Nicaragua or, surely, any support for the contras, whose advocates have languished in enforced silence.

Cruz Sr. and his associates also offer other typical Reaganite fantasies with no harm to their reputations. Thus the South American governments only pretend to be opposed to the contra attack; "usually they act in Central America in terms of their own extreme left constituencies" (Cruz), fearing their "Marxist-Leninist minorities" (Alfonso Robelo).[21]

Similarly, U.S. supporters of the contras complain that "Left-wing opponents of *contra* aid have thrashed the administration in the propaganda battle on campuses, in churches, *and in the press*" (Morton Kondracke) and tell us that "the American public is caught in a bitter propaganda war over Nicaragua," between the Reaganites and the Sandinistas' "well-organized network of 'opposition' figures, 'witnesses,' 'correspondents,' and professional writers of letters to editors" (Robert Leiken). No less frustrated over the awesome power of the Sandinista lobby, A. M. Rosenthal denounces "the pro-Sandinistas in press and politics" who are "contemptuous about the goal of political democracy in Nicaragua" because "they are more interested in continuation of Sandinista rule than in peace," and who act "as if it were a damnable sin to suggest that the United States should not immediately destroy the contras, whose existence brought about the opportunity for negotiations"[22]—in the manner that we have reviewed.

In short, the extraordinary constraints on expressible opinion just illustrated and the virtually unswerving loyalty of the media and Congress to the fundamental doctrines of Operation Truth are not sufficient. Even the tactical objections raised to the pursuit of the "noble cause" by bitter opponents of the Sandinistas are intolerable, a proof that the media are controlled by pro-Sandinista "mercenaries of ideas" and that the critics are so committed to Sandinista rule that they prefer it to democracy or peace. As long as no way has been found to stop talks in churches or letters to the editor by people who have lived and worked in Nicaragua, and are therefore naturally to be dismissed with sneers drawn from the familiar litany, as long as the slightest deviation from total servility to the state is still visible, then that proves that the enemy is within the gates and all is lost.

The totalitarian mentality is revealed with much clarity in such pronouncements.

Notes Chapter Eleven

1. See my articles in Morley and Petras, *Reagan Administration and Nicaragua*, and Walker, *Reagan vs. the Sandinistas*, for a closer analysis, including some qualifications ignored in this brief review and a description of some of the techniques used by contra supporters, notably Ronald Radosh. See the same articles for review of *New York Times* editorials on Nicaragua and El Salvador through the 1980s, illustrating the same conformity to state propaganda. See Jack Spence, in Walker, *Reagan vs. the Sandinistas*, for detailed analysis of news coverage of Nicaragua through the 1980s, with essentially the same conclusions. Also *TTT*, particularly pp. 140f.

2. *Oxfam America Special Report: Central America*, Fall 1985; Melrose, *Nicaragua: The Threat of a Good Example?*, 26, 14.

3. *BG*, Feb. 9, 1986.

4. The latter, the conclusion of the Dutch government observers, who are so committed to Reaganite atrocities that they see no problem in the exclusion of the left from the Salvadoran elections by massive terror; for quotes and references, including the misrepresentation of their report by Robert Leiken in the *New York Review*, see my introduction to Morley and Petras, *The Reagan Administration and Nicaragua*; also *TTT* for citation of commentary on both elections; and for more extensive discussion, Herman and Chomsky, *Political Economy of the Mass Media*, chapter 3. Also Smith, "Lies About Nicaragua," noting that even "an American observer delegation led by former Ambassador to Bolivia Ben Stephansky and former Ohio Republican Representative Charles Whalen pronounced [the elections] reasonably fair and an important step towards democracy." An Irish Parliamentary Delegation dominated by center-right parties was even more positive, and totally ignored, along with others with the wrong conclusions to impart.

5. Lord Chitnis, spokesman of the British Parliamentary Human Rights Group; see *TTT*, 117, for this and other foreign reactions.

6. Lars Shoultz, *National Security and United States Policy toward Latin America* (Princeton U. press, 1987), 320, 323.

7. "This year, amid mounting evidence of widespread political repression and human rights violations by the Sandinista government, nearly every lawmaker is on record as expressing distaste for the Nicaragua regime" (Peter Osterlund, *CSM*, March 21, 1986)—exactly as in the past. There is no such reaction—quite the opposite—to the vastly worse repression and human rights violations in U.S. client states such as El Salvador and

numerous others. For a review of congressional opinion, see William LeoGrande's chapter in Walker, *Reagan vs. the Sandinistas*.

8. R. W. Apple, *NYT*, March 12, 1986. Leiken, *New York Review*, Dec. 5, 1985; Statement before the Committee on Foreign Relations, United States Senate, March 4, 1986; *New Republic*, March 31, 1986; *Soviet Strategy in Latin America* (Praeger, 1982), 87-88. The rhetoric is drawn from the Maoist cult literature. According to its principles, the sturdy Nicaraguan peasants of northern Jinotega province, though illiterate and uneducated apart from the influence of the most reactionary elements of the clergy, nevertheless feel "anti-hegemonist sentiments" (in translation, anti-Soviet passion), as a result of the understanding of Soviet behavior in Eastern Europe and of the Soviet threat looming over the rest of the world that is instinctive among the masses. The same healthy instincts inform the peasants of Central America that their neighbor to the north is a lesser threat to their freedom and well-being. As noted earlier, the affinity between Maoist and "conservative" (or "neoliberal") opinion, and the easy transition from one to the other, is an interesting cultural phenomenon.

9. Interview, COHA's *Washington Report on the Hemisphere*, Oct. 1, 1986. On comparison of censorship and other rights violations in Nicaragua with the U.S. and Israel, under far less dire circumstances, see *TTT*, 72f., and my chapter in Walker, *Reagan vs. the Sandinistas*. Similar comparisons can be drawn elsewhere, but the power of the U.S. doctrinal system is revealed by the fact that Nicaraguan violations are virtually the sole topic of impassioned commentary, among critics of U.S. policies as well, in a burst of narrowly focused and—with rare exceptions—quite novel libertarian sentiment.

10. *The Listener*, Feb. 26, 1987.

11. Jaime Daremblum, "Costa Ricans Don't Have High Hopes for Peace Plan," *WSJ*, Aug. 21, 1987.

12. UPI, March 18, 1987; cited in *Central America News Update*, April 12, 1987.

13. See Preface, and *TTT*, chapter 2.

14. CIIR, *Nicaragua*, London, Feb. 1987.

15. *Comunidad* (Argentina), Aug. 1985; translated in *The Cry for Peace in Central America* (LADOC, Peru), June 1987.

16. *Central America Report*, May 22, 1987, with the text of the "Summary of Resolution Approved by the Interparliamentary Union Regarding Central American Conflict."

17. Stephen Kinzer, *NYT*, April 28, 1987.

18. *Amenecer*, Dec. 1985, cited in a March 1986 paper by Joseph Mulligan, SJ, Instituto Histórico Centroamericano (Managua); Doug Huss, *Guardian* (New York), April 16, 1986; Council on Hemispheric Affairs press release, April 12, 1986. Father Mulligan's paper also cites the pastoral letter by the Baptist Convention in Nicaragua (addressed to the Baptist Churches of the U.S. and the World Council of Churches)

supporting "our government's legitimacy" as shown by the November 1984 elections and denouncing U.S. measures against it, eyewitness testimony by a Jesuit priest working in the northern countryside on hideous contra torture and massacre of civilians and kidnapping of hundreds of peasants, and other important material unreportable here.

19. Cover story, *LAT Magazine*, April 19, 1987; *New Republic*, March 10, 1986.

20. Marshall Ingwerson, *CSM*, July 15, 1987.

21. *WP*, March 9; *CSM*, March 12, 1986.

22. Kondracke, *New Republic*, Dec. 29, 1986 (my emphasis); Leiken, *New York Review*, June 26, March 13, 1986; Rosenthal, *NYT*, Aug. 21, 1987.

PART THREE

The Current Agenda

12

The Threat of a Good Example

Concern over "the threat of a good example"—the well-chosen subtitle of the Oxfam pamphlet cited earlier—has always been a leading feature of U.S. policy.[1] It is illustrated once again by the satisfaction of Reagan administration officials over their success in impeding Sandinista social reforms. What concerns them is that the perception expressed by the founder of Costa Rican democracy, that "for the first time, Nicaragua has a government that cares for its people," might come to be widely shared among the dispossessed, who might draw unacceptable conclusions. The central problem was outlined by the commander of U.S. forces in Latin America, General John Galvin, explaining why enlarging armies in neighboring countries and stationing more U.S. troops in the region "would be barking up the wrong tree," an inappropriate means to counter Sandinista aggression. The problem is that "the Sandinistas would attack with ideological 'subversion' rather than conventional warfare, and 'You cannot contain that by putting military forces on their border'."[2]

The editors of the *Wall St. Journal* issue similar warnings, decrying the blindness to reality on the part of House Democrats and European parliamentarians, who "wrote a joint letter to members of Congress, opposing aid to the contras fighting what the Europeans called, 'the democratically elected government of Nicaragua'." "At least the Europeans have a plausible excuse for this preposterousness," the editors add: "Much of their junta aid [i.e., support for what they absurdly take to be the "elected government" of Nicaragua] is no doubt a sop to the left in their own countries," just as South America and the American media are dominated by the left, as the official Nicaraguan democrats and their supporters lament. But the *Journal* editors, not subject to such illusions about Nicaragua, see that diplomatic measures will not do the job:

> If the Sandinistas remain in power, they will surely carry out their promise to spread revolution throughout Central America. The U.S. will have no choice but to invoke the Monroe Doctrine and spend more of its defense budget securing its southern flank by blockading or finally invading communist Nicaragua.[3]

Presumably, the editors are not anticipating direct conquest of neighboring countries by the Nicaraguan superpower while the U.S. stands by helplessly (though this reading may be too charitable). It must be, then, that the Sandinistas will achieve their nefarious ends, thus threatening our security, even without invading their neighbors, by "ideological subversion."

The concerns are also felt—for good reasons—by the leadership in U.S. client states. They don't like the contras, "but they don't trust the Sandinistas, either," the *Wall St. Journal* reports accurately, also offering the reason: "Few seriously believe the Sandinistas will invade a neighbor, but officials are concerned that Nicaragua can cause trouble by training radical union and peasant leaders as well as guerrillas"[4]—thus threatening the monopoly of the U.S. government, which, with the cooperation of the U.S. labor bureaucracy, trains labor and peasant leaders and offers them extensive funding and resources in pursuit of its traditional efforts to install compliant business unionism in the Third World, trains and supplies the proxy forces it calls "guerillas," and pretends not to notice paramilitary training camps for mercenaries and international terrorists in the southern states. Given the nature of the U.S. client regimes, there is good reason for them—like their master—to be concerned over Nicaraguan training of union and peasant leaders, and even more reason if the Sandinistas were given the opportunity to continue with the quite frightening progress and reforms of the early years, thankfully aborted by Reaganite terror.

The purpose of the American military maneuvers is "to deter the Sandinista government in Managua from exporting its leftist ideology," the *New York Times* reports in its news columns with no trace of irony, expressing its understanding that since the U.S., once again, is politically weak but militarily strong, it must rely on violence to prevent the spread of unwanted ideas.[5] U.S. allies in Honduras are particularly concerned. "'We don't have a wall to stop Sandinista ideology or subversives,' complains William Hall Rivera, the Honduran president's chief of staff. 'It won't be a fight over land, but over minds'"—just the kind of game that the U.S. and its allies know they cannot win, unless the cards are properly stacked. The reporter, Clifford Krauss, describes such fears throughout the region. But "things could be worse," he concludes, employing a phrase that expresses the commitments of the media that are sometimes better concealed behind a mask of "objectivity"; fortunately, "left-wing movements in Central America have lost strength over the past few years, and revolution doesn't seem to be brewing in the region"—thanks to the successful use of terror to destroy "popular organizations," as he fails to observe. Still, there is the danger that "the Sandinistas will infiltrate [neighboring] countries with Marxist-trained student, union and peasant leaders promoting Nicaragua's 'revolution without frontiers'."[6]

The *New York Times* editors, contemplating the likely failure of the U.S. military option, propose that Washington take a "calculated risk" and "tolerate a Marxist neighbor, if it is boxed in by treaties and commitments to rudimentary human rights." The Sandinistas would have to agree "to keep Soviet and Cuban bases, advisers and missiles out of Nicaragua," and to observe human rights, a major issue standing alongside of U.S. security concerns, because Washington and its Central American allies "rightly see a connection between internal and external behavior."[7] One hardly knows which of these two ideas is more bizarre: the demand that Nicaragua adhere to treaty limitations barring foreign bases and advisers and missiles (the missiles added gratuitously by the *Times* editors to induce the proper hysteria)—agreements that Nicaragua has consistently supported along with controls to prevent cross-border operations, in vain, since the U.S. will accept no such constraints; or the concern over human rights violations in Nicaragua, real enough to be sure, but slight in comparison with those conducted by *Times* favorites, whose atrocities apparently raise no problem about a "connection between internal and external behavior," and are of little significance in any event, being directed against the poor majority who are the natural enemy of the Free Press.

The real fears of U.S. planners, and the services of the media to power, are well-illustrated by the brilliant exploitation of a speech by Sandinista commandante Tomás Borge,[8] in which he expressed his hopes that Nicaragua would be an example that would be followed by others, explaining that Nicaragua cannot "export our revolution" but can only "export our example" while "the people themselves of these countries...must make their revolutions." In this sense, he explained, the Nicaraguan revolution "transcends national boundaries." These remarks were converted by Operation Truth into the threat of military conquest, in pursuit of a "revolution without borders." The fraud was conscious and purposeful; the State Department document *Revolution Beyond Our Borders* (Sept. 1985), constructed on the basis of this gross misrepresentation of Borge's speech, cites as its source the Foreign Broadcast Information Service (FBIS) translation, which contains the relevant text, as Wayne Smith observes. The fraud was at once exposed publicly by the Council on Hemispheric Affairs, just as earlier similar frauds had been. But the device was far too useful to abandon and Borge's call for a "revolution without borders" is now a staple of U.S. disinformation, regularly cited by reporters (e.g., Krauss, cited above, and innumerable others) and by columnists who warn that "Sandinista Stalinism" may be serious about "waging a 'revolution without borders'."[9]

As noted, the fraud provided the framework for the State Department's pathetic attempt to support its allegations about Nicaraguan arming of Salvadoran guerrillas. Secretary of State George Shultz informed the Senate Foreign Relations Committee that just as Hitler spelled out his goals in *Mein Kampf*, so the Sandinistas had revealed their true intentions in "calling for a revolution without frontiers," yet another exhibition of his refreshing "candor." Asking rhetorically why there is such a "formidable buildup" of military forces in Nicaragua, Shultz testified that Borge had given the answer when he said "This revolution goes beyond our borders."[10] The same phrase has repeatedly been quoted by Reagan and other officials, though sometimes the formulations are more careful, as when Reagan explains that Nicaragua is far worse than South Africa because they seek "to impose their government on other surrounding countries" (see p. 100), by means left unspecified: in reality, by "ideological subversion," the force of their example.

The most interesting use of this brilliantly executed operation of the Office of Public Diplomacy was in Reagan's speech on the eve of the House vote on contra aid in June 1986, considered to be an outstanding triumph of "the great communicator," or "the great prevaricator," as he is now sometimes described.[11] After warning of the threat to our existence posed by Nicaragua, Reagan worked his way to the final climactic flourish: "Communist Nicaragua," he declaimed, is "dedicated—in the words of its own leaders—to a 'revolution without borders'." In short, they themselves admit that they intend to conquer and destroy us.[12]

Reagan's invocation of this dramatic Communist admission of their aggressive intent was reported by the press without comment, including the anti-Reagan liberal press. The editors of the *Boston Globe* wrote that "the State Department has never been able to document any arms shipment to back up the Sandinistas' boast about 'a revolution without borders'," adding that "their failure to spread their revolution, and their humiliating silence about it, should be taken as a sign of reassurance, but is ignored in Washington."[13] Thus the Sandinista failure to realize their hopes of social reform in the interests of the poor majority thanks to U.S. terror is "a sign of reassurance" for liberal humanists. "Conservative" commentators naturally were delighted with the successful fraud perpetrated by Operation Truth.

Apart from this intriguing illustration of the U.S. disinformation system at work, it is worthwhile to ask just what would be the significance of an actual Sandinista "boast" that they intend to conquer the hemisphere—a threat before which we must obviously quake in terror.

The fears about the demonstration effect of Sandinista achievements are real, and it is understandable that they should be masked in hysterical rhetoric about Soviet missiles and military bases, and a sudden, unprecedented and very narrowly focused concern over peasant discontent and human rights and democracy. These fears explain why the media and Congress adopt the framework of Reaganite doctrine virtually without exception, tactical judgments aside. There is, after all, broad agreement that the U.S. cannot tolerate any threat to the rule of the brutal and repressive elements that prevent the establishment of "nationalistic regimes" that are responsive to the needs and concerns of their own populations, the guiding policy principle laid down in secret planning documents; the traditional U.S. hostility to democracy and human rights remains without challenge. The media serve their function by defining carefully the range of expressible views, framing news reporting within the assumptions laid down by Operation Truth and simply excluding facts that are inappropriate, a highly consistent practice as has been illustrated throughout.[14] Congress serves its function by restricting its investigations to narrow procedural issues while proclaiming its support for the "noble objectives" of the Reagan administration. Once the basic doctrinal framework is adopted—U.S. benevolence and devotion to democracy, Sandinista totalitarianism[15] and service to their Soviet masters, Central America as a stage for the East-West conflict, the fledgling democracies, and the remainder of the familiar claptrap—there is no longer any danger of sane discussion informed by fact or guided by conditions of rationality. Within the bounds set by the doctrinal system, debate can rage in the Free Press, the more the better, since it serves only to reinforce the principles that are adopted across the spectrum because they serve the needs of the powerful and the privileged, while helping preserve the required illusions about American society and its internal openness.

Notes Chapter Twelve

1. See *TTT*, 2.4.

2. Richard Boudreaux and Marjorie Miller, *LAT*, May 20, 1987.

3. Editorial, *WSJ*, March 10, 1987.

4. Clifford Krauss, *WSJ*, Dec. 5, 1986. Note that training of guerrillas would be dangerous to states where guerrillas have a popular base and can operate internally without massive air supply and direct superpower intervention to protect them and enhance their effectiveness.

5. Richard Halloran, *NYT*, March 22, 1987.

6. Krauss, *WSJ*, May 18, 1987.

7. Editorial, *NYT*, March 15, 1987.

8. For additional details, see *TTT*, chapter 3, note 3, *PI*, 86f.; Morley and Petras, *The Reagan Administration and Nicaragua* and my introduction; Eldon Kenworthy, in Walker, *Reagan vs. the Sandinistas*; Smith, "Lies About Nicaragua."

9. George Will, *BG*, March 16, 1986. The same lie is featured by Ronald Radosh, *WSJ*, November 13, 1987, among many others.

10. Cited in Kenworthy, *op. cit.*

11. Imprecisely, in my view, for reasons discussed in *TTT*. To lie requires a certain competence, specifically, mastery of the concept of truth. We do not describe the babbling of an infant or the oratory of an actor reading his lines as lies, even if the statements are false. In this case, the poor man barely seems to understand the words on his note cards. It is necessary to pretend that he is "in charge" in order to maintain the illusion that this is, after all, government "by the people," who elected him.

12. *NYT*, June 25, 1986.

13. Editorial, *BG*, July 14, 1986. For further examples and more extensive discussion, see *PI*, 86f., and my article in Walker, *Reagan vs. the Sandinistas*.

14. To select further examples virtually at random, the Nicaraguan government announced on Feb. 10, 1987 that *Radio Católica* could reopen and that Bishop Vega and another clergyman expelled for supporting the contras could return if they agreed "to obey the law" (*Latinamerica press* (Peru), Feb. 26, 1987; *MacLean's* (Canada), Feb. 23, 1987). This was barely reported in the U.S. (there was a tiny item in the *Dallas Morning News*, Feb. 11), though these issues are among the major proofs of Sandinista "totalitarianism." Speaking at the American Society of Newspaper Editors annual convention, Nicaraguan UN Ambassador Nora Astorga stated that freedom of press will be restored and the suspended journal *La Prensa*

will reopen "as soon as the war ends" (AP, April 10, 1987). The *Times* covered the convention, but not these remarks, nor has it ever compared censorship in Nicaragua to the measures taken by the U.S. and its clients. On the general background of Church-state relations in Nicaragua, see Andrew Reding, *Monthly Review*, July-August, 1987. *Radio Católica* was closed after it failed to broadcast an address by President Ortega (a requirement that is standard practice in the Latin American democracies). Earlier broadcasts calling for the Virgin Mary to "liberate Nicaragua from Sandinista oppression," implicit support for the contras, attempts to boost its signal without a license, etc., had been overlooked. Bishop Vega was expelled after the U.S. "declaration of war" against Nicaragua in June 1986; on the eve of the vote for contra aid in March 1986, he had lied about Sandinista murder of priests in a talk in Washington at the right-wing Heritage foundation, as he quietly conceded later, among other examples of pro-contra activities. Bishop Vega's lies were suppressed by *New York Times* Managua correspondent Stephen Kinzer, who cerrtainly knew about them, since they were front page news in the Nicaraguan press, along with refutations by priests in Nicaragua.

15. On this matter, see particularly Abraham Brumberg's articles in *Dissent* through 1986.

13

The Fledgling Democracies

As discussed earlier, U.S. intervention in Central America is unpopular, but the potential costs to the United States are minimal, apart from Nicaragua. Correspondingly, only in the case of Nicaragua do elite groups articulate popular concerns, to a limited extent. The far more savage attack against the population of El Salvador imposes no serious costs for the supervisors of international terrorism. There was rising concern and a corresponding increase in honest reporting in 1981-83, when it appeared that the resort to violence by the U.S. and its mercenary forces might not be successful. But elite concerns were stilled, and reporting virtually ceased, as soon as it appeared that state terrorism might achieve its goals. El Salvador barely exists in the consciousness of the media and Congress, except as a demonstration of the U.S. commitment to democracy and human rights, and the successes achieved in the pursuit of these noble ends.

The situation was much the same in the 1960s. The primary target of U.S. aggression was always South Vietnam, but protest over that "noble cause"—as it is now regularly described—was limited until the popular movements gained force, because the destruction of South Vietnam was not perceived in elite circles as harmful to their interests. The extension of the aggression to North Vietnam, in contrast, was controversial from the start, because of the risks of a confrontation with China or the USSR. So pervasive was this cynicism that the U.S. doctrinal system recognizes no such event as the U.S. attack against South Vietnam, though it certainly occurred, surely from 1962, obviously from 1965. The extraordinary subordination of world opinion to U.S. power is illustrated by the fact that throughout most of the world, there is no recognition or awareness of the U.S. attack against South Vietnam. One finds no reference to this historical event in standard histories; the United Nations never condemned this attack or recognized that it took place, nor did it prepare documents on the war crimes carried out during the U.S. aggression in South Vietnam (or elsewhere, for that matter), in marked contrast to the reaction at the UN and elsewhere to the Soviet aggression in Afghanistan. The final illustration of the subservience of Western opinion to the United States is the common pretense that the world ignores the Soviet aggression in Afghanistan,[1] while it bitterly protested the U.S. "intervention" in Indochina "in defense of South Vietnam." In the real world, the Western governments supported the U.S. aggression in Indochina, either tacitly or openly, providing ample reason for their populations to protest, and strenuously so. The Soviet aggression, in contrast, is universally denounced.

The pattern is a familiar one, in many other cases as well, and by no means only in the United States.

Returning to El Salvador, we may rejoice that political killings by the security forces reduced to over four a day,[2] now that the government death squads have "decapitated the trade unions and mass organisations," a conservative British correspondent observes, so that "numbers are down and the bodies are dropped discreetly at night into the middle of Lake Ilopango and only rarely wash up on to the shore to remind bathers that the repression is still going on."[3] Few know—or would care if they knew—that "government agents routinely torture prisoners in their custody, conduct 'disappearances,' and commit political killings in attempts to eliminate opposition to the government," that "Salvadorans who allegedly violate human rights remain virtually immune from investigation and prosecution," and that "most victims are non-combatant civilians, including women and children," the primary targets being "refugee workers, trade unionists, and university staff and students" subjected to "arrest, torture, and killing."[4] Now that Duarte's U.S.-organized terror has "decapitated" and demolished labor and the popular organizations that might have laid the basis for meaningful democracy, the editors of the *New Republic* inform us that "The real model for supporting the push toward democracy in our sphere" is El Salvador, exulting in the success of their advice to Reagan to continue with the assault "regardless of how many are murdered," since "there are higher American priorities than Salvadoran human rights."[5] They are joined in this admiration for the successful terror carried out under Duarte's aegis by many others within mainstream liberalism, as cited earlier.

There is no reaction here to the report by the Salvadoran Church that its social workers are receiving death threats and that the government, with the aid of the U.S. Embassy, "appears to be engaged in a major confrontation with church officials after repeated accusations by police informers that churches have knowingly aided leftist guerrilla groups." The head of the Lutheran church, "who was arrested and tortured by the police three years ago," expressed concern over the campaign to bar social projects and work with refugees, noting that the charges virtually amount to a death sentence. On the basis of charges by a woman who says "that she had confessed only because the police had threatened to harm her 18-year old daughter," the Duarte government renewed its longstanding efforts, with the cooperation of the U.S. Embassy, to undermine human rights groups, arresting rights workers who say "they were beaten and threatened by the police for almost two weeks." In July 1986, "the government deported 23 foreign religious activists, including 19 Americans, who sought to accompany" refugees back to their homes. In June, the mutilated corpse of a young man was found after he had appealed to the Red Cross to prevent the army from once again displacing returnees from their homes—by "burning of our houses, our crops, our lands," peasants recounted. Meanwhile, the Council on Hemispheric Affairs reported that a U.S. "police training program" in Washington in June and July "included three of the most notorious death squad members in San Salvador" who will "have their techniques upgraded," and that in the same weeks "more than 10 independent human rights activists have been arrested by Salvadoran Security forces," some tortured according to the Archbishop, in actions defended by the U.S. Embassy.[6]

It does not merit even a single word in the national press when five imprisoned members of the Human Rights Commission CDHES, the only UN-recognized Human Rights Group in El Salvador, produce a carefully documented 160-page study, described as credible by Amnesty International, on the "routine" and "systematic" use of torture in a survey of over 400 political prisoners, fellow inmates at the Mariona prison almost all of whom report torture. Their study provides a detailed record of tortures, with names, dates and careful description, including sworn testimony that a U.S. army major administered electrical torture. The study was widely distributed to the press, but ignored, apart from the *San Francisco Examiner.*[7] In contrast, reports of harassment of human rights activists in Managua, not remotely approaching the atrocities documented in El Salvador, merit a front-page story in the *New York Times.*[8]

The Treasury Police had arrested virtually all members of CDHES in May 1986; of the 8 Salvadorans who founded the Commission in 1978, four have been killed, two have "disappeared," one is in exile, and the status of the eighth is unknown. Its president, Marianela Garcia Villas, was murdered by a U.S.-trained elite battalion while gathering evidence on the use of napalm.[9] The Marin County religious task force sent volunteers to El Salvador after the May arrests to offer some protection to the remaining human rights workers and help them continue their grim work. They describe the regular procession of peasants and urban poor who find their way to the Commission's unmarked office to tell their stories and seek information about missing family members. Continuing their work in Mariona prison after their arrest, the members of the Commission also succeeded in smuggling out a videotape with testimonies of torture; this too was distributed to the media, with no response. The tape also includes a segment made by a European journalist who entered an area from which journalists are excluded and filmed interviews with villagers whose houses had just been destroyed and families killed by bombing in January 1987, also unreported.[10]

Atrocities continue regularly, occasionally reported. In April 1987 the Confederation of Cooperative Organizations reported army murders and rapes in the San Carlos cooperative. A few days later, a law student, a member of the executive committee of the student association, was murdered in Santa Ana by a death squad. Labor leaders reported that five workers were killed and two women sexually abused in a police raid on a cooperative federation, while 20 union members were seized by police and the secretary general of the National Association of Agricultural Workers in San Miguel province was tortured and murdered by soldiers, then beheaded, after being captured on his way to arrange a loan for a peasant cooperative.[11] On May 15th a woman leading a CoMadres demonstration was run over by a car apparently driven by the national police. Five alleged guerrilla "collaborators" were murdered by the elite Arce battalion, notorious for human rights violations, on May 22, eliciting a condemnation from the Archbishop. On the 27th, five carloads of men in civilian clothes broke into the office of the Lutheran church at gunpoint and stole their records after issuing death threats to human rights workers. The following day, the CoMadres office was destroyed by bombing, with four people injured, and a refugee group demonstrating at the Cathedral was fired upon. A day later, three truckloads of men with machine guns broke into the CDHES office, fleeing when it seemed that journalists might arrive. On the 30th, the secretary-general of the teachers union was shot at a demonstration outside the Mariona prison calling for amnesty for political prisoners, by guards within the prison according to union leaders.[12]

In June, CDHES reported 14 political assassinations and more than 100 disappearances in the first 5 months of 1987. In mid-July, it reported that at least 13 corpses had been found in and around the capital during the preceding week in "the silent resurgence of the death squads." The Commission alleges that "victims are left "with signs of torture," while judicial authorities say that they have no concrete information.[13] The increase in visible atrocities—as distinct from those in more remote areas—also led foreign human rights analysts and diplomats to suspect that death squads are returning to regular operations in the urban centers. Growing opposition to the increasingly isolated Duarte government may be a factor in the resurgence of urban terror. Army operations chief Col. Emilio Ponce observes that "the guerillas are returning to the first phase of clandestine organization" in the cities, and to "mobilization of the masses." "This isn't new," the director of the Catholic Church human rights office observes:

> The death squads always appear when opposition increases and the government can't control it. We have no doubt that there's a military structure behind the death squads, given the level of intelligence they have, and their resources and infrastructure. Only people linked to military structures could have this kind of organization—a private group couldn't do it.[14]

Another reason for the death squad resurgence in urban areas may be that the State of Siege declared in March 1980, as Duarte joined the government and the terror began in full force, lapsed in January 1987. The military no longer have the "legal" right to carry out repressive actions and as a result, "human rights officials and diplomats say they fear that the security forces will now be tempted to kill rather than arrest people suspected of being leftists."[15] The lapse in the State of Siege was purely technical, resulting from a boycott of the National Assembly by the conservative parties, but *Times* correspondent James LeMoyne prefers to see it as a consequence of the decision of the Duarte government to "normalize" the situation, reporting that Duarte "lifted a state-of-siege law" to enhance a "political opening" and forgetting what the *Times* had published on the back pages a few months earlier.[16]

The State of Siege announced in Nicaragua in October 1985 elicited outraged denunciations and calls for a renewal of overt aid to the contras to overcome these abuses, so offensive to our libertarian passions. In contrast, there was total silence when El Salvador *renewed* its State of Siege two days later, as it had done monthly since March 1980. The Salvadoran State of Siege has been next to unmentionable in the press. The *New York Times* never mentioned it in its numerous editorials on El Salvador, which also succeeded in avoiding most other ongoing atrocities, preferring fables about "reformist democrats led by Mr. Duarte" who are unable to stem the violence of "the left and right."[17] There is not the slightest comparison between the repression under the State of Siege in Nicaragua and the massive atrocities conducted by the U.S.-installed government in El Salvador under its own unmentionable State of Siege, and media coverage and outrage is inversely related to the extent of atrocities, though directly related to U.S. government priorities.

It is necessary to maintain the atmosphere of terror in El Salvador to ensure that the "popular organizations" do not recover from the savage onslaught conducted by the U.S. mercenary forces to establish the proper conditions for "democracy." Meanwhile "illiterate 16-year-old kids [are] wrenched from their villages or shantytowns, rounded up by the police" and forced into the army to become mercenary killers, while "the BMWs and the Mercedes have never been more numerous," "the chic restaurants and nightclubs of the *Zona Rosa* are filled," and "the city's upper crust, high on violence and money and dulled by a servile press and television, dance the cha-cha and make small talk."[18] In the cities, popular protest is increasing, attributed by authorities to guerrilla subversion; and in the countryside, Chris Norton reports, the rebels "exude a new confidence" as they carry out regular attacks against military outposts and "have made significant progress over the past two years in winning support among the cautious, normally conservative townspeople," while their "slow, patient political work" is also paying dividends among the peasantry. They "are busy building an infrastructure" in rural areas, where people "still seem to feel more comfortable with the presence of the guerrillas rather than with the army":

> Interviews in different parts of the country reveal that support for the guerrillas, expecially in the countryside, appears to be holding firm... 'People see that the guerrillas are more humane, and there is an intuitive sense that they're on the people's side,' notes one Catholic church official. Adds an old-time labor leader: 'The *campesinos* know whose interests the army really represents'.[19]

According to the U.S. government, the guerrillas are able to sustain their operations only because of support from Nicaragua. This claim is necessary, as part of the important pretense that the guerrillas operating in El Salvador without visible external support, having been driven to the countryside by U.S.-organized terror, are comparable to the U.S. proxy army attacking Nicaragua, which cannot survive or "maintain its morale" without its daily air drops and other U.S. sustenance. Accordingly, the claims of Operation Truth are echoed by the national media: "The rebels deny receiving such support from Nicaragua," James LeMoyne asserts, "but ample evidence shows it exists, and it is questionable how long they could survive without it."[20]

Assuming this charge to be accurate, we are left with a question that he does not address: even if we are willing to grant the incompetence of U.S. intelligence and the *New York Times*, can it be so extraordinary that they have never been able to provide any credible evidence for this crucial support, though Nicaragua has never had any problem in providing ample evidence for U.S. support for the proxy army? A curious paradox indeed.

Recall also the impermissible question raised in note 12, p. 23.

The center-right Christian Democrats who constitute Duarte's political base, meanwhile, have succumbed to the usual temptations. "While PDC officials self-consciously set about to displace the oligarchy," Chris Norton writes, "they seem to have decided to replace it with themselves." Duarte's son Alejandro sports two new haciendas; the executive director of the U.S. Chamber of Commerce alleges that PDC officials "are making hundreds of thousands of colones a day in profits" by diverting basic foods, intended for the poor at affordable prices, to private outlets, along with many similar practices. Ignacio Martin Baro, vice-rector of the Jesuit-run Central American University, comments that "The tradition in this country is for whomever comes to power to take advantage of the situation. We expected the Christian Democrats to be different, but they haven't been. They've been the same." "This should come as no surprise," Norton comments. "Despite their Christian moralizing (based on their claim to be inspired by the social teachings of the Catholic Church), the PDC is a party of middle-class professionals who saw themselves and the country as being held back by some of the semi-feudal aspects of Salvadoran capitalism." They put themselves "at the helm" to remedy these defects, promising reforms as "a populist party with mass support from the poor," but quickly taking on the traditional role of corrupt oppressors. They have also used their control of U.S.-funded food and work projects for the nearly 1/2 million displaced persons to compel participation in government marches and rallies, under the threat that benefits will be cut if they do not.[21] As we have seen, the government's policies are perceived by the general population as welfare for the rich, and most regard "democracy" as a generally meaningless charade (see p. 102). But with the possibility of a genuine movement "with mass support from the poor" eliminated by successful state terror, the large majority of the population can only watch the farcical workings of "democracy," now properly functioning as a game among various privileged sectors, under the watchful eyes of the security forces and the American Embassy, who reign unchallenged.

While the Christian Democratic professional elites are demanding their share of privilege and power, the traditional oligarchies have hardly suffered under U.S. tutelage in "democracy." "The wealth of the country is now concentrated in fewer hands than before agrarian reform," and "the rich have more control than before," according to Dean Héctor Marroquín Arévalo, dean of the University of El Salvador, a conclusion confirmed by others. "The oligarchy is more powerful now," adds Juan Garcia, a professor of sociology at the University of Central America who has studied the effects of the reform: "If anything, the reforms aggravated the wide differences in wealth." The agrarian reform, instituted by the U.S. in 1980, generated "windfall profits for the wealthy people who were supposed to shoulder the burden of the economic restructuring," Times correspondent Lindsey Gruson observes, and "saddled the cooperatives with debts" that they cannot repay because of the provisions for compensation to landowners, while "many of the cooperatives were illegally stripped by landowners of their machinery and livestock." A USAID report "found that as many as 95% of the cooperatives were unable to pay interest on their debts, which totaled an estimated $800 million." Dean Marroquín estimates that 98% are "in effect bankrupt." Production has fallen sharply in export crops apart from sugar cane, and Salvadoran agriculture has been "immeasurably damaged," a USAID consultant comments. Worse, peasants are confined by the reform to small and unproductive plots, which rapidly become exhausted and unfertile, saddled with debts they cannot pay and lacking technical assistance, not to speak of the "1.8 million peasants who were overlooked in the 1980 program."

Gruson's report fails to observe that these are exactly the consequences predicted from the start by U.S. and Salvadoran government critics of the U.S.-initiated reform, which was imposed without any effort to engage or organize the poor and even bypassed Salvadoran government specialists. Like the Alliance for Progress, Reagan's Caribbean Basin Initiative, and similar programs generally, the U.S.-imposed plan was a completely cynical effort; these programs are not instituted because of a sudden recognition of the suffering of the poor, but out of fear that they might respond to organizing appeals that would impel them to seek to extricate themselves from their misery in ways incompatible with the Fifth Freedom (so-called "Communism"). Nor do we hear derisive commentary on the "failures," "mismanagement" and "incompetence" of the American supervisors of this failed effort, as is standard media fare with regard to the "Marxist-Leninist managers of misery," though the resources available to the United States are not notably less than those of its Nicaraguan enemy.[22]

The signing of the peace accords in early August 1987 was followed by an upsurge of repression in the urban areas, evoking no interest here as usual. In commentary rare to the point of near uniqueness, Chris Norton observes from San Salvador:

> Electoral posturing aside, diplomats say peace is harder to achieve here than in Nicaragua because the Salvadorean guerrillas, in contrast to the US financed Nicaraguan rebels, are an indigenous revolutionary movement, independent of external outside support from one source.
>
> Political analysts say the continuing arrests and disappearances of labor leaders and members of other opposition groups does not

bode well for national reconciliation. More than a dozen labor activists have been arrested since the peace plan was signed Aug. 7. The head of the university workers union was kidnapped Aug. 31. And the government still refuses to talk with the labor opposition.

"If this were going on in Nicaragua, [international observers] would be going crazy," says one political analyst.[23]

What was "going on in Nicaragua" did not compare to this record. Again, reporting and outrage were inversely proportional to degree of repression, and quite in accord with U.S. government priorities; the usual pattern.

The enhanced repression in El Salvador during the spring and summer of 1987 did not pass entirely without reaction here. The Reagan administration informed Congress on August 31 that it intends to provide over $9 million in equipment and weapons to the Salvadoran police, certifying to Congress that El Salvador "has made significant progress during the preceding six months in eliminating any human-rights violations, including torture, incommunicado detention, detention of persons solely for nonviolent expression of their political views or prolonged detention without trial." An accompanying report states that the U.S. assistance program "has met, or exceeded, expectations across the board and has uniformly fulfilled the criteria of human-rights improvements on the part of the public security forces"; this statement may very well be true, considering the expectations of Ronald Reagan and George Shultz, and the criteria that would satisfy their administration, which was providing exactly the same kind of upbeat certification to a docile Congress while the terror they organized in El Salvador reached its crescendo a few years earlier. Americas Watch issued a report on August 29 stating that the security forces continue to commit murder and other rights abuses, and is thus failing to meet the requirements of the Central American peace plan.[24] It was barely mentioned in the media, and in fact the whole issue is only of marginal interest. The state has determined that human rights violations in Nicaragua are the only topic of concern; the Free Press can hardly be expected to challenge these priorities.

Like El Salvador, Guatemala too is generally regarded as a great success of the U.S. dedication to fostering democracy—a tolerable pretense, now that the population has been thoroughly intimidated by U.S.-backed terror on a scale that reached near-genocidal proportions.[25] But now all is well, with death squad killings continuing and the newly-elected President acknowledging frankly that he can do nothing given the roots of actual power in the military and the oligarchy and that the civilian government are merely "the managers of bankruptcy and misery."[26] The Campesino Unity Committee, which had more than 100,000 members in 1981, "today does not dare to begin openly organizing in the countryside" and "the union movement proceeds with great caution" as a result of the terror of the past years. In its "year of promises" (1986), the Christian Democratic government failed to undertake social reforms though it did pursue policies for the benefit of the private sector, supported by the wealthy and the military, while "socio-economic conditions continued to worsen for the majority of Guatemalans." The military closely supervise "virtually every aspect of government." The effective control by the military and the business interests linked to them is illustrated by the fact that even more so than in El Salvador, the government would not dare to prosecute military officers for horrendous human rights abuses.[27]

The head of the armed forces, defense minister of the elected government, when asked about human rights abuses, says that the Army "defended the state of Guatemala," and the "casualties suffered by the Guatemalan people" were not its fault, since the Army merely "reacted against the terrorists in order to control the seizure of power by them." President Cerezo, in a television interview in August 1987, indicated that most of the "disappeared" had gone to live abroad or joined the guerrillas, "a measure of his [quite understandable] reluctance to confront the human rights issue in Guatemala and thereby antagonize the army," *Mesoamerica* comments.[28]

The civilian government remains "a project" of the military, as the armed forces explained when they allowed it to take office. Stephen Kinzer reports that President Cerezo "has not managed to wrest significant power from the army, in the view of diplomats and Guatemalan officials, and describes his government "as 'a transition regime' in which civilians will not be able to consolidate true power, but will be able to survive in office, gradually managing to curb the armed forces," he hopes. Nineth Garcia, the director of the leading human rights organization (the Mutual Support Group; GAM), states that "Here democracy is a coverup....the military is the real power..." A Western diplomat observes that the death squad apparatus "is still in place, it is simply not working at the moment" except for occasional incidents as "the squads are indulging now in more selective repression"—all that is required, as "democracy" functions in the intended manner.[29]

So do the U.S. media, where GAM reports are dismissed because it "represents only a tiny minority, mostly peasant Indians from the countryside long ignored by the political process anyway." This "minority" in fact is the majority of the population. It is, however, correct to say that they have been "ignored" by the political process, ever since the U.S. succeeded in overturning Guatemala's experiment with democracy in 1954; and it is instructive that this is sufficient reason to ignore their plight.[30]

TV journalist Elizabeth Farnsworth describes "the shadow of fear" that is "evident" in Guatemala. Seeking subjects for interviews, she found "that only people who already had a high profile, such as Church or elected officials, dared speak for attribution"; "the sense of fear is almost palpable in the hesitant and carefully chosen words of Bishop José Ramiro Pellecer," who consented to be interviewed, "though I think he fears for others and not for himself," she adds. Asked to "describe the changes that have taken place in Guatemala" under the elected Cerezo government, he says that "We are making a try at democracy but, in reality, there has not been much change." Exactly as in El Salvador, according to the perceptions of the public, though not Operation Truth and its minions. Bishop Pellecer agrees that the civilian government is "just a mask or façade for the military to hide behind." The death squads "are lying in wait, making certain things do not get out of hand," with violence increasing "the farther from the capital you get." "Things are more or less as they were before." The press has barely changed: "A civilian government is being attacked, but that was done before. There is still no criticism of the military," who retain effective power.[31]

The Council on Hemispheric Affairs continues to characterize Guatemala, along with El Salvador, as "currently the hemisphere's worst human rights violator." Inforpress Centroamerica in Guatemala reports political killings at the rate of one a day in May-June 1987, a small part of a rising tide of violence; what happens in the countryside is little known. The Mexican press reports that "the practice of repression and intimidation against workers" continues, though "more selectively" than before, and "since the inauguration of President Cerezo, the Security Forces, disguised as the Death Squads, have continued kidnapping and assassinating labor union leaders," citing a series of examples, while "the Christian Democratic authorities have found new methods of intimidation and pressure." The U.S. press meanwhile reports, accurately no doubt, that the guerrillas have lost support because they "were unable to protect the Indians from the military." Ken Anderson, a lawyer for the International Human Rights Law Group monitoring conditions in the countryside, says that "The Indians have been signed over to the army. With a hundred or more killings or disappearances a month since January [1987], I'm not optimistic that things have changed much."[32]

Economic conditions continue to deterioriate for the poor, with "oppressive poverty" so severe that in Guatemala City, "drivers look straight ahead with calculated indifference, dispirited by the exhibition of such misery." There is a new austerity program designed to salvage the faltering economy. Its "principal victims have been members of the shrinking middle class and the urban and rural poor. Most Guatemalans' living standards have dropped to levels surpassed 15 years ago. More than 50 percent of the economically active population are unemployed," while the civilian president has "devoted his energies to attacking the labor movement."[33]

Turning to Honduras, it merits no attention when the Honduran Human Rights Defense Commission releases a document reporting that hundreds of Honduran peasants were driven from their homes and forced into refugee camps in a joint operation of the contras and the Honduras 6th Army Battalion, their homes and possessions commandeered by the contras who killed peasants suspected of being Sandinista collaborators; mass kidnappings and other means of intimidation have led to the flight or removal of some 16,000 peasants from an area turned over to the contras by the Honduran government and wealthy Cuban-Honduran tobacco magnates who own vast estates near the border, according to the Commission and other sources. The minority leader of the Honduran Congress, Nicolas Cruz Torres, reports that 35 villages have been forcibly evacuated by the contras, a situation "not created by Honduras but by the government of the United States which is financing the counterrevolutionaries."[34]

The chief of staff of the Honduran military from March 1984 to February 1985, General Walter Lopez Reyes, told a news conference in Tegucigalpa that the CIA has bribed Honduran politicians so that they will continue to back U.S. aid to the contras, that in Honduras the contras have been involved in assassinations and disappearances of "numerous people for being against their mode of operation," and that the CIA "is prepared to control even the secret services of the Honduran police and to infiltrate all the government" of President Azcona. The Honduran Committee for the Defense of Human Rights reports that 300 people have been killed for political reasons and another 130 have disappeared in police custody.[35]

Young men are forcibly press-ganged into the army, dragged "out of theaters, buses and off the street for immediate induction into the Armed Forces," while "the sons of the wealthy are generally exempt"; "the general practice is to seize three times as many males as are needed, select the best for induction, and return the others to the families for a price."[36] The practice is the same, though apparently still more brutal and more sharply class-based, in El Salvador; and in Guatemala, the other "fledgling democracy," where Defense Minister Gramajo confirmed in an August 1987 television interview that the army does not recruit from the upper strata of society and that one-fourth of new recruits are impressed into the army.[37] This practice, common in U.S. domains, elicits no comment. In contrast, the resort to a civilian draft in Nicaragua, as is standard in democratic states in wartime or conditions of perceived threat, elicited massive outrage among a new breed of extreme civil libertarians who denounced this further demonstration of totalitarianism, with much fevered reporting of protests against the draft in Nicaragua. This enthusiasm was supplanted by muffled annoyance when the protests stilled after the government instituted such typical totalitarian measures as transporting groups of mothers to visit soldiers in the field and organizing Mothers' Councils to deal with personal problems, and when it became clear that as in such states as Israel, military service appears to function as a device of national integration; "these boys have come back proud," a Western European diplomat comments.[38]

The U.S. role in Honduras was adequately characterized by Ambassador John Ferch, removed from his post in June 1986 because he insisted on treating the civilian government, rather than the military command, as the country's highest authority, a signal failure of perception from the point of view of George Shultz and Elliott Abrams. He commented to *Newsday* that he was removed "because they wanted somebody down there to be strong enough and proconsul enough that no Honduran government is going to object to anything."[39] Another factor in his removal appears to have been his objection to State Department trickery in using the pretext of an alleged Nicaraguan "invasion" to induce Honduras to accept military aid, apparently funnelled to the contras as part of the illegal supply operation in March 1986. As for the CIA role, apart from training the battalion implicated in death squad activities and torture, it is also reported by a Honduran army defector to have arranged a fabricated forced "confession" by a kidnapped prisoner that he headed a "guerrilla front" and had planned attacks against U.S. installations; having learned his lines under appropriate inducements, he was to be displayed by the genocidal Guatemalan generals backed by the U.S. (as he was), in a further contribution to Operation Truth.[40]

Food First Central America analyst Medea Benjamin, working in the area, uncovered "a food crisis of frightening proportions in the southern part of the country" in 1986. "We alerted the national media in the United States," Food First reports, "but the story went uncovered." They report that hundreds of thousands of peasants are starving while President Azcona refused food aid, though other regions have food surpluses and the government announced that Honduras was self-sufficient in corn and beans in 1986 and is exporting beans to El Salvador. The Archbishop in the southern region protested the government's refusal to recognize the crisis: "We've seen scenes of misery like never before," he said, "children with swollen bellies, old people looking like corpses, women and children begging for food, men roaming the streets searching for work," lacking money to buy the food that is available, including thousands "displaced by the contras," according to a physician researching malnutrition at the National University.[41]

Recall the derisive commentary on the "Marxist-Leninist" dogma and "gross incompetence" of the Sandinista *commandantes*, which impels them to interfere with market mechanisms in an effort to ensure that the poor will have something to eat, one element of the flood of abuse directed against these appalling criminals who remind us of Hitler and Stalin. The Free Press is wise to keep its eyes averted from areas of Honduras on the Nicaraguan border, though it hardly needs notification from Food First of the critical conditions in the region through which reporters traipse in pursuit of encouraging news about the military prowess of "the resistance." Inspection of Honduras would yield unwanted conclusions about the application of market principles in a state organized for the needs of the oligarchy and the military, following the lessons taught them by their benefactor from the North. Better to look the other way, much like the drivers in Guatemala City.

Travelling to southern Honduras and Nicaragua to advance his political aspirations, presidential candidate Senator Robert Dole was deeply affected by "the suffering in Central America," which, as he saw first-hand, "is widespread." He was particularly moved, he says, by the suffering he saw "when I visited Miguel Cardinal Obando y Bravo, the Archbishop of Managua, and Violetta Chamorro, the publisher of the censored opposition paper La Prensa—courageous reminders that we are working for something very precious: freedom and dignity." He also saw "widespread suffering" in southern Honduras: "in the hollow eyes of thousands of Nicaraguan refugees." That is all. No Honduran "children with swollen bellies, old people looking like corpses, women and children begging for food, men roaming the streets searching for work" while the wealthy enjoy "democracy" in Tegucigalpa; no victims of U.S. terror in Nicaragua, no peasants in Honduras wandering through the countryside after having been "displaced by the contras," in our "pursuit of the goals that nearly all Americans share: democracy and an end to Soviet intrusion in Central America" (Dole). In short, a worthy candidate for the office of President.[42]

The visit by Senator Dole and his delegation to Managua was a "circus," in Dole's words, because President Ortega insisted that the meeting be public, saying "it was better that the interviews take place in the presence of witnesses, so there could be no false posturing afterward," Stephen Kinzer reports. Senator John McCain opened the meeting by informing Ortega breezily that he had just met with contra military commander Enrique Bermúdez of Somoza's National Guard: "Colonel Bermúdez sends his very best regards," Senator McCain told Mr. Ortega as the meeting began. "Colonel Bermúdez and Ronald Reagan should stop killing Nicaraguan children," Ortega responded. He also asked "Why doesn't President Reagan receive me or my congressmen? We receive you whenever you want. You don't even consult us in advance, which is a lack of respect. You just say there's a flight, and we're coming."[43]

Ortega understated the point. While it is taken for granted that U.S. supporters of the proxy army should have free access to the territory under U.S. attack, even giving public talks and press conferences where they call for renewed attacks against Nicaragua by the "freedom fighters" they praise for helping the CIA defend liberty, the Godfather's own turf is under stricter control. Thus, when a delegation of Nicaraguan parliamentarians including six opposition delegates sought to visit the U.S. to present Congress with a formal protest against contra aid, their visas were delayed in order to force them to cancel their visit, an event considered so normal in a terrorist culture that it passes without notice or comment, along with the barring of mothers tortured by Duarte's security services from our sacred soil, because they might tell the wrong stories to a few people in churches, threatening American democracy.[44]

When Senator Dole protested the jailing of two opposition lawyers for 30 days for participation in an unauthorized protest rally, banned by the emergency regulations, Ortega responded by producing "a photograph of an American priest, the Rev. Roy Bourgeois, being arrested in the United States in April during a protest against American support for the contras." He offered to free the two lawyers immediately in exchange for the freedom of Father Bourgeois, a Navy veteran wounded in the Vietnam war and now a Maryknoll priest, who is serving a nine-month sentence in Federal Prison in Louisiana for trespassing after a demonstration at a military base; in Ortega's words, "held in your jail for protesting your president's immoral policy of killing Nicaraguans." The two opposition leaders were released in the custody of Rep. Thomas Harkin; Rev. Bourgeois remained in prison, with no further comment here, as there had been none before this odd point was raised by the totalitarian Sandinistas. Senator Dole's press aide described the exchange offer as "a gimmick," adding that "It is ludicrous to compare our system with theirs." Shown a photo of the priest being dragged off by two policemen at the moment of his arrest, Dole responded: "You have us mixed up with the Soviet Union."[45] The press treated the matter of Rev. Bourgeois's incarceration, previously unreported, as a curiosity. Dole's brilliant and courageous performance at the "circus," as he perceives it, promises to be a centerpiece for his presidential campaign.

The incident and others like it, and the reaction here, reflect a form of imperial arrogance that is remarkable in the late 20th century, though perhaps King Leopold's delegates behaved similarly in the Congo a century ago. One might ask how Japanese fascist legislators would have been greeted in Washington in 1942, when the national territory was not under attack, bringing greetings from General Tojo.

Meanwhile the U.S. government proceeds to convert Honduras into its major base for subversion and aggression in the region, taking over the role that Nicaragua filled under Somoza. Apart from its favorable location for these ends, Honduras offers other advantages, as explained by Colonel Joseph Lucas, director of operations for the Southern Command:

> The airfields we build give us training we couldn't get anywhere else; there is not a place in the United States where you can go and build an airfield. There is not a place in the United States where the National Guard can go and build a long road without running afoul of the unions and contractors and all that ["The environmental impact statements alone could kill you," another Southern Command spokesman said.] So we benefit in the training aspect and training for every point from deployment to employment to redeployment to country [sic].[46]

There is no concern here over Honduras, not a country but rather a region to be robbed by the traditional oligarchy and their foreign associates along with the new super-rich, the military and politicians on the U.S. aid gravy train, while much of the population is reduced to ever greater misery. The country is a "democracy," under effective military rule, the overwhelming majority of the population playing the approved role of passive onlookers. As U.S. influence increased in the early 1980s, so did human rights violations, corruption, prostitution, economic decline for much of the population, ecological destruction in the interests of export-oriented agribusiness linked to U.S. corporations, and the takeover of parts of the country by U.S. Nicaraguan mercenaries. These developments elicit virtually no commentary, no protest, no public meetings, no congressional inquiries—in fact, nothing, except for the normal self-adulation in elite circles about this further demonstration of our impressive dedication to democracy and human rights.

Escaping the confines of the culture of terrorism, one might also detect other topics worthy of some concern, not only in the "fledgling democracies" but even in the functioning democracy of Costa Rica. Consider, for example, the problem of treatment of the indigenous population. In the early 1980s, Operation Truth succeeded in evoking a passionate concern over the Miskito Indians in Nicaragua after reports that several dozen had been killed by the Sandinista army and thousands forcibly removed in conflicts related to the early stages of the U.S. attack against

Nicaragua. This was an intriguing phenomenon in a society that is erected upon genocide of the native population and is not famous for its commitment to right these wrongs or for its attention to the fate of indigenous peoples elsewhere. In his Kennedy parody during his visit to the Bitburg cemetary to honor the memory of the war dead, including Waffen SS, Ronald Reagan solemnly announced that "I am a Jew..., a Miskito Indian in Nicaragua," and Elie Wiesel flew down to witness their plight and evoke the conscience of the nation over it; in contrast, the revered moralist and Nobel Peace Prize laureate found himself unable to manage even a private communication to the government of Israel to ask that they cease their contribution to ongoing genocide in Guatemala, with tens of thousands of Indians slaughtered.[47]

Concern over the Miskitos abated when it could no longer be exploited for the cause of mobilizing public support for the war against Nicaragua,[48] but it is striking to observe that this unprecedented passion for justice for Native Americans did not extend beyond the narrow confines of the Atlantic Coast of Nicaragua, to Guatemala for example, where the Indian population was being massacred wholesale and driven to concentration camps called "model villages" with enthusiastic support from the United States, or to other regions where the normal conditions of life persist. Journalists and humanitarians do not, for example, wring their hands in dismay over the life of the Guaymí Indians in plantations run by U.S. corporations in Costa Rica and Panama to the present day, where they are assigned such tasks as cleaning drainage ditches, which "requires wading—often up to one's chest—through snake-infested, muddy, stagnant water contaminated by pesticide and fertilizer runoff." This is a task that is appropriate for them because "foremen claim that the Guaymí, unlike the Latins or Blacks, 'don't mind' cleaning drainage ditches," and an assignment that is cheap for the companies because the Indians can be denied health care, are readily exploitable and constantly degraded, and can be replaced easily by others when they die of disease and overwork.[49] Nor do we organize proxy armies to pressure the governments to relieve these conditions, or even raise questions at board meetings in New York.

All such questions are off the agenda, useless for the service of power and privilege in the United States, on a par with the ecological destruction and starvation in Central America in the beans-and-forest to hamburger-and-pet food racket. Also off the agenda is the spraying of extensive areas of northern and western

Guatemala with highly toxic defoliants by the U.S. Drug Enforcement Agency in May-June, 1987, with 14 people killed, halted after protests by the Guatemalan Congress, in regions that are not known for drug producing but are "conflict zones" in the guerrilla war, leading "some observers to conclude that the anti-drug program had been incorporated into the counter-insurgency strategy of the Guatemalan army."[50] Or, putting speculation aside, it was never a matter of concern that by the 1970s about 40% of U.S. pesticide exports went to Central America, "making the region the world's highest per capita user of pesticides," an environmental as well as human calamity as pesticide poisoning takes a further toll among the suffering population. The issue is confronted nowhere apart from Nicaragua, where the government in 1979 "initiated a bold new experiment in environmental policy to combat decades of ecological destruction," a commitment "rarely seen anywhere in the world," but now, thankfully, undermined by the U.S. crusade for freedom.[51]

The same cynicism was illustrated with regard to Nicaragua before the overthrow of the Somoza dictatorship. The worst polluter in Nicaragua was the U.S. Penwalt corporation, which poisoned Lake Managua with tons of mercury while operating in Nicaragua to evade U.S. environmental laws.[52] During the 1960s and 1970s, Nicaraguan GNP nearly tripled—a triumph of the Alliance for Progress. Meanwhile child malnutrition doubled—a triumph of the particular mode of development sponsored under the Alliance. In 1970, half the population consumed about 70% of the recommended caloric allowance, 56% of children under five were malnourished and over a quarter of these suffered severe malnutrition, a factor contributing to the extremely high infant mortality rate.[53] None of this aroused concern. On the contrary, it was the efforts of the government to overcome this human disaster after the 1979 revolution that evoked fear and horror in the United States, disguised under the sudden conversion to the cause of "democracy" and "human rights."

Notes Chapter Thirteen

1. Not only in the United States, where one has become accustomed to such antics. The most frequently used headline in the Swedish press in 1984 was: "Why is there so much silence over the war in Afghanistan?" *Jyllands-Posten*, May 11, 1985; Alexander Cockburn, *Nation*, Aug. 31, 1985.

2. For 1985; see Americas Watch, *Settling into Routine*, May 1986. The nongovernmental Human Rights Commission CDHES (Comisión de Derechos Humanos de El Salvador), whose figures are generally about the same as those of other human rights organizations for earlier years (actually, somewhat lower), reports 4-5 murders a day for 1986, along with 213 recorded disappearances (CDHES Annual Report, January 1987). The Council on Hemispheric Affairs estimates "government sponsored assassinations" (including disappearance and abduction) at about a dozen a month; *News and Analysis,* Nov. 10, 1987. Both CDHES and Americas Watch record an increase in "those imprisoned for politically motivated offenses or associations," to 1100, 90% of them never tried, many claiming that confessions were obtained by torture; Watch Committees and Lawyers Committee for Human Rights, *The Reagan Administration's Record on Human Rights in 1986*, Feb. 1987. Recall that El Salvador, like Guatemala, has succeeded in radically reducing the number of political prisoners by assassination and disappearance.

3. Ambrose Evans-Pritchard, *Spectator* (London), May 10, 1986.

4. Amnesty International, *Amnesty Action*, Jan.-Feb., 1986.

5. *New Republic*, editorials, April 7, 1986; April 2, 1984. See *TTT*, 167-8, for further details, including the attempted coverup when these statements were exposed beyond the circle of *New Republic* readers, who apparently found nothing remarkable about them.

6. Reuters, *BG*, June 30; James LeMoyne, *NYT*, Aug. 3; Julia Preston, *WP Weekly*, Aug. 11; Chris Norton, *CSM*, July 10; COHA *News and Analysis*, July 28, 1986; Doyle McManus, *LAT*, Aug. 7, 1986. Also *Settling into Routine*. For details on the U.S. training of death squad leaders described by a Salvadoran official as "some of El Salvador's worst killers," see Vince Bielski and Dennis Bernstein, "Inviting Death Squads to Tea," *In These Times*, Aug. 20, 1986.

7. CDHES, "Torture in El Salvador," Sept. 24, 1986; distributed by the Marin Interfaith Task Force, 25 Buena Vista, Mill Valley CA 94941. Ron Ridenhour, "In prison, Salvador rights panel works on," *San Francisco Examiner*, Nov. 14; Ridenhour is the U.S. combat veteran who tried vainly for almost a year to publicize the My Lai massacre. Also Nov. 18, 1986,

with further details, and Larry Maatz, Nov. 10, on the Marin County religious group and its association with the CDHES. See Alexander Cockburn, *Nation*, Feb. 21, 1987, noting also confirmation of the CDHES findings in extensive interviews by a research team of the Los Angeles-based El Rescate relief organization; its report was also ignored. There is a brief reference to abuses in prison buried in an article by James LeMoyne, *NYT*, Feb. 16, 1987, possibly an oblique recognition of the existence of the important CDHES study.

8. Stephen Kinzer, "Managua Cracks Down on Group That Presses for Prisoners' Rights," *NYT*, April 5, 1987.

9. Professor Jorge Lara-Braud, San Francisco Theological Seminary, Marin Interfaith Task Force (MITF); see *TTT*, 123f.

10. See *Central America Report* of MITF, April, 1987; MITF report, 1987.

11. *Excelsior* (Mexico), April 14 (*Central America News Update*, May 10, 1987); NECAN Regional Student Program report, Northampton Mass., April 15, 1987; COHA News Release, April 29, 1987; *WP*, May 12, 1987.

12. Information received from El Salvador by the Marin Interfaith Task Force, and transmitted by them to the media in the U.S. Reuters, *CSM*, June 4, 1987. These events merited 38 words in paragraph 14 of an article by James LeMoyne on rebel activities in San Salvador, where CoMadres is identified simply as "a human rights office sympathetic to the rebels" (*NYT*, June 4, 1987). Frank Smyth, "El Salvador's Forgotten War," *Progressive*, Aug. 1987; Marjorie Miller, *LAT*, July 6, 1987. See also Julia Preston, *WP*, June 5, 1987.

13. *Excelsior* (Mexico), June 6, July 19, 1987.

14. Peter Ford, *CSM*, July 15, 1987; Chris Norton, *In These Times*, June 1987; *Latinamerica press*, July 23, 1987. For more on the June atrocities, attributed in part to the Arce battalion, see special, *NYT*, June 22, 1987.

15. *Ibid.*

16. AP, *NYT*, "Salvador State of Siege Lapses," Jan. 18, 1987, p. 22; LeMoyne, July 17, Aug. 13, 1987.

17. For details, see my article in Walker, *Reagan vs. the Sandinistas*.

18. René Backmann, *Nouvel Observateur* (Paris), translated in *World Press Review*, Aug. 1987. See p. 92, above.

19. Chris Norton, *CSM*, April 14, 1987; Nov. 26, 1986; and in *Latinamerica press*, Oct. 9, 1986.

20. *NYT*, Aug. 13, 1987. Few independent scholars take any of this seriously. See, e.g., the review by Jerome Slater, "Dominos in Central America," *International Security*, Fall 1987.

21. Chris Norton, "Salvador: Charges of rampant corruption damage Duarte's Christian Democrats," *Latinamerica press*, Sept. 3, 1987. Norton is one of the very few U.S. journalists reporting regularly from El Salvador. See also Clifford Krauss and Robert S. Greenberger, "Peril to Democracy," *WSJ*, Sept. 14, 1987, warning that the corruption under Duarte, more

"rampant" even than under his predecessors, is "threatening one of President Reagan's few foreign-policy successes," namely "foster[ing] democracy in this tiny Central American nation." See p. 92.

22. Lindsey Gruson, *NYT*, Sept. 28, 1987. On early criticisms of the land reform by Oxfam, Salvadoran land reform specialist Leonel Gómez, and others, and sources, see *Towards a New Cold War*, 43ff.; reprinted in Peck, *Chomsky Reader*.

23. *CSM*, Sept. 15, 1987. The Mexican Press reports that the union leader was kidnapped "by five elements of a security body." On the same day, the government announced the arrest of 12 union leaders. A week earlier, the leader of the agricultural workers union was murdered by members of the armed forces, one of the 46 cases of reported political violence that week. *Excelsior*, Sept. 1 (Also AFP, Reuters), Aug. 23, 1987. *Central America News Update*, Oct. 1, 1987.

24. John Goshko, "U.S. to Equip Salvadoran Police Despite Rights Charges," Sept. 9, 1987, p. 17; "Human Rights Group Says Salvador Fails Peace Plan," *Christian Science Monitor*, Sept. 1, 1987, 60 words. See Americas Watch, *The Civilian Toll: 1986-1987*, Aug. 30, 1987.

25. See *TTT*, chapters 1, 3.

26. COHA's *Washington Report on the Hemisphere*, April 16, 1986. Alan Nairn and Jean-Marie Simon, *New Republic*, June 30, 1986.

27. *Guatemala: the Year of Promises*, Inforpress Centroamericana, Guatemala City, Jan. 1987; see also *Human Rights in Guatemala During President Cerezo's First Year* (Americas Watch and the British Parliamentary Human Rights Group, Feb. 1987), confirming the "terrible" human rights situation and continued military domination of the government. See James Painter, *Guatemala: False Hope, False Freedom* (Catholic Institute for International Relations, Latin America Bureau, London, 1987), for more general discussion.

28. Kathryn Leger, *CSM*, July 23, 1987; *Mesoamerica* (Costa Rica), Sept. 1987.

29. COHA, *News and Analysis*, Feb. 6; Kinzer, *NYT*, May 13; Philip Bennett, *BG*, Jan. 20; Peter Ford, *CSM*, March 23, 1987.

30. Kathryn Leger, *CSM*, July 23, 1987. See the discussion of "worthy" and "unworthy" victims, in Herman and Chomsky, *Political Economy of the Mass Media*, chapters 2, 5, 6.

31. *World Policy Journal*, Summer 1987.

32. COHA press release, May 11, 1987; *Central America Report*, July 31, 1987; *Excelsior*, July 3, 1987; Crystal Nix, *NYT*, Aug. 12, 1987.

33. Julio Godoy, *Latinamerica press*, July 23, 1987.

34. Dave Todd, "Contras uproot 16,000 from Honduras homes," *Montreal Gazette*, Dec. 3, 1986; AP, April 29, 1987. See William Long, *LAT*, Sept. 25, 1986, citing the Honduran press figure of 16,000 displaced and quoting the vice president of the Honduran Association of Coffee

Producers who says that "the cause of this whole problem is the policy of Reagan"; cited in Americas Watch, *Human Rights in Honduras: Central America's 'Sideshow'*, May 1987, 84f.

35. AP, April 1, 1987; March 29, 1987, interview on CBS, "60 Minutes." Americas Watch plausibly regards Lopez's attribution of atrocities primarily to the contras as "disingenuous," an effort to exculpate the Honduran security forces, while observing that "the acknowledgement by an official as knowledgeable as Lopez that death squads were run by *contras* on Honduran soil is significant" (*Human Rights in Honduras*, 65). There had been accounts for years of contra atrocities in Honduras, rarely reported in the media, though a front-page story by James LeMoyne in the *New York Times* on May 2, 1987 reports that the Honduran army is linked to the death of 200 suspected leftists according to testimony of a Honduran army defector on torture, death squads, and "'elimination' techniques." His American trainers, he says, recommended "use of such techniques as sleep deprivation, cold and isolation," but opposed "physical torture" that was carried out in secret. His accounts appear in detail in the Americas Watch report cited, 126ff.

36. Americas Watch, *Human Rights in Honduras*, 46.

37. *Mesoamerica*, Sept. 1987.

38. June Erlick, *MH*, Feb. 19, 1987, describing the "propaganda" that has reduced draft resistance to a "trickle" by "allaying the concerns of mothers and providing special privileges for draftees," and other such insidious devices invented to control the population.

39. Reprinted in *WP*, Aug. 25, 1986; cited in Americas Watch, *Human Rights in Honduras*, 122-3.

40. *Ibid.*, 137f. On the "elaborate deception of Congress" in connection with the Nicaraguan "invasion," see Steve Stecklow, *Dallas Morning News*, Jan. 7, 1987; his account is based on Ferch's report to the General Accounting Office that contrary to U.S. government lies, the U.S. induced Honduras to accept the aid it "requested" to "defend itself" from the Nicaraguan operation. The State Department "did not dispute Ferch's account," Stecklow reports, "but said it would be 'cynical' to describe the administration's actions as deception." Recognition of the truth does tend to induce cynicism.

41. *Food First News*, Spring 1987; Medea Benjamin, *Links*, Spring 1987.

42. Bob Dole, "Arias's Hopes, Ortega's 'Circus'," *NYT*, Sept. 10, 1987.

43. Kinzer, *NYT*, Sept. 2, 1987.

44. UPI, *BG*, March 20, 1986; see pp. 171-172, 196.

45. Stephen Kinzer, *NYT*, Sept. 2, 1987. Special, *NYT*, Sept. 8; Douglas Farah, UPI, *WP*, Sept. 1, 1987. UPI, *BG*, Sept. 9, 1987, on the release of the prisoners in Nicaragua. Dole's response to the photo cited in B.C. Saintes, *Guardian* (New York), Sept. 16, 1987, in a transcript of a longer section of this exchange, broadcast live over Nicaraguan radio.

46. L. James Binder, Editor in Chief of *Army* magazine, *Army*, May 1987.

47. See *TTT*, 36. For more on his highly selective morality and the remarkable stated principles that underlie it, see *Fateful Triangle*, and a series of bitter condemnations in the Israeli press on the occasion of his Nobel Prize, some quoted by Alexander Cockburn, *Nation*, Nov. 8, 1986.

48. See Martin Diskin, "The Manipulation of Indigenous Struggles," in Walker, *Reagan vs. the Sandinistas*, for further discussion.

49. Philippe Bourgois, *Ethnic Diversity on a Corporate Plantation: Guaymí Labor on a United Fruit Brands Subsidiary in Costa Rica and Panama* (Cambridge: Cultural Survival, 1985).

50. *Mesoamerica* (Costa Rica), Sept. 1987. The DEA spraying is also considered a possible cause for many other deaths from shellfish contaminated with insecticide in areas nearby.

51. *Green Papers* 2, 1, Environmental Project on Central America (EPOCA), Earth Island Institute, San Francisco.

52. *Ibid.*

53. Dennis Gilbert; James Austin and Jonathan Fox; in Walker, *Nicaragua: The First Five Years*, 163, 399.

14

Restoring Regional Standards

The cultural scene is illuminated with particular clarity by the thinking of the liberal doves, who set the limits for respectable dissent. The *Washington Post*, for example, is generally considered a bastion of enlightened liberalism. Accordingly, its editors oppose support for the contras. Nevertheless, the basic thrust of the Reagan program is correct, they insist. In particular, Reagan is right to emphasize the importance of "containing Nicaragua." The idea that we must "contain Nicaragua" is not a topic of debate in the United States—though one may ask whether "debate" would be the proper reaction in circles that retain a measure of sanity. Rather, it "is now a given; it is true," in the words of the *Post* editors, on a par with the fact that "the Sandinistas are communists of the Cuban or Soviet school"; that "Nicaragua is a serious menace—to civil peace and democracy in Nicaragua and to the stability and security of the region"; that we must "contain ... the Sandinistas' aggressive thrust" and demand "credible evidence of reduced Sandinista support for El Salvador's guerrillas"; that we must "fit Nicaragua back into a Central American mode" and turn "Nicaragua back toward democracy," and, with the "Latin democracies," "demand reasonable conduct by a regional standard."[1] Recall that the source of these certainties is near the "dovish" end of the spectrum of expressible opinion, critical of the contras as "an imperfect instrument" to achieve our goals. These goals are laudable, by definition. That too "is a given; it is true," hence beyond the limits of discussion.

The editors do not expand on the nature of the "Central American mode" and "regional standard" to which we must "fit

Nicaragua back" as we turn it "back toward democracy."[2] To anyone familiar with the "Central American mode" that the U.S. has instituted and maintained and the "regional standard" it has set as it installed and backed some of the most violent terrorist states of the modern era after a long history of support for brutality and corruption, these words can only elicit amazement. We see again the utility of historical amnesia, and also of the tunnel vision that enables us to put aside unacceptable facts about the contemporary period.

Those who escape the indoctrination system and are capable of looking honestly at the facts of past and current history will recognize that the *Post* editors are quite right to say that the U.S. wants to "fit Nicaragua back" into the "Central American mode," though not quite in the sense that they intend the public to understand.

The "regional standards" advocated by the United States are illustrated in the Human Rights Report of the Council on Hemispheric Affairs for 1985, which designates Guatemala and El Salvador as the hemisphere's worst human rights offenders, the "only two governments in the hemisphere that abducted, killed, and tortured political opponents on a systematic and widespread basis," the sixth successive year that they achieved this honor, renewed for 1986-7, as noted earlier.[3] The only other candidate in Central America was the U.S. proxy army attacking Nicaragua. It will not escape notice that these three "prime human rights violators" are close U.S. allies and clients, and that our Honduran client would join the collection if "human rights" were extended to the right to work, to food, to health services, etc., as in international conventions. Could there be a lesson here about the United States? The answer within the ideological institutions is "No," since the United States stands for all good things, whatever the facts may be.

No less interesting is the *Post*'s demand for "credible evidence of reduced Sandinista support for El Salvador's guerrillas"—the necessary way to fix the burden of proof, given the inability of the U.S. government to provide credible evidence for its claims regarding such support. Recall that the World Court reviewed the publicly available evidence, dismissing it as of little merit and adding that even if the claims were valid they would be irrelevant to the criminal nature of the U.S. assault. A look at U.S. government documents explains their rather disdainful reaction.[4] But it is necessarily true that Nicaragua is aggressive, much as

Guatemala was aggressive in 1954; otherwise, how could we be defending ourselves by attacking it? Therefore "it is a given; it is true." Facts are the merest irrelevance.

Across the spectrum, it is agreed that we must "contain Nicaragua." "Nicaragua is a cancer, and we must cut it out," Secretary of State George Shultz thunders to "sustained applause" at Kansas State University, adding that "Negotiations are a euphemism for capitulation if the shadow of power is not cast across the bargaining table."[5] Shultz believes "that the Sandinistas had been hurt severely enough to make negotiations feasible," the former executive editor of the *New York Times* remarks approvingly with reference to Shultz's support for the Reagan-Wright plan, thus adding his personal endorsement to the resort to force to compel our victims to bow to our demands.[6] The pride and pleasure that Rosenthal feels in our success in "hurting severely" those who stand in our way, in administering sufficient pain and anguish to achieve our ends, are regarded as quite unremarkable in a terrorist culture, evidently unworthy of comment; none ensued. Richard Lugar, chairman of the Senate Foreign Relations Committee, "warned Nicaragua that unless it changes its ways the United States may consider using force against it." "We all lament the absence of freedom and pluralism" in Poland, he explains, but Nicaragua "is located in the Western Hemisphere," where, we are to understand, the U.S. has always fostered "freedom and pluralism."[7] The doves counter that the use of force might cause us problems; hence alternatives should be considered first.

These words evoke some historical memories. A high-ranking Western observer in Managua warned that on its present course, the U.S. "will be seen more and more as a kind of deviant democracy, with a kind of crypto-fascist foreign policy."[8] I am just old enough to recall Hitler's ravings about "containing Poland," protecting Germany from the "terror" of the Czechs and the "aggressiveness" of the Poles, excising "the cancer" of the Jews, casting the shadow of power over the negotiating table so that those who do not succumb will be hurt severely enough to sue for peace. Current rhetoric in Washington and New York, and its easy acceptance by elite opinion at home and among U.S. allies, teaches us something about ourselves—or would, if we cared to learn.

Notes Chapter Fourteen

1. Editorial, *WP Weekly*, March 31, 1986.

2. Not a misprint, but the regular demand, as illustrated by numerous earlier citations; see p. 124.

3. P. 236; *COHA's Human Rights Report* (Washington, Dec. 31, 1985).

4. See the references of chapter 6, note 8.

5. AP, April 14, 1986. Reference to Nicaragua as a "cancer" is standard; see, e.g., the President's March 16, 1986 address (*NYT*, March 17) and the remarks by Vernon Walters, cited above, p. 172. The reference to the "cancer" is excised from the sanitized official version of Shultz's talk; *Current Policy* No. 820, U.S. Department of State, Bureau of Public Affairs. People who attended the talk recall Shultz's reported remarks well, and deny the press account of "sustained applause," reporting rather a distinct chill as Shultz thundered on.

6. A. M. Rosenthal, *NYT*, Aug. 21, 1987; note that well after the government had conceded that this plan was offered in the firm expectation that it would be rejected by the Sandinistas, clearing the way for renewed military aid to the contras, Rosenthal is hard at work to portray it as a serious peace initiative. Note further that the Reagan-Wright plan was, in effect, a demand for capitulation, as discussed earlier.

7. AP, *NYT*, April 1, 1985.

8. Randolph Ryan, *BG*, March 10, 1986.

15

Standards for Ourselves

The task of restoring regional standards abroad can be conducted efficiently only if the rear base is stable and secure. Hence the importance of entrenching the values of the culture of terrorism at home.

History teaches terrible lessons about how easy it is to descend to unimaginable horror. Germany was the pinnacle of civilization, science, and high culture in the years when Hitler came to power. Famous as a "great communicator," he became perhaps the most popular political figure in the history of Germany as long as he was winning cheap victories abroad and carrying out the "Hitler revolution" at home: reinstating "traditional values" of family and devotion, revitalizing the economy through military production, stimulating pride in the nation's glory and faith in its mission. Nevertheless, despite Hitler's personal appeal, direct support for his genocidal projects was never high. In an important study of this matter, Norman Cohn observes that even among Nazi party members, in 1938 over 60% "expressed downright indignation at the outrages" carried out against Jews, while 5 percent considered that "physical violence against Jews was justified because 'terror must be met with terror'."[1] In the Fall of 1942, when the genocide was fully under way, some 5% of Nazi Party members approved the shipment of Jews to "labor camps," while 70% registered indifference and the rest "showed signs of concern for the Jews." Among the general population, support for the Holocaust would have surely been still less. The Nazi leaders required no popular enthusiasm in order to carry out what the Nazi press described as the "defensive action against the Jewish world-criminals," "the liberation of all non-Jewish humanity," "the mobilization of the German people's will to destroy the bacillus lodged in its body," and to purify the society, and the world, by eliminating the "bacteria, vermin and pests [that] cannot be tolerated." For these tasks, the leadership needed little more than "a mood of passive compliance," apathy, the willingness to look the other way, to concentrate on personal gain and to accept the symbolism of greatness and power with little skepticism—all of this enhanced, to be sure, by the knout that was never far from sight. The Nazi atrocities, needless to say, are vastly beyond any comparison even to what we have been considering here. But if we think we differ in fundamental ways from those who observed with passive compliance, we are mistaken.

In our far more fortunate case, the state is relatively limited, by comparative standards, in the capacity to control its population by force, and must therefore rely more heavily on the more subtle devices of imagery and doctrine. The culture of terrorism that has grown in our midst is a structure of considerable power, with an impressive arsenal of devices to protect itself from the threat of understanding and with a powerful base in the institutions that dominate every facet of social life—the economy and political institutions, the intellectual culture and much of the popular culture as well. Nevertheless, despite a solid foundation among the educated and privileged classes and the lack of any organized base of dissidence, the system of indoctrination and control is not without internal rifts, and it is far from omnipotent or all-pervasive; the inhabitants of "enemy territory" do not lack means of self-defense and effective counter-action. As discussed earlier, the problem of returning the population to the preferred state of apathy and obedience was consciously addressed during the latter part of the Vietnam war, and since, as it had been when earlier "crises of democracy" erupted, but this time with only limited success among the general population. The resort by the state authorities to clandestine terrorism, with the tacit acquiescence or overt and enthusiastic support of congressional and intellectual elites, was one of the means adopted to confront the persistent difficulties posed by the domestic enemy—with serious attendant problems for the state managers, as we have seen.

It is natural that privileged elites should be frightened and appalled by signs of intellectual independence and a real commitment to the moral values that are hypocritically professed within the doctrinal system. That is why the unmistakeable improvement in the intellectual and moral climate among students and many other popular sectors during the dread "sixties" aroused such paranoid fears, eliciting endless tirades in intellectual journals and best-sellers on the supermarket racks that offer their version of the ferment of those years. Suppressed throughout, and understandably so, are the most striking features of the period. These include the rise of sympathy and concern for the victims of our violence, and the awakening to some of the hidden realities of American life, such as the experience of those who had been left aside by the social contract on which the political order was founded and have since been marginalized or oppressed: the native population, women, blacks, working people without property, and other "persons forgotten," as they are called by historians celebrating the bicentennial of the Constitution, the "special interests" of contemporary political propaganda.[2] This is the authentic "counterculture" to the dominant culture of terrorism, and it remains a significant and perhaps growing force, though largely without an institutional structure to sustain it.

Even more dangerous than intellectual independence and moral integrity is a stable organizational framework that might convert these qualities into instruments of popular engagement in social and political life. Correspondingly, it has always been a high priority among elite groups to prevent the growth of popular organizations. In a properly functioning system of subordination to established privilege, there must be no effective unions with real worker participation that devote themselves to serious problems of the social order, groups dedicated to worker self-management and community control, information systems independent of private and state power, political clubs and parties based on active participation of broad constituencies, people of independent mind who choose to see for themselves what lies behind the curtain of propaganda, such as the "witnesses" in Nicaragua who try to build what their state is committed to destroy and are endlessly derided and abused for this sin of integrity and human concern, and so on. The success in restricting such developments is an important feature of American democracy at home. The same priorities have guided policy abroad, notoriously in the Third World, but also in the reconstruction of the state capitalist societies after World War II when it was necessary to dissipate the influence of the anti-fascist resistance worldwide, to undermine independent unions and pressures for workers control, even to "rescue Western zones of Germany by *walling them off* against Eastern penetration and integrating them into an international pattern of Western Europe rather than into a united Germany," as George Kennan successfully urged, so as to avoid the danger of "a unified, centralized, politicized labor movement committed to a far-reaching program of social change."[3]

Despite all efforts, the enemy at home has by no means been subdued. There is much disaffection and unease, and it has been lively enough in its manifestations to achieve limited but meaningful gains. The terror in Central America could have gone far beyond the frightening levels that it attained, to take just one example; and so it would have, had it been possible to rally the public to the cause. The constraints that have been imposed on state violence are not insubstantial achievements on the part of those who have exercised the effort and personal initiative to engage in serious work for freedom, democracy, and justice, in a society that offers limited means for such endeavors.

Organized and stable communities of solidarity and support make it possible for disaffection to become something more than cynicism and hopelessness. They can encourage independent thought, providing means of intellectual self-defense against the daily barrage of propaganda. They can allow people to find other ways to live beyond those chosen for them by established privilege, to pursue objectives that may be more attuned to their deeper needs and concerns. In the absence of such communities, individuals remain isolated, and often feel ineffectual and confused by what they see in process, far from their control or influence. The temptation to put the world aside and keep to personal concerns is high. People whose day-to-day existence offers them little in the way of satisfying work, control over the conditions of their lives, or even material security will be reluctant to face unpleasant realities and thus to abandon what little they have to give some meaning to their lives, to lose the comforting faith in the images devised to keep them subdued and acquiescent: the noble guardians of the gates, the enemy beyond, the benevolence of our intentions, and the whole array of devices concocted to show that we are wonderful and they are devious, evil and threatening. Others who have access to privilege may be no less reluctant to forgo the ample rewards that a wealthy society offers for service to power, and to accept the sacrifices that the demands of honesty may well entail. That many have nevertheless done so is a fact of much importance.

The standards we choose to set for ourselves will inevitably have far-reaching consequences, given American power and wealth and all that flows from these endowments.

Notes Chapter Fifteen

1. Norman Cohn, *Warrant for Genocide* (Harper & Row, 1967), 200-13. The samples of Nazi Party members polled are small, but Cohn concludes from other evidence as well that the figures are probably significant.

2. Richard Morris, *The Forging of the Union* (Harper & Row, 1987), 173ff. On the Orwellian usage of the terms "special interest" and "national interest" (the interests of the population, the interests of corporations, respectively), see *TTT*, chapter 5.

3. Carolyn Eisenberg, "Working-Class Politics and the Cold War: American Intervention in the German Labor Movement, 1945-49," *Diplomatic History*, 7.4, Fall 1983; Kennan, quoted by John H. Backer, *The Decision to Divide Germany* (Durham, 1978), 155-6; my emphasis. See my paper cited in note 23, p. 37, and sources cited, for further discussion of these policies, pursued worldwide.

16

Prospects

The United States plainly has the military capacity, and perhaps the moral capacity as well, to pursue its historical vocation of torturing Nicaragua while strengthening "democracy" in the standard Orwellian sense of the term in El Salvador and other dependencies. With regard to Nicaragua, the rational policy for a violent state with unparalleled resources and limited domestic constraints would be to refrain from outright invasion and to persist in the CIA program of 1981 outlined by David MacMichael at the World Court hearings, cited earlier (p. 121). The U.S. surely possesses the means to "'turn Nicaragua into the Albania of Central America,' that is, poor, isolated, and radical," as a State Department insider reportedly boasted in 1981.[1] Educated opinion will pose no problems, as long as the costs remain slight, including the domestic cost of an aroused public. Once "regional standards" have been restored by violence and we have fit the starving and miserable people in our backyard "back into their Central American mode," we may proceed to attend to their fate with the same solicitude we have shown throughout our history, meanwhile reveling in this renewed demonstration of our traditional benevolence.

This could be a winning strategy, given the balance of forces, and it already has achieved notable successes, both in deterring the threat of social reform in Nicaragua and, most dramatically, with regard to elite opinion at home. But even with efficient damage control operations, the disarray in Washington may influence this rational strategy. It may impede escalation to direct aggression, but it also might impel the policy-makers of the Reagan

261

administration, or their successors, to accelerate these efforts before constraints upon state terror mount to an unacceptable degree.

Reaganite "conservatives" no doubt hoped to leave a permanent stamp on American politics. They intended to prove that violence pays. Operation Truth and the Office of Public Diplomacy, their guidelines dutifully observed by our free institutions in their forays into "enemy territory" at home, successfully constructed a series of demons before whom we must cringe in terror. Fortunately, our leading thinkers tell us, "The Administration is trying to get rid of two scoundrels in Tripoli and Managua," along with their cohorts elsewhere.[2] If these miserable creatures could be destroyed by violence, whatever the human cost, then, it was hoped, the long-term effects on American political culture might be significant. There would be no place for "wimps" in the political system, no room for those who toy with treaties and negotiations, political settlements, international law, or other such tommyrot; only violent thugs who relish the role of "enforcer," who delight in sending their military forces and goon squads to torture and kill people who are too weak to fight back, and "hurt them severely" enough so that they will submit to our terms—what is called "conservatism," in modern political jargon.

Just how firmly the culture of terrorism has been established we shall see, as the Reaganites attempt to consummate their project and other elements within the narrow elite consensus take up the cause, in their own ways, adapting policies to unchanging goals that are deeply rooted in our institutions, our historical practice, and our cultural climate.

Notes Chapter Sixteen

1. Cited by Thomas Walker, in Coleman and Herring, *Central American Crisis*, 172.

2. James Reston, March 26, 1986.

INDEX

Brings together some of the best writings of contemporary anarchists in one volume.

ANARCHIST PAPERS
revised edition
Dimitrios Roussopoulos, editor

Anarchism, with its emphasis on ethics, has always stressed the need for a counterculture against the prevailing one.

Essays contained within this volume of *Anarchist Papers* include an assessment of Germany's Green Party and a study of the anarchist thought of Paul Goodman by George Woodcock. Linguist Noam Chomsky examines the many ways in which the political powers rewrite history to suit their needs. Murray Bookchin theorizes on libertarian municipalism, and J. Frank Harrison discusses the politics of conformity and persuasion that shape the world of the average person. Both Alice Wexler and Marsha Hewitt present essays on Emma Goldman that show the links between her anarchism and her feminism.

> Wexler's article offers an acute portrait, drawing Goldman warts and all, showing her contradictions and inconsistences, as well as her strengths and passions. —*Choice*

> To find Noam Chomsky, Murray Bookchin, George Woodcock, and Cornelius Castoriadis between the same covers is a rare treat indeed. —*Canadian Book Review Annual*

Dimitrios Roussopoulos is an editor, writer and economist. He has written widely on international politics, democracy and social change. His most recent publications are *The Public Place* and *Legacy of the New Left*.

216 pages
Paperback ISBN: 1-55614-180-1 $24.99
Hardcover ISBN: 1-55164-181-X $53.99

complied and edited by DIMITRIOS ROUSSOPOULOS

THE ANARCHIST PAPERS 2

The question of the individual and his/her freedom is looked at through the feminist-infused existentialism of L. Susan Brown, and then, by Janet Biehl, through a critical examination of the relationship between ecofeminism and deep ecology. Ron Sakolsky analyses the continuing relationship between production and consumption — "toiling to live that we may live to toil" —and where, in the scheme of things, this leaves cultural creativity.

The fundamental assumption of anarchist theory that political representation is neither possible nor desirable is addressed by William R. McKercher, by Thomas S. Martin, by Karl Hess, and by Marie Fleming. Most theorists would, however, allow for some form of representation, and by far the most mature statement of principles and programmatic objectives is that of the Vermont and New Hampshire Greens. *Toward a* New *Politics* offers a sound beginning and represents a continuity with the best of the 1960s new Left.

> *Some of the more interesting aspects of contemporary anarchism...useful to the social and political debate.* —Choice

> 192 pages
> Paperback ISBN:0-921689-36-5 $12.99
> Hardcover ISBN:0-921689-37-3 $41.99

THE ANARCHIST PAPERS 3

George Woodcock's introduction to Kropotkin's monumental work on the French Revolution is followed by a piece by Brian Morris who raises the idea that the French Revolution was essentially not a permanent revolution but an unfinished one. Bruce Allen looks at Poland's new generation of oppositionists, Frank Harrison at the crisis of Soviet Statism, Raymond Wrabley at the conflicts inherent in neo-conservatism and social ecology, L. Susan Brown at the connection between feminism, anarchism and human freedom, and finally, the ideological position of a community disillusioned with a dictatorship is revealed through a selection of documents from witnesses to the Tiananmen Square massacre.

> *This collection further defines anarchist thought and practice in a modern environment...a stimulating compendium.* —Ottawa Citizen

> 211 pages
> Paperback ISBN: 0-921689-52-7 $12.99
> Hardcover ISBN: 0-921689-53-5 $41.99

DIMITRIOS ROUSSOPOULOS, editor, writer and economist, has written widely on international politics, democracy, social change and ecology. His most recent books are *Dissidence: Essays Against the Mainstream*, *Political Ecology*, and *The Public Place: Citizen Participation in the Neighbourhood and the City.*

complied and edited by DIMITRIOS ROUSSOPOULOS

RADICAL PAPERS

In this volume, Murray Bookchin, in a forty page critical, but affirmative review, focuses on the anarcho-syndicalist role during the fascist revolt in Spain. Other essays include a discussion on the limits of the peace movement; a detailed examination of the life and influence of Gustav Landauer killed during suppression of the 1919 Bavarian Soviet Republic; a refutation of alleged anarchist 'elitism'; a study of the relationship of Proudhon and Bakunin; a memorial to Lucy Parsons, widow of the man hanged in 1887 as one outcome of the Haymarket Affair that recalls her as one of the founders of the IWW who continued radically active into her eighties; and finally, an essay by Noam Chomsky wherein he shows that the only connection between socialism and the Soviet Union is that of contradiction.

> *Very good introductions…highly recommended. An interesting, and stimulating collection.* —Canadian Book Review Annual

> *A good read…pieces of our lives we would otherwise lose in the dust-heaps of history.* —Humanist in Canada

Contributors include: Murray Bookchin, Noam Chomsky, Russell Berman, Juan Gomez Casas, Tim Luke, Brian Martin, Arlene Meyers, Gary Prevost, William Reichert and Daniel Guérin.

    160 pages
    Paperback ISBN: 0-920057-86-1 $12.99
    Hardcover ISBN: 0-920057-87-X $41.99

RADICAL PAPERS 2

Contains an essay by Noam Chomsky on the Reagan administration, describing the underpinnings of American foreign policy in Central America, that illustrate the contradictions within the U.S. doctrinal system; the theory of the ecological movement by Murray Bookchin; an examination of Canada-U.S. free trade by Gary Temple; a retrospective look at Edward Carpenter's socialism by William Reichert; the Barcelona women's bread riots of 1918 by Martha Ackelsberg; and a painstakingly argued contribution to feminist theory on the origins of male domination by Rosella Di Leo.

> *…attempts to make up the ground the left has lost…the essays…reflect a post-Reagan urgency in left-wing debates. Chomsky's excellent essay succeeds in underlining the paradoxes surrounding Reagan's vision of democracy in Central America.* —Kingston Whig-Standard

    168 pages
    Paperback ISBN: 0-921689-12-8 $12.99
    Hardcover ISBN: 0-921689-13-6 $41.99

MANUFACTURING CONSENT
Noam Chomsky and the Media
Mark Achbar, editor

A primer in intellectual self-defense
This companion volume to the celebrated film of the same name charts the life of America's most famous dissident, from his boyhood days running his uncle's newsstand in Manhattan to his current role as outspoken social critic. Included are exchanges between Chomsky and his critics, historical and biographical material, filmmakers' notes, a resource guide, more than 270 stills from the film, and, 18 "Philosopher All-Stars" Trading Cards!

An invigorating introduction to one of the least soporific of American minds. *—The New York Times*

A juicily subversive biographical/philosophical documentary bristling and buzzing with ideas. *—Washington Post*

You will see the whole sweep of the most challenging critic in modern political thought. *—Boston Globe*

One of our real geniuses…an excellent introduction. *—Village Voice*

An intellectually challenging crash course in the man's cooly contentious analysis, laying out his thoughts in a package that is clever and accessible. *—Los Angeles Times*

…challenging, controversial. *—Globe and Mail*

…a rich, rewarding experience, a thoughtful and lucid exploration of the danger that might exist in a controlled media. *—Edmonton Journal*

Mark Achbar has applied a wide range of creative abilities and technical skills to over fifty films, videos and books. In 1986, he received a Gemini nomination for Best Writer on *The Canadian Conspiracy*, a cultural/political satire.

264 pages, 270 illustrations, bibliography, index, Trading cards
Paperback ISBN: 1-55164-002-3 $26.99
Hardcover ISBN: 1-55164-003-1 $55.99

BOOKS OF RELATED INTEREST BY

Culture and Social Change, *Colin Leys, Marguerite Mendell, editors*
Canada and Radical Social Change, *Dimitrios Roussopoulos, editor*
Decentralizing Power: On Paul Goodman, *Taylor Stoehr, editor*
Defending the Earth, *by Murray Bookchin*
Designing Utopia, *by Michael Lang*
Dissidence: Essays Against the Mainstream, *by Dimitrios Roussopoulos*
Fighting for Hope, *by Joan Newman Kuyek*
First Person Plural, *by David Smith*
Fugitive Writings, *by Peter Kropotkin*
Legacy of the New Left, *by Dimitrios Roussopoulos*
Nationalism and Culture, *by Rudolf Rocker*
Perspectives on Power, *by Noam Chomsky*
Previews and Premises, *by Alvin Toffler*
Public Place, *by Dimitrios Roussopoulos*
Rethinking Camelot, *by Noam Chomsky*
Words of A Rebel, *by Peter Kropotkin*
Year 501, *by Noam Chomsky*

send for a free catalogue of all our titles
BLACK ROSE BOOKS
C.P. 1258, Succ. Place du Parc
Montréal, Québec
H3W 2R3 Canada
or visit our web site at: http://www.web.net/blackrosebooks

To order books:
In Canada: (phone) 1-800-565-9523 (fax) 1-800-221-9985
email: utpbooks@utpress.utoronto.ca

In United States: (phone) 1-800-283-3572 (fax) 1-651-917-6406

In UK & Europe: (phone) London 44 (0)20 8986-4854 (fax) 44 (0)20 8533-5821
email: order@centralbooks.com

Printed by the workers of
MARC VEILLEUX IMPRIMEUR INC.
Boucherville, Québec
for Black Rose Books Ltd.